50⁰⁰
80E

D1072106

P O E M S

by

E P H E L I A

(c. 1679)

"Relentless caper for all those who step
The legend of their youth into the noon"

Hart Crane, "Legend" (*White Buildings*, 1926)

Set by Mel Powell, *Events* (1963)

Frontispiece, *Female Poems On Several Occasions. Written By Ephelia* (1679, 1682)
Included in the Exhibition *Engraved Portraits of Women Writers, Sappho to George Eliot*
The Grolier Club, New York City, 1895

POEMS

by

EPHELIA

(c. 1679)

THE PREMIER FACSIMILE EDITION

OF THE

COLLECTED MANUSCRIPT AND PUBLISHED POEMS

WITH A CRITICAL ESSAY

AND

APPARATUS

BY

MAUREEN E. MULVIHILL

SCHOLARS' FACSIMILES & REPRINTS
Delmar, New York
Second Printing, 1993

SCHOLARS' FACSIMILES & REPRINTS
ISSN 0161-7729
SERIES ESTABLISHED 1936
VOLUME 463

Published by Scholars' Facsimiles & Reprints
An Imprint of Academic Resources Corporation
Delmar, New York 12054-0344, U.S.A.

First Printing, December, 1992
Second Printing, December, 1993

Printed and manufactured in the United States of America

Library of Congress Cataloguing-in-Publication Data

Ephelia, fl. 1679

*Poems by Ephelia (c. 1679): The Premier Facsimile Edition of the Collected
Manuscript & Published Poems ... With a Critical Essay & Apparatus*
By Maureen E. Mulvihill.

278 p. cm. 14 x 22   19 ills.
(Scholars' Facsimiles & Reprints, ISSN 0161-7729; v. 463)

Includes bibliographical references and indexes.

ISBN 0-8201-1463-4

I. Mulvihill, Maureen Esther.   II. Title

PR3431.E57A124   1992
821'.4--dc20   92-15119
CIP
rev.

To my parents, Charles and Esther Mulvihill, and siblings

My husband, Daniel Harris, and the Jazz Cat from Brooklyn

Daniel Jones Conway and Alice Gaule Jones Conway

To the memory of John Gaule, Sir Colin McDuff, and Zoot

And to the newcomers to the clan Mulvihill:

Michael Daniel and David Ryan

Myles Vincent and Shanley Marie

Maria Elizabeth and John Damien

CONTENTS

all page references follow pagination at foot of page

CONTENTS

CONTENTS

———

CONTENTS

ILLUSTRATIONS

Frontispiece: Engraved frontispiece portrait of Ephelia, unsigned and undated, in *Female Poems On several Occasions. Written by Ephelia* (1679, 1682). John Verney copy, 1679 edition. Courtesy, Folger Shakespeare Library, Washington, D.C.

ILLUSTRATIONS

ꓕCKNOWLEDGMENTS

Reclaiming a 'lost' pseudonymous writer of the seventeenth century is a daunting project, one befitting a team of specialists. While independently conducting broad and interdisciplinary searches into Ephelia's writings, coterie, patronage, and concealed authorship, I nonetheless profited from the supportive interest and guidance of many specialists. It is a pleasure to record at last my gratitude to the following:

In the United States: In New York: Norman Mangouni and Margaret Mirabelli, Scholars' Facsimiles & Reprints; Ellen Chirelstein, art historian; James Cummins, Stephen Weissman, the late John F. Fleming, rare book dealers; Charles Hamilton, handwriting specialist; Daniel Harris, composer-musician; Robert Hayes, Brooklyn Public Library; Clem Labine, Publisher; Mary Ann O'Donnell, Manhattan College; Gunther Pohl, Barbara Hillman, Local History & Genealogy Division, New York Public Library; Leona Rostenberg and Madeleine B. Stern, authors, scholars, and antiquarian book dealers; Ralph Smith, *The Magazine Antiques*; G. Thomas Tanselle, John Simon Guggenheim Memorial Foundation, and Columbia University; Sharon Valiant.

Elsewhere in the United States & in Canada: Mark Livesay, Thomson-Shore, Inc., Dexter, Michigan; Mark R. Farrell, Curator, Taylor Collection, Firestone Library, Princeton University; Samuel J. Hardman, poet and art historian, Commerce, Georgia; Joseph C. Barnett, Jr., M.D., art collector; Cathy Henderson, Ransom Research Center, Austin, Texas; Nati Krivatsy, Folger Shakespeare Library, Washington, D.C.; Joanna Lipking, Northwestern University; Ralph Mathisen, Classicist, University of South Carolina; John Morrison, Wing Office, Yale University; Arthur Scouten, Emeritus, University of Pennsylvania; Susan Smith Nashe, publisher, *texture press*, Norman, Oklahoma; Thomas Lange, Alan Jutzi, Sara Hodson, Huntington Library, San Marino, California; Susanne Woods, Elaine Brennan, Women Writers Project, Brown University; specialists at the NEH Institute, The Johns Hopkins University, 1990; my colleagues at The Princeton Research Forum, Princeton, New Jersey. *In Canada:* Richard Morton, McMaster University, Hamilton, Ontario; Patricia Köster, University of Victoria, British Columbia.

In the United Kingdom: In England: Peter Beal, Sotheby's, London; E J Burford, author, London; D H B Chesshyre and the Herald Painter, College of Arms, London; L W L Edwards, Society of Genealogists, London; Sheila Edward, Clive Hurst, Paul Morgan, Paul Nash, Judith Priestman, Bodleian Library, Oxford; W J F Fenton, genealogist and heraldic painter, Surrey; Patricia Gill, Goodwood Papers, West Sussex PRO; J Max Griffin, Frances Harris, M J Jannetta, British Library, London; M T Halford, A M Carr, Shropshire County Council and Shrewsbury Public Library; Henry A N Hallam, Honorary Librarian, Lamport Hall Library, Northamptonshire (the Isham family); Eeyan Hartley, Archivist, Castle Howard, Yorkshire; R M Harvey, Guildhall Library, London; C R J Humphery-Smith, Institute of

ACKNOWLEDGMENTS

Heraldic and Genealogical Studies, Kent; Dorothy Johnston, Anthony Upton, Manuscripts, Nottingham Library; James Mosley, St Bride's Printing Library, London; D W Riley, Rylands University Library, Manchester; Sara Rodger, Arundel Castle Archives, West Sussex; C D W Sheppard, Brotherton Collection, Leeds University Library; Margaret Swarbrick, Victoria Library, Westminster; Janet Todd, University of East Anglia, Norwich; Muriel Tonkin, genealogist, Herefordshire; Rachel Watson, Northamptonshire PRO; H J R Wing, Christ Church, Oxford; Andrew Wright, St Julian's, Shrewsbury.

In Scotland: A. Hildago, Aberdeen Art Gallery; John Horden, editor, *Dictionary of Concealed Authorship*, Stirling; Alistair Cherry, National Library of Scotland, Edinburgh; J V Howard, Edinburgh University Library.

In Wales: John Owen, PRO, Dyfed; Graham Thomas, National Library of Wales, Aberystwyth.

In Switzerland: Gustav Ungerer, Universität Bern.

MAUREEN E. MULVIHILL
Bloomsday, 16 June 1992
New York City

$\mathcal{A}$ NOTE ON THE SECOND PRINTING

Within less than a year of its publication in December, 1992, *Poems by Ephelia* saw a second printing in 1993. Its editor-author and publisher are grateful for this opportunity to correct the inevitable errata and occasional editorial gaffe in the first printing; to acknowledge the warm reception of this volume in most circles; and to encourage the rising controversy it has stirred in others (see *TLS* 25 June 1993; 3 September 1993).

Ephelia introduces today's readers to one of the most baffling cases in the history of pseudonymous authorship. Since the 19th Century, several scholars and literary enthusiasts have attempted to find the woman behind the "Ephelia" mask; but not until now has anyone seriously tackled this intriguing case by bringing together in one volume all of the existing writings traditionally attributed to or associated with this interesting poet-playwright-songwriter, as well as the body of fictions and hypotheses which her concealed authorship has inspired. This edition reopens the Ephelia case anew. Exploiting tactics of both interdisciplinary and multimedia research, this investigation systematically probes complex textual, canonical, and attributive issues related to the Ephelia texts; it also offers several new formulations suggested by existing facts and heretofore overlooked circumstantial evidence in contemporary sources.

To date, the fortunes of *Ephelia* have been felicitous: In July, 1993, the edition was nominated by the distinguished specialist on 17th-century books, bibliography, and the book trade, Dr Leona Rostenberg of Leona Rostenberg and Madeleine Stern Rare Books - New York, for a book prize sponsored by The Modern Language Association of America. By October, 1993, sales and incoming orders justified the publisher's decision to proceed with a second printing. In December, 1993, the book was exhibited at the annual Small Press Center Book Fair, 20 West 44th Street, New York City. And throughout the month of January, 1994, *Ephelia* was the subject of a window display at the Center.

On this occasion, the editor-author and publisher gratefully acknowledge the good work of Lana Paton and Keith Reisinger at our printer, Thomson-Shore, Inc., Dexter, Michigan, who coordinated within weeks the second printing of *Ephelia* -- in all its fussy particulars.

I. CRITICAL ESSAY

———————

1

CRITICAL ESSAY

Let not young souls
be smothered out
before they do quaint deeds
and
fully flaunt their pride

Vachel Lindsay

Who was the elusive Ephelia? What circumstances led to her concealed authorship? Were specialists correct when they asserted, century after century, 'We simply don't *know* who Ephelia *was!*'?

Such lazy indifference roused the literary picklock in me. Opening the door on Ephelia's obscurity, I found myself in a large house of quiet, undisturbed rooms. My pleasureful tour soon became a long visit.

The subject of this book is pertinacious digging. It reconstructs the course of false starts, blind leads, and not a few startling discoveries.

GOALS, PROCEDURES, METHODOLOGIES

Editorial responsibilities in assembling a scholarly photographic facsimile edition are no less weighty than in preparing an old-spelling critical edition. In some respects, shaping a readable and intelligently organized facsimile edition is apt to present many unexpected challenges and creative opportunities unencountered in other editorial formats. Certainly, this has been the case in *Poems by Ephelia*.

3

CRITICAL ESSAY

In this ambitious enterprise, I was gathering a number of rare writings, inaccessible to most readers. I also was introducing to a postmodern readership a body of 17th-century manuscript and published poems, long obscured by over three centuries of concealed authorship and further muddled by longstanding canonical confusion. Before I identify this edition's procedural principles and my project's research methodologies, let me properly begin with the three overarching goals that set into motion this intriguing case in literary detection.

I. Edition Goals

Above all, this edition seeks to restore Ephelia to the record of English literature as an authentic personality of the later Stuart period, no matter how fixed her status as a minor figure. Contrary to a deeply embedded tradition of Ephelia as a mere hoax or literary fiction of the Restoration -- an unfortunate myth promulgated by those who failed to 'find' her, from Joseph Woodfall Ebsworth in 1883 down to the editorial team of *Kissing The Rod* in 1988 -- this edition demonstrates that Ephelia lived a life in London during the 1670s and '80s, and that contemporary references and facts about her life and work attest to this. My concern with her authenticity prompted me to drop the traditional quotation marks around her pseudonym. Not only are they typographically distracting and cumbersome, but they also reinforce the longstanding fictive reputation of Ephelia. As her small literary remains disclose, this was a young career writer with a following, who most assuredly coveted fame, as did most women writers of her day. Sometime in 1677-78, Ephelia won the sponsorship of Lady Mary (Villiers) Stuart, Dowager Duchess of Richmond and Lennox, a woman with powerful connections to the Villiers, Herbert, Stuart, and Howard lines. With a 50-line broadside addressed to Charles II on the volatile subject of the Popish Plot, Ephelia cautiously 'stepped the Legend of her Youth into the Noon,' to borrow a phrase from Hart Crane.

The corpus of her work gives us a versatile writer of plays, songs, and poems. Primarily, Ephelia was a poet. Certainly, she is a more skilled and enjoyable writer than most 19th- and 20th-century commentators are willing to acknowledge. She produced broadsides on sensitive affairs of state, as well as coterie verse, poems on social and feminist issues, many secular songs, and several amorous lyrics of vivid self-portraiture. Biographical truth, by way of unmasking Ephelia's enigmatic identity, was never the principal aim of this project: *locating her writings, researching their backgrounds and provenance, and getting her*

4

work back into circulation in an informative, attractive edition was the chief aim of this search.

It is entirely possible, of course, to appreciate a body of writings without knowing its author's full and complete biography. Traditions of ambiguity and controversy continue to surround Shakespeare. Aphra Behn's family background and apprenticeship remain shadowy even yet. And we know almost nothing about Elizabeth Polwhele, whose romantic farce *The Frolicks* (1671) was recently returned to the canon of Restoration literature in 1977 through the admirable recovery researches of Judith Milhous and Robert D. Hume. Regardless of limited information on the identities of these writers, their work can be valued for its craft and continuing historical value. No less the case with Ephelia.

Second, because this edition is a photographic facsimile, Ephelia's collected writings are now accessible in their original state and full contemporary dress, evidently as my poet wished them to appear during her own lifetime. In this one-volume, illustrated edition, a wider audience of students, generalists, and nonspecialists now have an opportunity to examine and enjoy my poet's collected writings as they looked to her own readers in the 17th century. This is an opportunity lost in a modernized reprint or in an "e-text" format. Specialists will observe in this edition that Ephelia's handsome publications of 1678, 1679, and 1681 suggest close authorial or patronal supervision. And enthusiasts in English printing history certainly will recognize that her published writings display some of the best features of contemporary typography and formatting, especially at a time when English book-design compared unfavorably with the lovely work of French and Dutch printers (*v.* Plomer *English Printers' Ornaments* 1924). In this edition, readers now can examine these aesthetic features of Ephelia's work, features which have made her a collectible author in British and American antiquarian circles. The appreciation of the artistic aspects of my poet's work among rare book collectors, print collectors, and literary specialists is documented in Appendix E of this edition's apparatus.

Poems by Ephelia also introduces an autograph manuscript, which I date to 1681, and which I attribute to my poet. Because of the existence of this manuscript, readers can now observe her script and signature, as well as her habits of composition, revision, and formatting. These physical characteristics of any writer's work are important categories of bibliographical information. Such valuable evidence is lost in modernized and electronic formats.

Third, this edition performs a service to the community of

literary scholars, textual specialists, and feminist recovery researchers. As this essay will demonstrate, my search has shed new light on Ephelia's canon, patronage, coterie, and potential family background. While my investigations did not consistently produce incontrovertible evidence for some of my arguments, especially those touching my writer's identity, many of my formulations and hypotheses intersected with fragments of hard, primary evidence in rather astonishing ways, so as to form new configurations and fresh lines of inquiry. Such instances of intersection and linkage sometimes led to further information, which then enabled me to proceed with some provocative yet plausible speculations.

With prudence tempering enthusiasm, I have moved cautiously on all fronts, phrasing some of my conclusions tentatively, lest future research require a published rescission of many painstaking efforts here. Yet I hasten to add that most arguments are supported by factual information and, oftentimes, a cluster of related contemporary references and allusions, which came to assume special weight and veracity over the course of my searches. As the respective editors of *The Roxburghe Ballads* and *Poems On Affairs Of State* have shown, there exists a large body of 'lost,' fugitive, and unascribed literature produced during Ephelia's day, whose authors have remained concealed or obscured for more than 300 years, in spite of deep researches conducted by senior literary specialists with convenient access to literary manuscripts, printers' ledgers, and social and legal documents.

While always proceeding with faith in the long-term historical value of this project, I strove nonetheless to remain objective and honest in the face of contradictory and divergent evidence. Reconfiguring my findings and reconnoitering tactics were integral to the process of synthesis, especially as this project began to gain momentum. It is in fragments, after all, that reconstruction begins. Over the course of this project, the chains of scholarly reasoning consistently began with fragile but telling evidence.

Consider these three pieces of intersecting contemporary fragments, which I later could refer to as persuasive 'evidence': First was Behn's reference to "a Poet Joan" in the Prologue to *Sir Patient Fancy* (1678). Second was Thomas Newcomb's reference in *Bibliotheca* (1712) to a poetess "Phillips," who "in verse her Passion told." And, third, was the identification of Delarivier[e] Manley's "Euphelia" as a "Miss Proud" in the *Key* to Manley's *Atalantis* (1714). This latter identification was most attractive, as it linked up with information from Joseph Woodfall Ebsworth in *The Roxburghe Ballads* that "One of Mulgrave's mistresses was 'humble Joan'" (IV:1883), a nickname which

CRITICAL ESSAY

I read ironically as "proud Joan" or "Joan Proud." (The second half of
the "Euphelia" identification, namely that this Miss Proud was an
attendant to Queen Anne, was irrelevant, as it was too late for my
author, and it was not corroborated in the standard documentary
sources, such as Strickland's *Lives of the Queens of England* 1902 and
Somerset's *Ladies-In-Waiting* 1984.) Perceived, then, as a cluster of
related contemporary allusions, consisting of Behn's "Poet Joan,"
Newcomb's female poet "Phillips," and Manley's "Miss Proud," this
otherwise motley gathering of informational fragments eventually fell
into place and assumed a particular relevance. What I had in such a
small unit of references was a nexus of intersecting information which,
in turn, pointed me in the direction of biographical and genealogical
researches. That path led me to an attractive speculative candidate for
Ephelia in the related Prowde-Phillips-Milton line of Shrewsbury and
London, as well as to the possible context of H.B. Wheatley's
identification of Ephelia in 1885 as one Joan Phillips. Such was the
pattern of intersecting clues and allusions which came to dominate
most of my researches.

Even though Ephelia's identity was one of the most closely
guarded secrets of the Restoration, her work is abundant in 'markers.'
These reference points in the primary writings proved to be quiet leads.
In time, they enabled me to establish relevant backgrounds for my
poet's work. They also invited me to sort out the status of Ephelia's
canon, beginning with the addition of three new poems and a
reasonable challenge to the longstanding attribution of her best lyric
"*Ephelia's* Lamentation" [c. 1674/5] to Sir George Etherege.

Even should stunning new developments presently come to light that
incontrovertibly identify Ephelia as someone other than the candidate
I offer later in this essay, it is hoped that this edition will be valued
nonetheless on its own merits as performing a fair amount of
indispensable spadework on this intriguing young writer. Readers will
find here newly excavated textual and bibliographical details on
Ephelia's work in poetry, drama, and song; the identification of her
patroness and coterie; reconstructions of her canon; and the amazing
though little-known provenance of her writings among the world's
most distinguished book collectors. If this edition also serves as a
working model for other enthusiasts of 'lost' writers and as a spur to
continuing research into my subject, then my labors will have been
worthwhile indeed.

CRITICAL ESSAY

II. Procedural Principles

A classical humanist by training, I turned first to models at the outset of this venture. It is a pleasure to acknowledge the editorial work of Vivian de Sola Pinto, James Thorpe, Earl Miner, John T. Shawcross, the editors of *Poems On Affairs Of State* and of the California *Dryden*, David Trotter, and Patrick Thomas. The methodologies and procedural principles employed by these editors of 17th-century English poetry were instructive.

Guiding my textual investigations were the theoretical writings and practice of Fredson Bowers, James Thorpe, G. Thomas Tanselle, D. F. McKenzie, and David C. Greetham.

In the knotty area of attribution, I benefitted from the work of Frederick Mosteller, D. L. Wallace, David M. Vieth, and J. W. Johnson.

While my publisher and I had planned to submit this edition to the Center for Critical Editions of the Modern Language Association for its approval and seal, and had made preliminary arrangements with Jo Ann Boydston and Gary A. Stringer of the Center, the publication schedule for this edition unfortunately worked against this desirable plan.

I prepared for this project by participating in two intensive seminars at the post-doctoral level in the late 1980s: "Scholarly Editing" led by G. Thomas Tanselle at Columbia University's Rare Book School; and "Stuart Portraiture" led by Duncan Robinson at The Yale Center for British Art. Also useful was a nine-lecture symposium I attended in 1988 at the Metropolitan Museum of Art, "Methods of Art Historians." All of these exposures proved invaluable over the course of this project.

Collation & Copy Selection. Surviving copies of Ephelia's published writings are identified, with locations, in Donald Wing's *Short-Title Catalogue*, the *National Union Catalogue*, and printed catalogues of major American and British libraries. To identify new acquisitions, potential manuscripts, and heretofore unidentified published writings, I consulted catalogues of manuscripts and printed books under the author headings "Ephelia," "Phillips" (all variant spellings), "Prowde" ("Proud"), "By a Gentlewoman," and "By a Lady." I soon found that my efforts were better served by relying almost exclusively on direct communications with curators at the principal research libraries and with rare book dealers. I also published several queries, in *The New York Times Book Review*, *Notes and Queries*, and in several specialized journals for the literary, antiquarian, and art markets, especially those which circulated on both sides of the Atlantic

8

(*v.* p. 260 of my Annotated Bibliography). All of these time-consuming procedures were fruitful in various ways.

The selection of copies of Ephelia's work for reproduction in this edition was a far less complicated process than it otherwise would have been, since the extant copies of my writer's published texts of 1678, 1679, and 1681, are in fact identical to one another. Surviving copies were evidently produced at the same time and printed from the same types.

For example, in the process of collating the first issue of her principal work, the small octavo *Female Poems On several Occasions. Written by Ephelia* (1679), I identified four distinguishing features of this book which consistently appeared in all surviving copies, namely three production errors and a curious typographical feature:

    (i) an incorrect catchword ("*Celadon*" p.31), suggesting printer error or a cancellation during production of a poem by Ephelia to or about a "*Celadon*" (he is probably the "Friend" whose "Reply" she sets to verse, pp.30-31);

    (ii) the omission of stanza numeral "1" in the love song "Neglect Returned" (p. 37);

    (iii) an inverted type ("Aud" for "And" p. 54, line 10); and

    (iv) a bold, upper-case "W" in several presentations of "World," "Woman," "Wit," and "Witty" (*e.g.* pp. 76, 77, 85, 107; other "W"s, on these same pages, are not set in bold). This curious typographical feature of the *Female Poems* may have been a clever encoding suggested by Ephelia or her patroness to the book's printer William Downing to identify Ephelia as a <u>w</u>orldly <u>w</u>oman of <u>w</u>it, qualities consistent with her literary persona.

My overall determinants in copy selection, therefore, were:

    (i) the physical condition of extant copies and their potential reproductive quality in the photo-facsimile medium;

    (ii) physical evidence in the copies -- inscriptions, ownership signatures, bookplates, dates, sale prices, identifications -- supplied by owners or book-sellers; and,

    (iii) the provenance of the copies as a clue to my writer's associations and as evidence of the appreciating value of her work over the centuries.

These, then, were my choices:

The copy of Ephelia's licensed broadside, *A Poem To His Sacred Majesty, On The Plot. Written by a Gentlewoman* (1678), preserved in the Elias Ashmole Collection at the Bodleian Library, held special interest for me because of its provenance in Ashmole. This copy, which also

CRITICAL ESSAY

happens to be in good reproducible condition, was selected over other extant copies of this poem, identified in Appendix A, because its provenance aligned with my probes into Ephelia's longstanding identification as one Joan Phillips. As my researches, and those of R. E. Hone, revealed, Ashmole had close ties to Milton's elder nephew, Edward Phillips, who in fact had served as Ashmole's researcher-secretary during the years of Ashmole's work on *The Order of the Garter* (1672) (*v.* Hone *N&Q* April 1956). My further delvings into Ashmole's collection turned up a copy of another broadside of Ephelia's, *Advice To His Grace*, addressed to Monmouth and published in 1681. This information was significant, as it strengthened my longstanding belief that the knowledgeable H. B. Wheatley, Recorder and Clerk to the Royal Society, was correct when he identified Ephelia in print in 1885 as a Phillips. Over the course of investigating several literary Phillips lines of Ephelia's day, relevant information came to light which galvanized the Ephelia-Edward Phillips connection, making the Ashmole copy of Ephelia's Popish Plot broadside an appropriate choice.

Provenance again became a determinant in copy selection in the case of Ephelia's second broadside, *Advice To His Grace* (1681). The Arthur M. Rosenbloom copy of this rare poem, his gift to Yale University's Beinecke Rare Book and Manuscripts Library in 1952, was selected because it illustrated Ephelia's continuing status as a collectible writer among antiquarian specialists and rare-book collectors (*v.* Appendix E).

The Folger Shakespeare Library copy of Ephelia's *Female Poems* (1679) was selected over my own copy and over other institutional copies for two reasons. First was its provenance in the Verney family. This was a prominent political and literary line of the 17th century, whose coterie included Rochester, the young amateur poet Anne Wharton of Behn's circle, and the Villiers-Isham-Duppa circle. As this essay will show, most of these individuals or their families are linked to Ephelia in various ways. The fact that a copy of the *Female Poems* was in the Verney family library strengthened my case for Ephelia's status as a minor career writer with some major connections. Moreover, this particular copy contained several informative inscriptions, evidently in a contemporary hand. These, and all other pieces of physical evidence in surviving copies of Ephelia's book, are identified in Appendix E.

The reissue of *Female Poems* in 1682 (Fig.2) was not considered for reproduction here. Reasonable grounds exist to support my belief that, far from being the most authoritative edition of my poet's book, this subsequent edition was a 'pirated' or unauthorized publication,

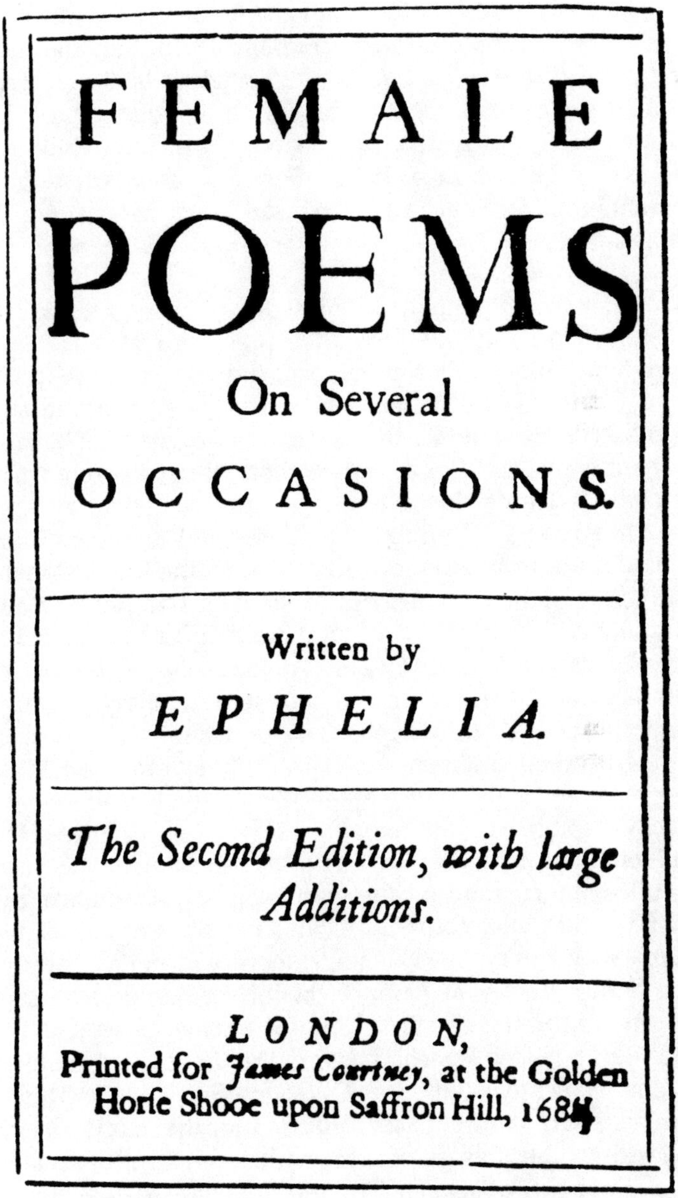

FEMALE

POEMS

On Several

OCCASIONS.

Written by

E P H E L I A.

*The Second Edition, with large
Additions.*

L O N D O N,
Printed for *James Courtney*, at the Golden
Horse Shooe upon Saffron Hill, 1682.

Figure 2. Titlepage, *Female Poems ... by Ephelia* (2d ed., 1682)
Courtesy, Huntington Library
Manual cancel in publication date unique to this copy

occasioned by Ephelia's death around this time. As illustrated by an embarrassing gaffe in Alastair Fowler's otherwise commendable *New Oxford Book of Seventeenth-Century Verse* (1991), even senior specialists of 17th-century English poetry are unfamiliar with the interesting textual background of the second edition of Ephelia's book. I, therefore, give the 1682 *Female Poems* special attention in Appendix A of this edition. In Appendix E, I provide a provenance list of the surviving copies of this now highly scarce book. For my annotation on Fowler's representation of Ephelia's work, see page 264 of my Annotated Bibliography.

Manuscript Materials. This edition takes special pleasure in publishing Portland MS PwV 336, preserved at The University of Nottingham Library. This manuscript bears the title "A funerall Elegie on the Death of S. Thomas Isham Barronet" and the subscription "Ephelia." (While some Restoration specialists may not be familiar with the Isham name, scholars of Boswell and Johnson surely will recognize it.) Details touching this manuscript's physical state and provenance appear in Appendix D. Internal evidence and the poem's background of linked families led me to believe that (i) the "Isham" manuscript is an authentic literary manuscript of the later 17th century; and (ii) it is an authentic autograph manuscript written by the same author who wrote *Female Poems ... by Ephelia*. To convenience the modern reader unfamiliar with 17th-century cursive styles, I have supplied in this edition an unedited transcription of the "Isham" manuscript.

I proceeded skeptically with such a dramatic addition to my writer's canon; and I must especially thank Dorothy Johnston and Anthony Upton at Nottingham, as well as Charles Hamilton, a prominent New York City handwriting specialist, for special attentions, as I culled information on the manuscript's provenance, cataloguing data, physical state, formatting, ink, paper, script, and watermark. Contacts with Henry A N Hallam, Honorary Librarian of the celebrated Isham family library at Lamport Hall, Northamptonshire, also were useful in identifying extant family documents, as well as intersecting connections between Ephelia's coterie and that of the Ishams (*v*. Hallam "Lamport Hall Revisited" *Book Collector* Winter 1967). This leg of my researches into family backgrounds and the circle of individuals connected to the subject of this manuscript produced a linkage of staunch Stuart royalists and families: Ephelia-Isham-Villiers-Etherege-Duppa-Verney.

This edition also publishes an 18th-century manuscript pedigree of the Prowde family of Shrewsbury. Genealogical data in this manuscript were central to my hypothesis that Ephelia may well have been related to the Prowde-Phillips-Milton line.

Almost all of the illustrative matter in this edition, because of its original size, had to be reduced to accommodate the 6" x 9" format of this book. These reductions -- Ephelia's broadsides, portraits, manuscripts, Moses Snow's setting of Ephelia's poem "Neglect Returned," coats-of-arms, family pedigrees -- were managed thoughtfully by my publisher, so as not to compromise the legibility and aesthetic properties of these essential primary materials.

Apparatus. The (scholarly) pulse of this edition is its ambitious apparatus. There the reader will observe something of the challenging critical judgments and unanticipated creative opportunities involved in producing a responsible and useful editorial product. The overall goal of the apparatus is to introduce today's readers to a sizeable amount of virtually uncollected and new information on my subject, which I trust is transmitted here in intelligent formats. This edition's apparatus offers six discrete categories of information:

Appendix A, in lieu of a proper descriptive bibliography of Ephelia's canon, is a descriptive list of the writings, noting locations as well as such essential physical features of the writings as format, typography, watermark, chainlines, and, in the case of the "Isham" manuscript, paper quality, and quality of ink transmission. As more information on Ephelia comes to light, as it surely will after this edition begins to circulate, a descriptive bibliography will then be possible.

Appendix B offers speculative additions to Ephelia's canon, being two poems from Thomas D'Uffet's miscellany *New Poems, New Songs* ... (1676). These verses are preceded by a substantial essay, wherein I detail my grounds for adding these two minor verses to my writer's corpus.

Appendix C, a proposed chronological schedule of Ephelia's writings, was an adventuresome, perhaps premature, reconstruction at this early point in researches into my writer. Time will judge. This schematic tasked and tested my critical judgment more so than any other component of this edition. Following John T. Shawcross's "Chronological Schedule" of the poems of John Donne (*Donne* 1967 411-417), this table includes an "Evidence" category for the dates I assign to Ephelia's poems. While the veracity of many of these dates is unassailable, since many are based on recorded publication data or other firm 'markers' throughout Ephelia's work, the certainty of some others is challengeable, as they are adduced from external, circumstantial evidence. Nonetheless, it is my hope that this compilation will provide the preliminary structure for subsequent revised chronologies.

Appendix D identifies extant manuscripts of Ephelia's, being the "Isham" manuscript at Nottingham, mentioned above, and several scribal or scriptorium copies of my poet's signature poem, the popular "*Ephelia's* Lamentation," a virtuosic love-epistle cast in the ovidian mode and addressed to "*Bajazet*," namely John (Sheffield) Lord Mulgrave (1648-1721), whom Ephelia identifies as her first lover. As I explain in a preliminary headnote to this appendix, my list of manuscript copies of this poem is indebted to earlier collations conducted respectively by James Thorpe, David M. Vieth, and Peter Beal. Each of these scholars supports the traditional attribution of the "Lamentation" to Sir George Etherege, a tradition I challenge later in this essay. I am pleased to supplement their collations of this poem with additional information, resulting from my own research.

Appendix E, the first collective provenance record of Ephelia's *Female Poems*, was the most pleasureful component of this edition to prepare for any rare-book collector. My intention here is to show modern readers the longstanding, appreciating value of Ephelia's writings in the antiquarian market. Dating from Rawlinson and Verney in Ephelia's own day, down to Gerald E. Slater in the 1980s, the work of Ephelia claims a distinguished pedigree. Her book of '*female poems*,' only recently recognized by the academic community, has long been prized by collectors for its rarity, its loveliness as a physical artifact of its time, and its uniqueness as a collection of verses from a female perspective. My provenance list also identifies physical evidence in all known surviving copies. Such valuable information sometimes guided my hypotheses and substantiated my arguments. As Roger Stoddard has reminded us, there exists in books a "top layer" of physical evidence, which is readily available when we handle and observe books sensitively (*v. Marks In Books*, exhibition catalogue, Houghton Library, Harvard University 1985).

Of special interest in this section is my identification of Ephelia's book in the libraries of two print collectors, thereby documenting the value of the book's engraved frontispiece portrait in art circles. Given the scarcity of the portrait in surviving copies, it obviously has been coveted over the centuries (*v.* Mulvihill "Feminism and the Rare-Book Market" *Scriblerian* Autumn 1989).

Appendix F is a thematic and generic organization of Ephelia's writings. It was compiled principally for students and teachers of Ephelia, who may be interested in my poet's treatment of various subjects and her performance in a range of genres. Such a breakdown of the writings displays the public character of this highly private writer, as well as the range and versatility of her pen, the worlds she moved in, and her engagement in controversial issues of her day.

This edition concludes with an **Annotated Secondary Bibliography**, organized chronologically so that today's readers can observe the persistent (but mystified) interest in Ephelia over the centuries. This section documents a spectrum of dramatically differing opinion on my poet, offered by academic specialists as well as interested poets and playwrights. The alert reader will notice that my publications on Ephelia centered attention on this poet, resulting in her inclusion in several of the new feminist anthologies and reference books, listed in this section.

Also included in my **Bibliography** are publication data which document Ephelia's relative success as a Restoration song-writer, a facet of her talent completely overlooked by previous 'ephelians.' My searches located listings of 17th- and 18th-century settings of Ephelia's poems in Day and Murrie's *English Song-Books* (1940). My methodology at this point involved

(i) preparing a first-line index of all of Ephelia's known writings to date;

(ii) comparing and cross-referencing my prepared index against Day and Murrie's first-line index; and

(iii) identifying details about selected song-books in the new online *Eighteenth-Century Short-Title Catalogue* (*ECSTC*) (New York University, Bobst Library copy).

This edition includes Moses Snow's setting of one of Ephelia's songs, published by Henry Playford in a popular secular song-book of 1687, *The Theater of Music*. The appearance of her work in a song-book of 1687, and in 18th-century song-books, attests to the currency of her writings after their initial publication in the *Female Poems* of 1679. Based on Snow's setting, and others by Thomas Farmer and William Turner, her songs were single-voice tunes on traditional amatory themes, accompanied by the guitar, the bass viol, or the theorbo lute.

I am especially pleased to document in my **Bibliography** the inclusion of the spectacular engraved frontispiece portrait of Ephelia in an exhibition mounted at The Grolier Club, New York City, in 1895. As the record shows, specialists have made a place for Ephelia in the refined world of antiquarian tastes. With this edition, the scholarly and academic communities have an opportunity to do likewise. In sympathy with Ephelia's *Female Poems*, this book selects for its frontispiece the same portrait she chose for her own book in 1679.

This edition closes with three indexes. The first is an annotated

Index of Names in Ephelia's poems. This list of place names, proper names, and pastoral names serves as a window on my poet's social class, coterie, the field of her experience, and the environments in which she moved. This segregated Names index also will be useful to future researches into Ephelia and other writers of her day. The edition closes with the usual Index of Titles and Index of First Lines.

Cumulatively, these several appendixes, along with my annotated bibliography and indexes, stand on their own merits as a gesture of reclamation. It is hoped that my efforts on Ephelia's behalf will correct the longstanding historical ignorance and indifference which have blemished my writer's reputation and diminished her literary status since the 17th century.

II. Research Methodologies

As the first fruits of this investigation illustrate, the formulations and arguments introduced later in this essay follow from internal, external, and circumstantial evidence. The body of evidence which I came to identify throughout this project resulted from systematic probes into many areas. The information I culled, as well as the hypothesis and arguments I introduce in my discussions below, resulted from several layers of research:

Interdisciplinary Research. While giving priority to the literature of Ephelia's day, with its interesting arcana, curiosa, and many 'fugitive' pieces, my investigations were most productive in several adjacent areas, which became essential in a project of this scale and complexity.

For example, in my analysis of the autograph manuscript at Nottingham, which I attribute to Ephelia, I sought out the opinion and observations of Charles Hamilton, a prominent New York City handwriting specialist. While I was not always in full agreement with what Hamilton saw in the manuscript, I nonetheless appreciated his remarks, and I modified some of my conclusions because of them.

My researches into other areas -- heraldry, genealogy, watermarks -- were all fruitful in various ways. These probes, with accompanying illustrative matter, are discussed over the course of this essay.

Multimedia Research. "The medium is the message," proclaimed communications specialist Marshall McLuhan nearly half a century ago.

His thesis was well served in this project, which exploited several media in a wide search for information. My investigations were multimedia or transmedia to the extent that they went beyond printed books and manuscripts to include relevant sources in the pictorial, electronic, and photographic media (Fig.3).

The portraiture seminar at Yale, mentioned above, as well as my own researches into styles of Stuart female portraiture and frontispiece portraits, allowed me to offer a reasonable reading of the articulate iconography of Ephelia's frontispiece portrait in *Female Poems*. It also led me to Thomas Flatman of Edward Phillips's circle as the possible portraitist, and to Prince Rupert of Lady Mary (Villiers) Stuart's circle as its possible engraver.

A moment of 'quickening' in my researches occurred when a computer scanning of Ephelia's writings, by way of a concordance of her work, set up on WordPerfect 5.1, enabled me to identify multiple instances of "Proud" and its variants. Here were critical data to substantiate my developing hypothesis of Ephelia's connection to the related Phillips-Prowde-Milton line. I had been impressed with the statistical research methodologies employed by Eduard Sievers, Alvar Ellegård, C.S. Brinegar, and Judith Stanton; and with the computer-assisted research of Burrows and Hassall, who had electronically surveyed the writings of Henry and Sarah Fielding (*v. ECS* 21:1988).

Also useful was a demonstration-workshop I attended on the in-progress online *ECSTC*, mentioned above. This workshop was hosted by New York University's Bobst Library in April, 1989, and run by Henry Snyder, David Vander Meulen, and Richard Sher. Computer-assisted research through electronic databases for pre-1700 materials is still a developing area; and, so, this was the least productive avenue of my researches, overall. Nonetheless, I did profit from the *ECSTC* during my searches into secular song-books circulating in London during the early 18th century. This electronic database led me to sources, which included settings of Ephelia's songs. (See my research procedures at this point, outlined on page 15 above.)

Unfortunately, I was unable to submit some of my findings to sophisticated technical analyses. The University of Nottingham Library was (understandably) unwilling to send out its delicate "Isham" manuscript for ink or paper analysis. I had been persuaded to the benefits of such procedures in several interesting essays on beta-radiography and the otoscope in manuscript work, published in the journal *Direction Line*. To compensate for this critical methodological gap, I at least was able to obtain a hand-drawn tracing (facsimile) of the manuscript's watermark from Nottingham's helpful curatorial staff.

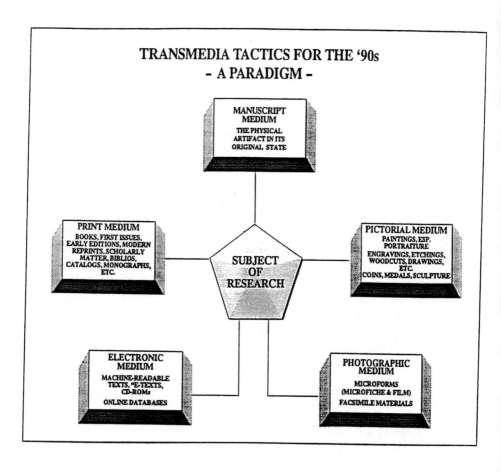

Figure 3. Transmedia Tactics for the '90s: A Multimedia Research Strategy
See Mulvihill, "The Multimedia Research Initiative" (*Studies in 18th-Century Culture* 1992)

CRITICAL ESSAY

My analysis of Ephelia's emblematic frontispiece portrait, which graces both editions of the *Female Poems*, was critically assisted by professional magnification of certain curious details in the portrait, supplied by the photographer Thomas Todd of Taurgo Slides, New York City, and of the Metropolitan Museum Of Art's Slide Library.

Deductive & Inductive Methodologies. A researcher needn't have the strategic genius of a Karl von Clausewitz to successfully manage a large project, but she had better have a systematic and flexible plan of action in place.

A researcher begins with first principles, namely with what already exists. In this case, that meant

(i) scouring my poet's work for names -- place names, proper names, coterie names, publishers, printers, patrons, acknowledged models -- as well as for allusions to her social class and environments;

(ii) examining textual and bibliographical traditions of her work that developed during her own day and beyond;

(iii) assembling available biographical, genealogical, and heraldic information on my subject and her potential kin;

(iv) identifying physical evidence in surviving copies of her writings; and

(v) respecting (mightily) the occasional speculative hunch, the intuitive guess, the wild rumor.

In this fashion, I was able to establish a broad base (or pool) of existing information on my subject, no matter at the outset its total veracity or pertinence. These fragments of information, as well as reliable factual data, served throughout the course of my search as 'markers' or reference points which in turn guided my procedures and formulations. Once this large pool or base of information took shape, the game was afoot.

Throughout 'the Ephelia chase,' I worked chronologically in both directions. I would select a piece of commonly recorded information about Ephelia, say, Wheatley's identification of her in 1885 as Joan Phillips, and then scout backwards with it, to contemporary sources, where I hoped to find references to a Joan or to a female poet "Phillips" (all variant spellings). Or I might take a piece of information from Ephelia's day -- say, the armorial badge in her portrait -- and trace it forward, into selected 18th-, 19th-, and 20th-century heraldic sources, most helpfully *Papworth's Ordinary of British Armorials* (1961). Then, with a short-list of targeted families in mind, I could begin scouring family pedigrees (ideally, in their manuscript state) for likely candidates.

Pictorial Research. Throughout this book, the reader observes my emphasis on the visual image as an essential adjunct to literary research. This edition includes both published and hand-traced facsimile sketches of 17th-century watermarks; original paintings of three coats-of-arms (Tilly, Phillips, Prowde), which I commissioned from heraldic painters in England; and photographs of selected portraits. All such pictorial matter became integral to my arguments.

With special pleasure, I include in this edition, with the gracious permission of Dr William C. Barnett, an American art collector, a photograph of Van Dyck's portrait of Lady Mary Villiers, Ephelia's patroness, which was painted about 1636 (Fig. 4, page 32). Locating this portrait, and then Samuel J. Hardman's published work on Van Dyck's portraits of Lady Mary, were memorable moments in this project. Heretofore, Ephelia's patroness has been identified rather vaguely, as one "Mary Stuart," when in fact she was the daughter of George Villiers 1st duke of Buckingham, and had married into three prestigious lines -- Herbert, Stuart, and Howard. While she retained her title of Duchess of Richmond and Lennox after the death of her second husband James Stuart (a first cousin of Charles I's), she was the widow of a Howard when she sponsored Ephelia's *Female Poems* in 1679. As demonstrated below, all of the illustrative matter in this edition involved specialized research, which consisted of consultation with specialists, background reading, and specific training.

Consider, for example, the bountiful research possibilities suggested by the dominant (red) cross of the Tilly coat-of-arms in the frontispiece portrait of Ephelia in *Female Poems*: Did it in fact relate to the Tilly line or to its cadet branches, Mowbray (later Howard) and Russell? Was it a Rosicrucian allusion? Might it refer to Madam Le Croix, the famous London fortuneteller? Might it suggest Adam Hare's bookshop in Red Cross Street? Could it refer to John Tilly, Deputy Warden of Fleet Prison? Was it a reference to the cross *flory* (*fleury*) on those broadsides which listed plague victims in 1665 (one of these, printed by Thomas Milbourn in Jewen Street, is preserved at The Guildhall Library)? And why is the coat displayed in a roundel, rather than on the conventional shield? And why is the roundel encircled with laurels? As researchers can appreciate, a level of familiarity with specialized adjacent fields, such as heraldry, genealogy, and emblemology, was critical, lest time be wasted in unfocused research.

———

Omissions are inevitable in a project of any complexity and originality. In this case, because of understandable space constraints, my extensive list of sources consulted and my endnotes on individual poems could not be included. Yet, these omissions should not be problematic in light of the extent of information offered throughout the front and back matter of this book.

As researchers know, there is a large body of primary materials at the major British libraries which has yet to be identified and catalogued. In due course, these manuscripts and documents will become available, and will shed further light on my subject. While I investigated a fair amount of contemporary sources, as this essay illustrates, I could not survey virtually all of the identified papers to date of Mulgrave, Etherege, and Colonel Thomas Howard; nor did I locate incontrovertible, hard evidence for some of my formulations. Nonetheless, I am reasonably satisfied with the overall results of my venture on two principal grounds. Above all, I found a forward-looking spirit in publisher Norman Mangouni, whose press, more so than most of the prestigious university presses, has done much to bring back into circulation the 'lost' writings of the early modern period. Over time, the editions he has published will gain in value. Moreover, I am satisfied that my diversified research methodologies were successful to the extent that they uncovered fresh information on Ephelia's life, work, and sponsorship. May such findings walk my writer out of the shadows of a long, oppressive obscurity.

*E*PHELIA IN HER CONTEMPORARY SETTING

Few pens remained still before such a tableau. When the young Ephelia made the decision to set up as a writer in London in the mid-1670s, she must have been struck by the volatile temper of the times. On the political front, the Monarchy and its subjects were stirred by the hysteria of the Popish Plot controversy. Government and the populace were further agitated by the Exclusion Crisis, which tested loyalties and fractured an entire nation. As Ephelia's celebrated contemporary Aphra Behn wrote:

> The World ran mad, and each distemper'd Brain,
> Did strange and different Frenzies entertain.
> Here Politick mischiefs, there Ambition swayed;
> The credulous Rest, were Fools and coward-mad.

CRITICAL ESSAY

The mood in the literary sphere was no less exuberant. The Restoration saw the rise of the professional writer, with John Dryden distinguishing himself as England's first great professional man of letters. The principal producers of literature at this time were mostly university-trained men of good lineage, broad contacts, and wide experience. In the main, their work was a distinctly "masculine" literature, dominated by strong loyalist poems on the Stuart monarchy, bawdry, biting satire, and brisk plays of sexual intrigue. It was "a lubrique and adult'rate Age," with a "venal Court" at the center, wrote Dryden. His chief adversary, the glamorous Court Wit, John (Wilmot) 2d Earl of Rochester, one of the best poets of the Restoration, wrote of the day's manners and verse: "My Lady she / Complain'd our Love was coarse, our Poetry / Unfit for modest ears." While professional writers, even of Dryden's elevated status, complained of low royalties, unpaid commissions, and the occasional "hack" piece that booksellers could readily vend to a rising market culture, no writer wanted for a subject to take the public taste.

During these vigorous years, Ephelia also would have observed something unprecedented in English cultural history: the rise of women in the literary and theatrical professions. With the re-opening of the theaters in 1660, English women of talent and ambition were given the first opportunity to penetrate the male stronghold of playwriting and authorship. A small group of courageous entrants tested their mettle before essentially three 'tribes' of male detractors: the "Criticks"; the "grave Gown-Men" of the universities; and professional male writers. Not surprisingly, this new breed of writer was promptly jeered and ridiculed as undomesticated slatterns, plagiarists, and hack-writers (v. Rochester "Artemisa to Cloe" Poems 1680; Robert Gould Satyrical Epistle 1691). The women responded sharply to such attacks in the prologues and epilogues of their plays. They engaged the enemy with humor, wit, and grace. Before Ephelia's amateur play "The Pair-Royal of Coxcombs" was mounted, probably in the mid-1670s, she doubtless was inspired by the example of several female contemporaries in drama who braved this hostile climate, such as Elizabeth Polwhele, Frances Boothby, Katherine Philips, and especially Aphra Behn, evidently a model of Ephelia's and, later, a collaborator. The pioneering efforts of these first professional English women writers carried cumulative historical force, and their achievement was singular: they laid the foundation for women in the professional theater throughout the English-speaking world (v. Mulvihill "A Feminist Link in the Old Boys' Network: The Cosseting of Katherine Philips" Curtain Calls eds. Schofield and Macheski 1991).

CRITICAL ESSAY

Complementing the efforts of English women on the London Stage were a number of feminist polemicists, such as Margaret (Cavendish) Duchess of Newcastle, Bathsua Makin, the little-known Clement Barksdale, Margaret Fox, Mary Astell, and Judith Drake. This militant group produced programmatic essays and tracts on the inequities to women of English institutions, particularly education, law, and marriage. Their admirable efforts gave intellectual muscle to the more sensationalistic image of public English feminism at this time. The never uninteresting Duchess of Newcastle who, preceding Mary Wollstonecraft in the 1790s, outlined the most "fundamentally radical assessment of institutional oppression of Englishwomen" (*v.* Kathleen Jones *Glorious Fame* 1988), wrote and published an amazing public letter to the faculties of Cambridge and Oxford, protesting that "We [women] are Shut out of all Power and Authority, never Imployed in Civil Affairs, and our Counsels Despised and Laught at by the Over-weening Conceit Men have of themselves" (*v.* Cavendish *Opinions* 1655).

Models for many of these early feminist tracts and pamphlets were to be found in the rational discourse of contemporary Dutch and French writers, such as the prodigy Anna Maria van Schurman, Poulain de la Barre, and the little-known Jacquette Guillaume, whose work circulated in English literary circles (*v.* Mulvihill "Van Schurman" *Dictionary* ed. Janet Todd 1987; Gerald MacLean *La Barre* 1988; Mulvihill "Guillaume" *Encyclopedia of Continental Women Writers* ed. K M Wilson 1991; Erica Harth *Cartesian Women* 1992).

While no one believes that these writers constituted an organized battalion of feminists, storming the patriarchal citadels with their manuscripts, one must appreciate the historical repercussions of the work they produced. Because of its sheer force, reasonableness, and contribution to the growth of a political feminism, these writings pointed the way for bolder pronouncements in the 18th-century by Mary Wollstonecraft and Anne Laetitia Barbould. Their writings, in combination with many cultural and economic factors of the time, led to a mobilization for feminist and social reform in the following century. When Cambridge University opened its gates to women in 1869 with the founding of Girton College, one of the earliest of women's colleges, the roots of such a victory are to be found in the writings of Margaret Cavendish, Bathsua Makin, Aphra Behn, Mary Astell, and certain male feminists, who deserve more of our attention.

Against such a background of agitation and deep cultural change, a young gentlewoman, new to town, was quietly producing a small body of literature: love poems, prologues and epilogues, songs, and occasional pieces. Her strong political broadsides to the Stuarts would come later, after she came to the attention of influential individuals at Court. She joined the ranks of this small literary underclass of aspiring women writers, calling herself only Ephelia. Her beat, as an urban newcomer, may have been the seedy district of Saffron Hill, where she would have met her future publisher John Courtney (Courtenay). For a time, he may have employed her at his shop, The Golden Horse Shoe, just as the publisher Joseph Johnson would later employ Mary Wollstonecraft at No. 72 in the northside of St Paul's Churchyard. After this brief interval, according to my speculative reconstruction, Ephelia's literary apprenticeship may have begun in Chelsea in the mid-1670s, at the new boarding-school for gentlewomen and theatrical ingénues, run by James Hart and Jeffrey Banister (v. Appendix B). Perhaps it was there that Ephelia received the "loud Applauses" she mentions in her telling poem "To A Proud Beauty." In due course, her networks broadened. By 1674/5, she attracted wide notice with a striking lyric on a failed love affair with an eminent man of letters. So popular was this poem that it inspired an answer-poem from Charles II's most amiable libertine and Court Wit. By 1678, this entrant had secured a patroness and reached print. She was now writing to a public, and had become a young player in the literary market.

The Writings & Coterie of Ephelia

My poet's career in London began in the mid-1670s and evidently concluded after August, 1681. Because of the existence of a manuscript version of "Ephelia's Lamentation" in the miscellany "Wit & Learning ... 1677" (Osborn b54: ff. 1180-1 Beinecke Library), we know that Ephelia was active on the literary scene before she published her first broadside in 1678. Biographical allusions to Lord Mulgrave's career in the "Lamentation" date that poem and Ephelia's affair with him to about 1674/5. Two pieces in D'Uffet's New Poems ... (1676), which may be her work, also date her apprenticeship to that time (v. Appendixes B, C). Her principal work was the lovely 112-page octavo Female Poems on Several Occasions. Written by Ephelia, Easter-term 1679. Two years later, she published a broadside against Monmouth. We hear no more from Ephelia after she penned an unpublished funeral elegy on Sir Thomas Isham, who was buried at Northhamptonshire in August, 1681.

As sections of Appendixes A and B in this edition document, Ephelia's published work positions her primarily as a poet, whose material was inspired by personal circumstance, political controversy, and rising feminist belief. But it is entirely likely that she began as a hired 'female Pen,' specializing in prologues, epilogues, and songs for the active theater circuit. These were uncomplicated forms a young literary amateur could dash off; they also were vendible in the hands of enterprising booksellers and compilers of miscellanies. Certainly throughout her work, especially in her better poems, Ephelia writes in the style of a dramatist, with a decidedly aural accent and immediacy. Writing for the ear, she effectively mimics the sound and tempo of living speech, with its uneven cadences and sudden starts and stops. Her style is typically direct and disruptive, and she almost always writes in the first or second person. Ephelia confronts her subjects, as an actor in a critical scene. David Trotter, in his book on the poems of Cowley, one of Ephelia's acknowledged models, calls such an ethos "locutionary truth" (*Cowley* 1979). Here are five excerpts from Ephelia's *Female Poems*, which display the aural accent of her work, as well as the several modes and styles her pen enjoyed:

> YOu wrong me *Strephon*, when you say
> Ime Jealous or Severe,
> Did I not see you Kiss and Play
> With all you came a neer?

> In him I center'd all my hopes of Bliss;
> For him I lost --- alas! what lost I not?
> Fame, all the Valuable Things of Life,
> To meet his Love by a less Name than Wife

> COceited Coxcomb! tho' I was so kind
> To wish to see you, think not I design'd
> To force my self to your unwilling Arms,
> Your Conversation holds no such Charms:

> OH cruel Fate, when wilt thou weary be?
> When satisfied with tormenting me?
> What have I e're design'd, but thou hast crost?
> All that I wisht to gain by Thee, I've lost:

> With joy [Sheldon] suffer'd for the Church and State,
> And bore with ease the weightiest stroaks of Fate.
> Stop! stop a while! fierce Rapture choaks my words.
> And no expression to my Thought affords.

25

CRITICAL ESSAY

No dispassionate witness to her life and times, Ephelia is the least nuanced of early English women writers. Her poems are rousing and full of commotion: she scolds, advises, confronts, interrogates, laments, and declaims. Autobiographical disclosures are not infrequent in Ephelia's verse; in fact, she is a skilled self-portraitist. While her amorous lyrics generously illustrate her talent in this vein, some of her coterie verse contains valuable biographical fragments. In an amusing poem to a female contemporary, "To a Proud Beauty," probably Barbara (Villiers) Lady Castlemaine, one of Ephelia's patroness's least favorite relatives (*v.* Pepys *Diary* 21 April 1662), Ephelia tells this "stately Piece of Vanity" that she herself has achieved "Fame," and that she has received "loud Applauses" for "a fine Face," "things that Nature gave," a "gen'rous Mind," and "pleasing Converse." Ephelia's claim to celebrity may refer to her apprenticeship years in Chelsea or, more likely, to the popularity of her best love-poem, "*Ephelia's* Lamentation," which began circulating in manuscript during the mid-1670s (*v.* Appendixes C, D). Other references to Ephelia's contemporary popularity and beauty exist in her poem "To my Rival," wherein she calls herself "a Prize." These casual remarks are useful for the insights they offer into Ephelia's temperament and literary status; they also lend veracity to the riveting image of Ephelia in the frontispiece of her *Female Poems*.

Robert Gould, a near-contemporary of Ephelia's, whose career in playwrighting and poetry was assured through the sponsorship of James (Bertie), Earl of Abingdon, and poets John Oldham and John Dryden, offers a wholly different view of Ephelia, which may combine the sore financial straits of her apprenticeship with the desperation of her declining years when she evidently lost her patroness, but gained a sometime-collaborator in Behn. In his *Satyrical Epistle*, published in 1691, though doubtless circulating much earlier in manuscript, Gould describes Ephelia as a "ragged" "Hackney [*i.e.* "hired"] Writer"; he also links her to Behn. In his unsavory lines, Gould portrays Ephelia and Behn as a literary team, who had once "Answer'd [him] in a more decent Style." This reference attractively suggests their collaborative authorship of *Sylvia's Revenge*, the most popular feminist answer-poem of the 17th century, which was precipitated by Gould's misogynistic *Love Given Over*. Gould's lengthy attack evidently circulated in manuscript a few years before its publication in 1683. *Sylvia's Revenge*, which did not reach print until 1688, though also circulating in manuscript well before that time, was published without ascription; yet, it includes a preface, signed "*M.P.*," which may stand for "Mrs Phillips" or "Mrs Prowde," identifications of Ephelia discussed later in this essay.

In his gritty sketch of Ephelia and Behn, Gould provides

striking details of their everyday life, which ring true. He depicts them as a sororal team from the London street culture, reduced to working the literary fringe for commissions, food, and drink. Gould could draw off a good scene as economically as, say, Ravenscroft:

> *Ephelia*! poor *Ephelia*, ragged Jilt!
> And *Sappho* [Behn], famous for her gout and gilt.
> Either of these, tho' both debauch'd and Vile,
> Had answer'd Me in a more Decent Style:
> Yet *Hackney Writers*; when their Verse did Fail
> To get 'em Brandy, Bread and Cheese, and Ale,
> Their Wants by Prostitution were suppl'd;
> Shew but a Tester, you might up and ride:
> For Punk and Poetess agree so Pat,
> You cannot well be this, and not be That.

Its distracting misogyny aside -- more modish than sincere, as Gould's circle included Anne Wharton and Sarah Gilly, both young amateur poets -- I give special weight to this outburst from Gould's splenetic pen. As my researches proceeded, I began to perceive this passage as an objective center in a project dominated by conflicting signs -- and so should other researchers on this subject. The intimacy of Gould's report, with its vivid details, seems persuasively truthful. If his sketch is sound, and I expect it is, as (i) Gould harbored no recorded animus toward Behn nor Ephelia, and (ii) many pro-Stuart writers, certainly Behn, were in fact quite "ragged" during the decline of Stuart power in the 1680s, Ephelia's employment as a hired hack-writer at the beginning and end of a brief career explains her facility with several genres and subjects, identified in Appendix F.

A companion piece to Gould's lines exists in a little-known manuscript poem, preserved in the British Library (B.L. Harleian MS 6913 folios 251-3) [c.1670-80], and conveniently available in Angeline Goreau's *Whole Duty Of A Woman* (1985). This interesting poem is principally a moral attack on a bawdy "Famous Poetress." The details in this poem intrigue me. They state that this "Poetress" had "an elder sister," who "fairly stuck to One [lover]." This poem may be a direct reference to Ephelia as "the Poetress," to Behn as "the elder [literary] Sister," and to Behn's principal lover John Hoyle as the "One" whom Behn "fairly stuck to." If such a reading is even remotely correct, this manuscript poem on the "Famous Poetress" strengthens my case for a contemporary perception of Behn and Ephelia as paired literary associates -- perhaps more.

We now turn to selections from Ephelia's "female Pen."

CRITICAL ESSAY

A POEM TO HIS SACRED MAJESTY, ON THE PLOT. WRITTEN BY A GENTLEWOMAN (1678). Ephelia's first publication must have been a sensitive and cautious affair. This much-overlooked poem on a major subject of the 1670s is remarkable on several grounds, beginning with its loyalty to the Stuarts and its author's direct engagement in the public sphere.

A handsomely produced broadside of 50 lines, Ephelia's inaugural publication is addressed to Charles II on one of the most volatile subjects of the later-17th century, the so-called Popish Plot controversy. The fact that this poem is written to the King and, moreover, licensed by the royal licensor of the press Sir Roger L'Estrange, whose name appears at the foot of the broadside, attests to its authenticity as a bona fide publication of its time and its sponsorship by influential, guiding hands.

Interestingly, this is the only known published work of Ephelia's to date which she did *not* sign. She identifies herself, nonetheless, in the poem's title as "*A Gentlewoman.*" This description is a disclosure of sorts, as it supplies a degree of information on the author's sex, social class, and education. Ephelia's claim to gentility in the title of her first publication is important because it establishes at the outset of her career the stance of personal privilege and entitlement which is so characteristic of her work. As Ephelia's by-line, choice of subject, and addressee in this particular broadside all suggest, she was no stranger at the gate.

Far from being a surreptitious publication, Ephelia's first printed piece entered the public domain through the capable hands of Henry Brome, an appropriate choice. Brome, a successful bookseller at the Gun in St Paul's Churchyard, had cornered the market as a royalist bookseller-publisher. His stock was predictably strong in anti-papal literature (*v. Stationers' Register 1640-78*, pp.87-93; 20 Oct.1679f). Joanna Brome, his wife and collaborator at the Gun, published Gould's *Presbytery* in 1683; and we know from my discussion thus far that a clear link exists between Gould and Ephelia. It interests me that the text of Ephelia's broadside is set entirely in italic type, an intriguing feature of the poem addressed below.

This poem, written "By a Gentlewoman" and published by Henry Brome in 1678, is most certainly Ephelia's work. She makes her claim to it when she publishes this broadside in a slightly revised state a year later in her small octavo, *Female Poems On several Occasions. Written by Ephelia* (1679), a title which emphasizes her pride of authorship and her proprietary claim to all of the poems in this book.

Ephelia's broadside to Charles Stuart on the Plot takes its contours, occasional phrasing, and royalist line from one of her four models, identified in *Female Poems*: John Dryden, the preeminent political writer of the 17th century and a skilled Stuart propagandist. By 1678, the year of Ephelia's broadside, Dryden had published two lengthy loyal poems: *Astraea Redux* (1660), on the restoration of the Stuarts and the English monarchy; and *Annus Mirabilis* (1666), an historical poem on the Second Dutch War and the Great Fire of London. In both poems, Dryden works in the allusive mode which characterizes the political writings of this future poet-laureate and historiographer-royal. In both poems, Dryden typically positions his subject against the larger background of Classical history, while animating the poem's foreground with contemporary historical details. Dryden also presents the newly restored Stuart monarch as an heroic figure of civic harmony and justice.

Ephelia selectively adapts Dryden's treatment. She follows his royalist line by depicting Charles as the great preserver of the commonweal in the face of pervasive national paranoia and hysteria. But typical of her poetic management of serious affairs of state, Ephelia personalizes her subject. In this case, she addresses Charles directly, in the second person. Where Dryden's subject is a commanding, but remote, figure of heroic scale, Ephelia's is a man with a "Self," "Soul," "Sufferings" "effects of Fate," and personal qualities of justice and prudence. And while Dryden's couplet-art is predictably elevated and oratorical to support the grand stature of his subject, Ephelia's is intimate and personal, almost conversational by contrast (*v.* Piper *The Heroic Couplet* 1969).

Sentiment, always a feature of Ephelia's poetic strain, is brought into her paean to Charles when she attempts to comfort the disturbed King. Ephelia reassures him of his continuing authority by emphasizing the love and loyalty he inspires in his subjects. Her point of view in this piece is tactically correct; for by November 1678, the date of Ephelia's broadside, Titus Oates, the architect of the Popish Plot, had disclosed his fabricated 'Plot' to Sir Edmund Berry Godfrey and other legal authorities in London. Ephelia's modification of Dryden's heroic ethos produces a sentimental and softer treatment of an already overcharged subject.

Touching the poem's structure and development, Ephelia begins the poem with the observation, "So many Virtues crowd Your [Charles's] Breast...We...almost question your Humanity." The poem then moves forward with instances of her subject's humanity. Ephelia makes of Dryden's oversized heroic King a credible human being.

CRITICAL ESSAY

So important was this first published poem to Ephelia that she publishes it again, in a slightly altered state a year later, in her book of *'female poems.'* The significant substantive variant which distinguishes these two surviving texts of Ephelia's Popish Plot poem is discussed below.

FEMALE POEMS ON SEVERAL OCCASIONS. WRITTEN BY EPHELIA (1679). One of the rarest and most elegantly produced books of the Restoration, the *Female Poems* is Ephelia's principal work. It also is a unique book in many ways. Its curious title calls attention to the fact that of the many poetic miscellanies of the later-Carolean period entitled *Poems On Several Occasions*, by Rochester, Katherine Philips, Aphra Behn, and others, Ephelia's adopts a distinctively 'female' perspective. While some 20 of the 65 poems in this collection reconstruct Ephelia's tormented four-year love-affair with a certain "J.G.," her book is a nicely balanced collection. In addition to many amorous lyrics, it includes acrostics, elegies, an epistle-dedicatory, a long verse-essay on the obsessions of wealth, dramatic verse, many songs, and delightful poems on manners and deportment between the sexes (*v.* Appendix F). The first issue of this book in 1679 sold for 1*s.* (bound) (*v.* Arber *Term Catalogue* I:350). In 1982, at the sale of the Gerald E. Slater library at Christie's, New York, the Slater copy of Ephelia's book fetched $1800 from Jonathan Hill, a New York City bookseller, who then sold the Slater *Ephelia* to the Clark Library at the University of California at Los Angeles. For details on the rarity of Ephelia's *Female Poems*, see Appendix E in the back matter of this edition, wherein I record the various owners of this book, from Rawlinson and Verney down to Chew, Huth, Huntington, and Slater.

Touching the sequence of verses in Ephelia's collection, her book reflects neither a chronological nor thematic organization. The poems follow no particular order, although her first two poems, to Charles II and to Archbishop Gilbert Sheldon, represent relatively recent work of the later 1670s; and several of the closing poems, such as the *"Bajazet"* and "To Madam G." (probably Nell Gwyn, as the manuscript note in the Verney copy in this edition suggests), are probably earlier efforts. The indiscriminate sequence of verses may have been a strategy of Ephelia's to further obfuscate her identity, since this apparently capricious sequence of verses makes it difficult to reconstruct the precise years of her movements in London on the basis of internal evidence. Nonetheless, I have worked out a tentative chronological schedule of her writings in Appendix C.

The Epistle-Dedicatory. The dedicatee of Ephelia's book is the powerful Lady Mary (Villiers) Stuart, Dowager Duchess of Richmond and Lennox (1622-1685) (Fig.4). When she sponsored Ephelia's *Female Poems* in 1679, Lady Mary was aged 57 years, and had recently lost her third husband, Colonel Thomas Howard of the Catholic Howard line.

A member of Queen Henrietta Maria's inner circle and, later, Lady of the Bedchamber to Catherine of Braganza in 1662, Lady Mary was the sole daughter of the powerful George Villiers 1st Duke of Buckingham, and the elder sister of the Court Wit, George Villiers 2^{d} Duke of Buckingham. After the assassination of her father in 1628 and the subsequent remarriage of her mother, the young Lady Mary Villiers was taken in by Charles I, and raised in the royal nursery as a ward of the Court. As documented in Samuel J. Hardman's beautifully produced monograph, *Sir Anthony Van Dyck's Portraits of Lady Mary Villiers* (1976), her interesting life included marriages into three impressive lines: Her first husband was Charles (Herbert), 5th Earl of Pembroke, who died in 1636. When she married, in 1637, James Stuart 4th Duke of Lennox, later Duke of Richmond, a direct kinsman (cousin) of Charles I, she was given away by the King with a portion of 20,000*l*. Lady Mary retained her title of Duchess of Richmond and Lennox until her death. It is with respect for her patroness's most senior rank in the nobility, as well as her relation to the royal Stuarts, that Ephelia identifies Lady Mary in the dedication of *Female Poems* as "the Most Excellent PRINCESS MARY." After James Stuart died in the Civil Wars in 1655, Lady Mary wed Colonel Thomas ("Northern Tom") Howard in 1664. He died in 1678. According to Robert Harley, Lady Mary died a Catholic (Portland MS III:391; see also Henry Howard, *Howard Family* 1834).

It interests me that both Lady Mary and her *protégée* suffered the loss of parents. It is commonly documented that Lady Mary was raised in the royal nursery; and Ephelia mentions the loss of both parents in her important autobiographical poem "My Fate." This circumstance may have been an early point of connection between these two intriguing figures.

Ephelia's 45-line dedication to Lady Mary is not written in prose, but in heroic couplets, my poet's characteristic measure. One of the best pieces in the *Female Poems*, the epistle-dedicatory is a nicely written, finished piece, whose beginning lines illustrate the four-line unit in Restoration couplet practice; later in the poem, it displays the 11- and 12-syllable longer line. Eager to establish authorship throughout her poetic collection, Ephelia publishes her dedication as a signed poem. After the last line of verse, we observe the printed subscription *"Ephelia"* set in italic type. While her dedication to Lady Mary bears the conventional features of the contemporary dedication --

Figure 4. *Lady Mary Villiers, Duchess of Richmond & Lennox* (1622-1685)
Dedicatee of *Female Poems ... by Ephelia* (1679, 1682)
By Sir Anthony Van Dyck, *c.* 1636
Courtesy, Barnett Collection

effusive gratitude for the patron's "protection," the author's self-effacing humility, *etc.* -- it is particularized by several references to Lady Mary's biography. As in her broadside to Charles II in 1678, Ephelia personalizes her subject by alluding to some of the crises in Lady Mary's life: the assassination of her father, the death of her second husband James Stuart during the Civil Wars, and the recent arrest of her relative William Howard, 1st Viscount Stafford during the Popish Plot hysteria (he would be executed the following year). Far too painful for Ephelia to mention is Lady Mary's two recent losses: the death of her third husband, Col. Thomas Howard (d.1678), and the death of her only daughter, by James Stuart, Lady Mary (Stuart), Countess of Arran, who died in 1668 at Chapelizod (*v.* Burghclere *Ormonde* 1912 II:97). In view of the mutual personal losses of patroness and protégée, this may have been a sort of surrogate mother-daughter relationship.

My poet may have come to her patroness's attention through Lady Mary's younger brother, George Villiers ("Buckingham"), a prominent poet-playwright and Court Wit with broad connections. He may have heard of Ephelia's work in the mid-1670s, resulting from her affair with Mulgrave and the popular poem that marked that affair, "*Ephelia's* Lamentation." Acting as Ephelia's literary agent and conduit, Buckingham's sister, Lady Mary (Villiers) Stuart, probably coordinated the licensing and publication of Ephelia's first published poem, the broadside to Charles II on the Plot (1678). She may have advised the young writer not to disclose the pseudonym she had been using as early as "*Ephelia's* Lamentation" until she had first cultivated a small following and a receptive climate for more of her work. The fact that the text of Ephelia's broadside to Charles II in 1678 and her epistle-dedicatory to Lady Mary are both set in italic type may be more than coincidental. The similar typography of both poems may have been a strategy to identify Ephelia as the author of the earlier poem, which was published anonymously ("*By a Gentlewoman*") in its first state.

A telling link between Ephelia and her patroness exists in the similarity between the pseudonym "Ephelia" and the coterie name of Ephelia's patroness, "Eugenia" (etymologically "high-born"): both are four-syllable coterie names, beginning with "E." The links between writer and patroness are attractive. Ephelia could have been a ward of Lady Mary's at some point, or even an illegitimate child of her patroness's or of one of Lady Mary's female kin in the Villiers, Herbert, Stuart, and Howard lines. Such a connection would place Ephelia at the Court. The wording of one of her poetic titles, "*To A Gentleman, that durst not pass the door while I stood there,*" suggests a designated post of Ephelia's at Court. Yet, no one resembling Ephelia, such as an attendant named Proud or Phillips (all variant spellings), is mentioned in Strickland (*Lives* 1902), Somerset (*Ladies-in-Waiting* 1984), or contemporary sources, such as Lady Mary's few surviving papers preserved in West Sussex (Goodwood Collection), which fail to mention a young female writer who might have been Ephelia. Many personal papers of Lady Mary's reportedly went down with a baggage ship in the late 1640s (*v.* Hamilton *Henrietta Maria* 1976 187). In any case, Ephelia's identity, if it is ever to be known for certain, rests with Lady Mary: She is the strongest link.

The most interesting of Ephelia's three poems to Lady Mary in *Female Poems* is "To the Angry *Eugenia*." In this piece, Ephelia mentions a breach in their relationship. Evidently, Ephelia had carelessly identified her patroness before a "Crowd." While one can only speculate as to the meaning behind this information, it suggests that Ephelia had inappropriately alluded to her sponsor at some official ceremony or public gathering, perhaps a small court production of a play, whose prologue or epilogue Ephelia may have written or delivered. In any case, sometime after 1681, Ephelia evidently lost her patroness. Had she enjoyed a brief stay at Court, Ephelia's preferment was short-lived due to some misunderstanding or breach in protocols involving Lady Mary. Interestingly, we hear no more from Ephelia after 1681. Without Lady Mary's 'protection,' my poet was at the mercy of her publisher James Courtney at the Golden Horse Shoe in Saffron Hill, who published an unauthorized and enlarged second edition of her book in 1682. It is my belief that this reissue was most probably occasioned by my poet's death around this time (*v.* Appendix A). Gould's lines, cited above (p. 27), suggest that toward the end of Ephelia's brief career, *c.* early 1680s, she, as Behn, had fallen into sore financial straits, and provided Gould the unsavory details he seized upon in his *Satyrical Epistle*.

A POEM Presented to His Sacred Majesty, On the Discovery of the PLOT. Following the Epistle-Dedicatory in *Female Poems*, we are given two poems on affairs of state which merit special attention, beginning with the collection's inaugural piece, "A POEM Presented to His Sacred Majesty, On the Discovery of the PLOT."

Evidently, when this poem was originally published as a broadside in 1678, discussed above (pages 28-30), it was so well received at Court that a slightly altered version of the poem was presented to the King in 1679, to mark its second appearance in Ephelia's *Female Poems* (1679). The text of Ephelia's Popish Plot poem of 1679 exists in a slightly altered second state from its first printed appearance in the 1678 broadside. In addition to some 12 stylistic variants, the major substantive variant is the addition of a significant verb in the title, "*Presented*." (The other new word in the title, "*Discovery*," should have been part of the original title in 1678, since Titus Oates swore to the truth of his newly discovered "Plot" in June, 1678, before magistrate Sir Edmund Berry Godfrey. The "Plot" had been 'discovered' a full five months before Ephelia published her broadside in November, 1678. "*Discovery*" in the title of the 1679 version of the poem, therefore, represents a desirable refinement of the 1678 title, and nothing more.)

It is unlikely that Ephelia herself would have personally given the King a presentation copy of this particular poem; but this action would not have been inappropriate for a kin of the Stuarts, such as Ephelia's patroness Lady Mary (Villiers) Stuart.

The Elegy to Sheldon. Ephelia's panegyric to Charles II in *Female Poems* is followed by another poem on a serious political subject, the death of Gilbert Sheldon, the Archbishop of Canterbury, one of the chief architects of the Restoration. David Loggan's portrait of Sheldon literally depicts him as Charles II's right-hand man (*v.* Staley *Sheldon* 1913 112).

Ephelia's elegy on Sheldon's death was written earlier than its printed appearance in *Female Poems* in 1679; it would have been composed in 1677, the commonly recorded year of Sheldon's death. The poem merits our attention on several grounds. First, Ephelia emphasizes Sheldon's celebrated munificence (amounting to a recorded 72,000*l.* in charities [*DNB*]). Moreover, she describes his bereft congregation with the appropriate image of the abandoned orphan. This is pertinent, as Ephelia identifies herself as an orphan in "My Fate." Sheldon's generosity, according to his biographer Staley, extended to orphans and writers (*v. Sheldon* 208-9, 213, *passim*). In light of this background, perhaps Ephelia was materially assisted by Sheldon after the death of her parents, which my speculative reconstruction dates to the mid-1660s, judging from the probable timeframe of Ephelia's apprenticeship in Saffron Hill and later Chelsea in the early 1670s, shortly before she fell into the quick hands of Lord Mulgrave.

My supposition of personal ties between Sheldon and Ephelia gained credibility during biographical researches into Ephelia's concealed identity. This leg of the search began with H B Wheatley's identification of her in 1885 as one Joan Phillips. As my searches uncovered, Wheatley's "Joan Phillips" was corroborated by contemporary allusions from Behn, Manley, and Newcomb, identified above (pages 6-7). As discussed below, over the course of this investigation I surveyed selected literary English Phillips families. The John Milton-Edward Phillips line naturally beckoned. An examination of several pedigrees of this related line identified the Prowde family of Shrewsbury as in-laws of the Phillipses.

This discovery of a Phillips-Prowde connection lined up with earlier information I had culled. In *The Roxburghe Ballads*, for example, I found that Joseph Woodfall Ebsworth had contributed the invaluable information that "One of Mulgrave's mistresses was 'humble Joan'," which I read ironically as "proud Joan" or "Joan Proud" (1883 IV:568). Ebsworth's 'clue' then intersected with another earlier find, namely the identification of one "Euphelia," in the published *Key* to Manley's novel *Atalantis* (1714), as a "Miss Proud." Integrating these fragments was pivotal information I found in 17th-century legal documents on the related Prowde-Phillips families, preserved at Shrewsbury; these primary materials identified none other than Gilbert Sheldon, Archbishop of Canterbury, as a legal witness to some property transactions involving the Prowde and Phillips families (Shrewsbury Public Library document 567, 2F 2-3; document 1230). Moreover, information in Staley's *Sheldon* further connected the Archbishop to Shrewsbury: (i) Shrewsbury had been a sanctuary for royalists during the Civil Wars; and (ii) Sheldon's father had been employed by Gilbert earl of Shrewsbury, after whom this future Archbishop of Canterbury was named.

Here, then, was a plausible personal background behind Ephelia's impassioned elegy to Sheldon. This background also lent weight to my developing hypothesis of Ephelia as one of the Shrewsbury Prowdes, taken up later in this essay.

The elegy to Sheldon is also important for its display of one of Ephelia's characteristic poetic effects: the momentary muteness of the poet before overwhelming emotion. Such an inarticulate moment in the Sheldon elegy appears in the fifth excerpt from Ephelia's verse quoted at the beginning of this section (page 25). This sentimental device also appears on two other occasions in Ephelia's verse, in *"Ephelia's* Lamentation," taken up at length below, and in her elegy to Sir Thomas Isham, examined closely at the end of this essay.

The J.G. Poems. Ephelia's 20-odd verses to or about one "*J.G.*" in *Female Poems* are remarkable for their achievement in the self-portrait as an expressive form of the Stuart lyric.

This tormented love affair, which dominated four years of Ephelia's life (*v*. "My Fate"), began about 1675, shortly after the demise of her maiden affair with Lord Mulgrave. Based on internal evidence in Ephelia's collection, *J.G.* was not a slave-trader, as Moira Ferguson, Elaine Hobby, and several others who have searched for Ephelia have adduced, but rather a principal in the Crown's gold-coast venture in Tangier. He may have been affiliated with either The Royal Africa Company, chartered in 1672, or the Merchant-Venturers (*v*. C T Carr "Trading Companies" *Selden Soc*. 28 1913). Isobel Grundy in *The Feminist*

Companion, and others, have described *J.G.* as a "Captain" in the Tangier trade. This is challengeable, as it derives, evidently, from a misreading of a reference to "the Brave Captain" in Ephelia's "Intended Farewel to *J.G.*" in *Female Poems* (page 61, line 17).

As Ephelia discloses, it is *J.G.*'s love of gold that precipitates his abandonment of her and her rival "Mopsa" to marry, instead, a wealthy young beauty in Tangier. (I shall leave it to Judith Page at The University of Oklahoma-Norman to tell us more about *J.G.*'s wife.) His greed most probably inspired Ephelia's longest poem "Wealth's Power," a fine early effort by an English woman in the verse-essay. Its subject is materialism; appropriately, "gold" dominates the poem's imagery.

Ephelia's unit of verse on *J.G.* supplies many biographical details on this man, touching his manner, appearance, age, occupation, movements in and out of London, and his Stewardship of a club called "The Society," possibly The Society of Merchant-Venturers or perhaps The Society of Sea-Sergeants, a Welsh royalist group (*v.* Francis Jones *Cymmrodorian* 1967 57-91). The weight of so many details about *J.G.* authenticate him as a real person in my poet's life, rather than a mere fictional vehicle for Ephelia's many styles in love poetry, as some 'ephelians' have suggested.

Tracing *J.G.* would be a large and probably fruitless task, since the initials themselves may be entirely fictional. Yet, I did locate several attractive Grahams, Gwynnes, and Grays in available membership rolls of the Sea-Sergeants and the Merchant-Venturers; and the Grafton and Gerard families also held my attention at an earlier point.

The value of the *J.G.* unit in *Female Poems* is its display of Ephelia's principal *métier* in poetry: the self-portrait. Through the medium of language, she impressively transmits the play of memory and time on the mind. This ability to convey in language the complexity of conflicting and obsessive mental states is Ephelia's particular strength in lyric verse. While she names Cowley as one of her models (his popular collection *The Mistress* of 1656 would have been among her favorite reading matter), it is more likely Cowley's source in Sidney which inspired Ephelia's poetic interest in the fluctuating psychological states of lovers.

Because of the appearance of the name "Mopsa" in Ephelia's verse (a name she takes from Sidney's *Arcadia*, though its less memorable first location is in Shakespeare's *Winter's Tale*), we can be assured that Ephelia was familiar with Sidney's work. His *Arcadia*, which saw thirteen editions during the 17th century, drew a strong female readership. Given her talent in self-portraiture, Ephelia must have been influenced by Sidney's best work in lyric, the *Astrophil to*

Stella sonnet-cycle. Astrophil says of himself to Stella: "Then think, my deare, that you in me do reed / Of Lover's ruine, some sad Tragedie. / I am not I, pitie this Tale of me." How very like Ephelia to her perfidious lovers. The phrasing and sensitive treatment of delicate states of mind and heart in the *J.G.* lyrics, as well as in Ephelia's quintessential lyric of feminine regret, the lamentation to *Bajazet*, recall Sidney's manner with such material. Echoing Sidney, she says to *Bajazet*: "Think then, thou greatest, loveliest, falsest Man, / How you have vow'd, how I have lov'd, and then, / My faithless Dear, be cruel if you can ...." As for her talent in reconstructing obsessive states in lovers, Ephelia's lyric "Love's Cruelty" persuasively serves.

No other woman poet of Ephelia's century, with the single exception of Louise Labé in Lyon, whose verse circulated in London in Robert Green's English-language edition of 1608, was producing romantic verse of such an affecting ethos. Ephelia's skill in reconstructing states of intimacy and obsession is impressive. These are depths of female sensibility unexplored in the verse of her immediate predecessor, Katherine Philips. And Aphra Behn's love-poems to "*J.H.*" (John Hoyle) seem mere effusions by comparison. My poet's achievement in what might be called a female psychological portraiture is one of her distinguishing talents, and her special contribution to the Stuart lyric.

Ephelia's Lamentation to "Bajazet." It is now time to speak of a knotty issue, the love poem known as "*Ephelia's* Lamentation."

A lengthy verse-epistle of 54 lines, the "Lamentation" was first printed in Ephelia's *Female Poems* (1679) under the title "In the Person of a Lady to *Bajazet*, Her Inconstant Gallant." This poem introduces a whole different order of discussion in this appreciation of my poet.

Ovid's *Heroides*, that timeless collection from Antiquity of fictive letters from abandoned or jilted women to absent husbands or unfaithful lovers, is the larger parent-text behind the "Lamentation." The popularity of this forceful lyric, which survives only in several lovely scriptorium copies, some entitled "*Ephelia to Bajazet*," others "*Ephelia's* Lamentation" (*v.* Appendix D), may have inspired one of Dryden's principal projects in translation, his *Ovid* (1680). Dryden's project included contributions from two of Ephelia's circle, Aphra Behn and *Bajazet* himself, John Sheffield, Lord Mulgrave, one of Dryden's patrons (Fig.5).

Ephelia's poem is not a satire, as most Restoration scholars have long held, but a complaint and lament from a newly-deflowered *naïf* (Ephelia) to her libertine lover (Mulgrave). Ephelia's name for

Figure 5. *John Sheffield, 3d Earl of Mulgrave (1648-1721)*
Ephelia's *"Bajazet"* and Rochester's "My Lord All-Pride"
By Sir Godfrey Kneller, *c.* 1680
Courtesy, National Portrait Gallery, London

Mulgrave, "*Bajazet*," in the title of the version of the poem in *Female Poems* and in several scribal and printed texts of the "Lamentation," is entirely appropriate, as it associates this unamiable libertine with the imperious Turkish emperor and womanizer Bajazet in Marlowe's play *Tamburlaine the Great* (1590). The name Bajazet was brought into currency during the later years of the Restoration by the popularity of the Ephelia-*Bajazet* poem and by various adaptations of Marlowe's play, by Racine (*Bajazet* 1672), Charles Saunders (*Tamerlane* 1681), and, somewhat later, Nicholas Rowe (*Tamerlane* 1701). Ephelia's popular poem may have helped to sustain the commercial appeal and market for Marlowe's play after 1679.

My poet's subject in this lament is universal. Recalling her female prototypes in Ovid's *Heroides* and, closer to her own day, in Shakespeare's *Hamlet*, Ephelia writes of maiden virtue rudely strumpeted. James Thorpe, who prints a version of the "Lamentation" in his edition of Etherege's verse (1963), suggests that the pseudonym "Ephelia" is but a variant of "Ophelia" (*v*. Annotated Bibliography). While Ophelia and Ephelia certainly conform to the literary prototype of the deceived, abandoned woman, there are many unappreciated complexities in my poet's pseudonym which distinguish her name choice; and this intriguing subject receives dedicated attention a bit later in this essay.

The immediate occasion of Ephelia's poem may well have been Mulgrave's abandonment of Ephelia for Barbara (Villiers) Palmer, Countess of Castlemaine and Duchess of Cleveland (1642-1708), the great promiscuous beauty of the Restoration and a principal mistress of Charles II's. The received reading by such Restoration specialists as Wilson, Thorpe, and Vieth identifies Mary "Moll" Kirke as the 'other woman' behind this poem. Castlemaine is the more plausible candidate, I suggest, as she had been instrumental in Mulgrave's election to The Order Of The Garter in 1674 when the "Lamentation" evidently was written and began circulating in manuscript (*v*. Aiken *Nottingham* 1941 43-44; Wilson *Court Satires* 1976 269). An Ephelia-Mulgrave-Castlemaine love triangle as primary context for the "Lamentation" would also explain Ephelia's animus in "To A Proud Beauty," a poem which bears all the characteristics of bitter female rivalry. The object of Ephelia's attack in this poem suggests a woman of Castlemaine's reported qualities and status.

The "Lamentation is one of the finest products of Ephelia's pen; yet it presents some deeply embedded textual problems and a longstanding tradition of attribution to Sir George Etherege, which now can be challenged. Its authorship in Etherege has been maintained by

40

most Restoration specialists. Ebsworth, Verity, Pinto, Thorpe, and Vieth have respectively discussed this poem, as "most probably" Etherege's. The line traditionally taken, beginning with Ebsworth's in *The Roxburghe Ballads* (1883 IV:573f), is that the "Lamentation" is one of several satires on Mulgrave by his male contemporaries; and that, furthermore, these satires form a dedicated unit of verses (*v.* Section IV: Annotated Bibliography).

On the face of it, this traditional reading of the "Lamentation" can no longer be sustained. First, the poem is not a satire, but an impassioned lament, written in a decidedly female voice, and from a decidedly female point of view. Moreover, Etherege was a longstanding acquaintance of Mulgrave's; as demonstrated below, they were on amicable terms with one another, to the point of sharing mistresses. What would be "Gentle George" Etherege's motive for ridiculing Mulgrave? To date, no recorded reason exists.

Predating Ebsworth's attribution of this poem to Etherege in *The Roxburghe Ballads* (1883 IV:574), a curious tradition of ambiguous authorship was associated with the "Lamentation." Surviving 17th- and 18th-century scribal copies credit the piece variously to Etherege *and* to Rochester (*v.* Appendix D). And, amusingly, in the 1707 and 1709 reissues of Rochester's *Poems* (1680), the "Lamentation" is ascribed neither to Etherege nor to Rochester, but to a certain "Lady *K.S.*" This must be Katherine Sedley, Duchess of Dorchester (1657-1717) and mistress of James II when duke of York. Her authorship of the "Lamentation" is highly unlikely: temperamentally, she was not a lyric poet, nor was she attractive enough to sustain Mulgrave's interest ("even for a Day," as he would say). Though a Court Wit, lampoonist, and 'songster' in her own right, Katherine Sedley did not conform to contemporary standards of female beauty, according to descriptions of her (as "Dorinda") in Dorset's lampoons. This 18th-century tradition of Katherine Sedley's authorship of the "Lamentation" is nonetheless useful on two grounds: (i) it identifies the author of this lyric as a living female wit and personality of Rochester's time, who was active in Court circles; and (ii) it suggests that the author of the "Lamentation" was unknown except to a small circle of close friends.

In the 19th century, when Ebsworth reprinted a version of the "Lamentation" in *The Roxburghe Ballads,* he expressed the opinion that Etherege was most likely the author behind the Ephelia pseudonym (*v.* Annotated Bibliography). In fact, Ebsworth's remarks on the "Lamentation" are accompanied by a 19th-century illustration of a man in female dress, removing a female mask (IV:573). Regrettably, this tradition has held. But now, with my new information on Ephelia and her coterie brought to light, this 'old' attribution of the "Lamentation" to Etherege finally can be tested with attractive external and internal evidence, and with some intersecting pieces of contemporary information. Here is my formulation:

As Ebsworth claims, this lyric was originally entitled "*Ephelia's* Lamentation." This is corroborated by the presence of such a title in several surviving scribal copies of the poem. In Ephelia's *Female Poems*, however, where the poem receives its first printed appearance, it appears under the new (and contrived) title, "In the Person of a Lady to *Bajazet*, Her unconstant Gallant." In light of Ephelia's efforts to obscure her identity, and especially in view of the poem's popularity before it reached print, it seems reasonable to suggest that its author chose not to call the poem "*Ephelia's* Lamentation" in *Female Poems* in an effort to disassociate or distance herself from the poem, from Mulgrave, and from the deep emotional trauma which precipitated this poignant lyric.

Thorpe and other Restoration specialists have judged the text of this poem in Ephelia's book to be truncated and unreliable, as compared to the text of the poem in many surviving manuscript copies. This observation is challengeable, since most manuscript copies of the "Lamentation" in fact follow the text of the poem in *Female Poems* fairly closely, with only minor variants, and include moreover *only two lines* which do not appear in the version of the poem in Ephelia's book: "O! Can the Coldness which you show me now, / Suit with the gen'rous Heat you once did show?" (lines 48-49 in most manuscript copies). Reasonably, these two lines were excised by the printer of Ephelia's book on the simple and obvious ground of formatting and page-layout. Had this couplet been printed, this already-lengthy lyric would not have conveniently concluded at the foot of page 106. These two particular lines were selected because they were simply redundant. Virtually all subsequent printed versions of this poem, dating from Ebsworth's text of the poem in the 19th century, follow the full text of the poem as it appears in surviving manuscript copies. Nonetheless, I say that the reader is justly served with the version in *Female Poems*.

So popular was the "Lamentation" that it drew a companion poem (or answer-poem) entitled *A Very Heroical Epistle from My Lord All-Pride to Doll-Common*. This verse, originally printed without ascription as a broadside in 1679 and, then, as "A very Heroical Epistle in Answer to *Ephelia*" in Rochester's *Poems* (1680), is now attributed to Mulgrave's bitter adversary Rochester on completely persuasive grounds (*v.* Vieth *Attribution* 1963 Ch.13; 468f.). Rochester's answer-poem humorously displays the two principal qualities of Mulgrave's character: his conceit, nicely transmitted in Kneller's portrait (Fig. 5, page 39); and his sexual exploitation of naïve young women, which Rochester found especially repugnant. In light of the well known enmity between these two powerful men of letters, one imagines Rochester's delight when "Ephelia's Lamentation" came into circulation around 1675. Here was an open invitation to embarrass and ridicule Mulgrave with a facetious reply from a cast-off mistress. The allusion to a duel at the close of Rochester's companion poem is commonly thought to refer to the duel which took place between Mulgrave and Percy Kirke. My reconstruction, however, suggests that this allusion brings to mind a far more relevant circumstance: the duel between Mulgrave and Rochester himself, in 1670. So violent were the potential repercussions of this confrontation that Charles II stopped the duel (*v.* Wilson *Court Satires* 1976 269).

Appreciating my suggested contexts behind these two interesting lyrics, with their colorful cast of characters and high emotional voltage, one is not surprised that the Ephelia-Bajazet poems soon became the most popular companion poems of the Restoration. As Appendix D in my apparatus shows, they frequently traveled together in many 17th- and 18th-century miscellanies.

When James Courtney at the Golden Horse Shoe in Saffron Hill published in 1682 an unauthorized second issue of *Female Poems On several Occasions. Written by Ephelia,* now very scarce, he included Rochester's reply under the title, "An Answer to *Ephelia*'s Letter to *Bajazet.*" The wording of Courtney's title is important, I suggest, because it identifies Ephelia as the author of the "Lamentation," both in its manuscript state of *c.* 1675, as well as in its slightly abridged state, which Courtney himself published in the first edition of the *Female Poems* in 1679. While Ephelia coyly attempted to conceal her authorship of this verse-epistle in her collection by retitling "*Ephelia*'s Lamentation" with the completely neutral title "In the Person of a Lady to *Bajazet,* Her inconstant Gallant," her subterfuge fails; for, as the very wording of her book's titlepage states, these are "*Female Poems On several Occasions. Written by Ephelia*" (my emphasis).

Restoration specialists, dating from Joseph Woodfall Ebsworth in the 19th century, have continued to rely on a single piece of evidence to make a case for Sir George Etherege's authorship of the "Lamentation." It is one couplet from the popular Restoration lampoon, "A Familiar Epistle to *Julian,* Secretary to the Muses" (*c.* 1677). The "Julian" poem is thought to be the work of George Villiers 2d Duke of Buckingham, a brother of Ephelia's patroness, Lady Mary (Villiers) Stuart (*v.* Vieth *Attribution* [1963] 350-2). This interesting and ambiguously worded couplet, as it appears in many 17th- and 18th-century manuscript copies, is:

Poor *George,* grows old, his Muse worne out of fashion,

CRITICAL ESSAY

> Hoarsly she sang *Ephelia's* Lamentation.
> (Osborn Col., Beinecke, +Case bl05, f.353; also Osborn b54, f.1184)

Interestingly, in the version of Julian's "Epistle" printed in *Poems On Affairs Of State*, and in several 19th- and 20th-century collections of Restoration poetry, the operative phrase "she sang" appears as "he sang" to support, evidently, the longstanding attribution of the "Lamentation" to Etherege (I:388 1963, ed. Lord). Almost all Restoration specialists associate this poem with Etherege, including (surprisingly) some feminist specialists, who have not sufficiently investigated the textual backgrounds of this poem (*v.* Greer *Kissing The Rod* 1988; Grundy *The Feminist Companion* 1990).

This important couplet from *"Julian,"* in its various printed versions, results in a highly problematic reading. Let me introduce an attractive potential background to this curious and ambiguously worded couplet, which heretofore has not been entered into the record: an intimate relationship between Etherege and Ephelia. Such a relationship clarifies the meaning of Julian's couplet, overturns its traditional reading, and properly returns the authorship of the "Lamentation" to Ephelia. Here is my line:

As Peter Beal at Sotheby's, London, reminded me, Mulgrave wrote to Etherege from Whitehall on 7 March 1687 about a tantalizing young beauty whom both writers had respectively enjoyed at various times in their youth. Mulgrave calls her only "the Lady in the Garret." Mulgrave writes to Etherege: "The Remembrance of her [is] very sweet, both as a pleasure enjoyed and a danger escaped" (*v.* Etherege "Letterbook" B.L. Add. MS 11518 ff.180ᵛ-181). The redoubtable John Harold Wilson also mentions this woman, but he admits that she has eluded him (*v. Court Wits* 1976 198). If in fact Julian's reference to "George" is to George Etherege (not to George Villiers), and if Mulgrave's "Lady in the Garret" is Ephelia, then the allusion to Etherege's "Muse" who hoarsly sang *"Ephelia's* Lamentation" refers to Ephelia herself as a kept woman of Etherege's and as the author of the lyric that bears her name.

This provocative hypothesis gains credibility in light of intersecting circumstantial evidence I ferreted out on the background of Ephelia's elegy on Sir Thomas Isham [1681], which is introduced in this edition. Isham was a member of Etherege's circle. In view of the fact that Isham was a theater enthusiast, he may have sponsored Etherege at some point. In any case, a specimen of their correspondence has been preserved at the Northamptonshire PRO (MS IC 4558). While this surviving piece of correspondence is entirely unremarkable, it nonetheless serves as hard, primary evidence of a direct link between Etherege and Isham. Moreover, this documented association between

Isham and Etherege would suggest a link between Ephelia and Etherege through Isham. A further intersection along these lines exists in Ephelia's acrostic to Rachel Powney in the *Female Poems*, who may be one of the Powneys of Berkshire, which happens to be Etherege's maternal line.

Some attractive internal evidence also comes to hand: A sensitive comparison between the "Lamentation" and Ephelia's poems illustrates a consistency in poetic habits and imagery. First, as mentioned above, there is a moment in the "Lamentation" where language breaks down altogether, leaving the speaker temporarily speechless:

> In him I center'd all my hopes of Bliss:
> For him, my Duty to my Friends forgot;
> For him I lost -- alas! what lost I not?
> (*Female Poems*, 1679,p.105,ll.21-23)

Such a moment also appears in Ephelia's elegy to Sheldon, excerpted above (page 25). A somewhat similar moment, though less dramatically presented, appears in Ephelia's "Isham" elegy: "And even the Muses too are stricken dumbe: / None breath their sorrows in a murmuring verse / but all in awfull silence waite his Hearse."

Further internal evidence exists in Ephelia's manner of reconstructing romantic intimacy and non-verbal communication between lovers. She also describes something more subtle: their perception of time. Consider these parallel passages which illustrate this special ethos in my poet's amorous verse:

> He met my Passion with an equal Fire.
> Both sweetly languisht in a soft Desire:
> Close put in each other's Arms, we sate all Day,
> Each Smile I gave, he'd with a Kiss repay.
> In every Hour an Ages Bliss we reaped,
> And lavisht favours on each other heap'd.
> ("My Fate," *Female Poems...by Ephelia*, 1679)

> Fix'd on my Eyes, how often wou'd he say,
> He cou'd with Pleasure gaze an Age away.
> When Thought, too great for Words, had made him mute,
> In Kisses he wou'd tell my Hand his Suite:
> ...
> Nor was my Love weaker, or less than his;
> In him I center'd all my hopes of Bliss
> ("*Bajazet*," *Female Poems...by Ephelia*, 1679)

45

Equally striking is Ephelia's characteristic language of betrayed love and feminine regret. In the process of creating the state of woman *in extremis*, she relies on a particular imagery. Nowhere is it more fiercely presented than in the *Lamentation* (virtually any version), which pointedly draws upon "vows," "cold," "neglect," "false," "bliss," "falsest Man," "faithless Dear," "first Look," *etc* . We see this same imagery throughout Ephelia's many verses to *J.G.* in *Female Poems*. This consistency in phrasing, imagery, and ethos seriously challenges the claim of Vieth, Thorpe, and Hobby that Ephelia's plaint to "*Bajazet*" in the *Female Poems* is "out of keeping" with the rest of the collection.

A final point of interest in my analysis of this compelling lyric is the curious change in the speaker's point of view. In the printed version of "*Ephelia*'s Lamentation" in *Female Poems*, the first 34 lines refer to *Bajazet* in the third-person, beginning with line 9, "So kind <u>he</u> look'd, such tender Words <u>he</u> spoke" (my emphasis). But by line 35, the speaker can no longer sustain the poetic fiction of writing a letter to her 'unconstant Gallant.' She suddenly shifts from platitudes to intimate details ("to you I brought/My Virgin Innocence"), and begins to address *Bajazet* directly, in the second person, Ephelia's typical preference in point of view. Beginning with line 35 of the *Bajazet* poem, Ephelia's whimsical catalogue of regrets suddenly becomes an angry frontal attack. Reproaching the man who jilted her, she challenges, "Think then thou greatest, loveliest, falsest Man, / How you have vow'd, how I have lov'd, and then / My faithless Dear, be cruel if you can."

Interestingly, the text of the Ephelia-*Bajazet* poem printed in later collections of Restoration poetry (*e.g.*, *Miscellaneous Works of Lords Rochester, Roscommon ...* 1707; *Roxburghe Ballads* IV 1883) does not follow this inconsistency in point of view. Many later texts of the poem change Ephelia's third-person references ("he"/"him") to second-person references ("you") throughout, possibly to reconstruct the poem from lyric to satire, as modern-day supporters of the Etherege authorship of the "Lamentation" might explain. The second-person perspective in later texts of this problematic and rich lyric strategically shifts attention from the distress of the speaker (Ephelia) to the "you" of the poem, namely Ephelia's addressee, the heartless and indifferent "Inconstant Gallant," Lord Mulgrave.

It is possible that <u>all</u> references to *Bajazet* in the 'lost' holograph of the "Lamentation" were originally cast in the second person, and that Ephelia introduced this shift in point of view from third to second person in the first printed version of this piece in *Female Poems* in order to candidly display her inability to dispassionately fictionalize the subject-matter of this poem, making the subterfuge of the poem's neutral new title especially unsuccessful. Even after a lapse of some four years, the memory of the Mulgrave affair was painful enough to undermine Ephelia's skill as an editor of her own work, a skill she capably displays in 1681, in the "Isham" elegy, discussed below.

Related to this issue of point of view is the interrogative mode of this lyric as it is punctuated in Ephelia's *Female Poems*. It begins with a question: "How far are they deceiv'd, that hope in vain / A lasting Lease of Joys from Love t' obtain?" But Ephelia's interrogation of her 'inconstant Gallant' shifts, along with the shift in point of view, to the imperative mode when regret and nostalgia are replaced with anger: "Then think thou greatest, loveliest, falsest Man, / How you have vow'd, how I have lov'd ...." Regrettably, this dramatic shift in the speaker's psychological state is lost in most modern versions of the poem because editors, from Verity to Thorpe, have replaced the question mark which punctuates the poem's opening couplet with an exclamation point (*v.* Thorpe *Etherege* 1963 9). This emendation, I suggest, is unfaithful to the dark ethos of the poem as it is printed in Ephelia's *Female Poems*, Rochester's *Poems*, and in many surviving scribal copies (*v.* "Wit and Learning ... 1677," Beinecke Library, Osborn b54, ff. 1180-1). The theme of the "Lamentation," established in its opening couplet, is answered as the speaker proceeds to the brink of collapse, for this is a serious poem on the mental and emotional anguish of betrayal. As its incipit emphasizes, it is a portrait in despair and the sting of deception. I suggest that the force of the introduced exclamation mark cancels the interrogative mood and direction of the beginning section of the poem, and subverts its opening plaintive ethos.

These observations and the intersecting information brought to bear on this lyric would seem to have cumulative force: at the very least, they lend strength to a plausible case for Ephelia's authorship of "*Ephelia*'s Lamentation" and its subsequent printed appearance in *Female Poems .. by Ephelia*. It has been the absence of incontrovertible primary evidence of Ephelia's authorship of the "Lamentation," rather than proof positive of Etherege's, that has permitted this most 'female' of the *Female Poems* to remain in Etherege's canon since the 19th century.

Ephelia's Acrostics. Of lesser interest in *Female Poems* are four acrostics, to Venitia Cooke, Ann Bury, Rachel Powney, and Anne Gilbert. These women were probably friends from Ephelia's girlhood or adolescence. Based upon this poetic form (a rather dated one by 1679) and the unsophisticated level of the verses themselves, these acrostics must be juvenilia, composed at a time when Ephelia would have been impressed with the friendship poems of the celebrated "Orinda" Philips. One notices that Orinda's signature phrase "sacred

Friendship" appears twice in Ephelia's book (*v.* "Vindication ..." and "Twin Flame").

In light of her guarded identity, Ephelia must have felt that nothing was revealed by naming her women friends in these poems; for, by the date of their publication in 1679, her acrostics had named individuals who probably were no longer traceable under the surnames Ephelia disclosed. There is also the possibility that she scrambled her friends' surnames to confuse readers. As her pseudonym, portrait, and delight in acrostic all suggest, Ephelia, unlike her celebrated female contemporary "Orinda" Philips, was playful, witty, and amusing.

My searches into the surnames of Ephelia's women friends nonetheless pointed to certain literary families. Venitia Cooke brings to mind the literary Cooke women of Gidea Hall, Essex, noticed in Ballard's *Memoirs* (1752), as well as the Restoration actress, Sarah Cooke. Ann Bury suggests the 17th-century diarist Anne Bury and the learned lady, Elizabeth Laurence Lloyd Bury, also mentioned by Ballard. Rachel Powney suggests the Powney-Ethereges of Berkshire, mentioned above. Anne Gilbert could be kin to Ephelia's *J.G.*, assuming his surname actually began with "G." and could have been "Gilbert."

Relations between the Sexes, and Libertine Verse. Several verses in *Female Poems ... by Ephelia* center on two related subjects: deportment between the sexes, and Ephelia's attitude to libertine verse, which had been brought into vogue by Charles II's Court Wits, especially Rochester, who, upon visiting Paris in 1662 and '69, found the verse of *libertin* poets, especially Regnier, just to his taste (*v.* Foxon *Libertine Literature in England 1660-1745* 1965; Griffin *Rochester* 1973).

With regard to Ephelia's views on deportment between the sexes, she can be harshly critical of her female contemporaries when their behavior is deceitful and mercenary, as in "To a Proud Beauty," "To a Lady who (tho Married) ...," "To my Rival," and in "Song" ("Obscure the Glories of your Eyes"). She is equally abrupt with her male contemporaries, when their behavior is rude, as in "To one that affronted the Excellent *Eugenia*," and "To *Coridon*, on shutting his Door against some Ladies (*v.* Appendix F). But generally Ephelia is a writer of sympathetic 'female poems,' and certainly an exuberant feminist whose beliefs do not preclude affectionate relations with men, as in "To *Phylocles*, inviting him to Friendship."

Yet, Ephelia's feminism could be artistically problematic. On one occasion "a Friend" requested (or commissioned) a poem on the subject, maidenhead. This "Friend" may have been one of the Court Wits, who relished "impromptus" on rakish subjects. As specialists

CRITICAL ESSAY

appreciate, maidenhead poems were in vogue throughout the 17th century. Heywood, Cowley, and the Court Wits exercised their pen on the subject. While obliging her "Friend" with an amusing trifle, Ephelia admits her discomfort with his choice in subject-matter, as well as her hesitancy in meeting his request: "AT your Intreaty, I at last have writ / This whimsey, that has nigh nonplust my wit" (my emphases).

Unlike the coarse lyrics of her day, this small product of Ephelia's apprenticeship, written evidently before she surrendered her virginity to Mulgrave *c.* 1674/5, is not "risqué" (*v. Feminist Companion* 1990), but rather a feminist reworking of a traditional *libertin* theme; as such, it bears comparison to Behn's "Disappointment," which recasts from a feminist perspective Catenac's and Rochester's poems on male sexual performance. Ephelia's "Maidenhead" concludes with feminist musings on virginity as an imposed cultural value, a digression she suddenly realizes is not at all what her bawdy-minded friend had in mind: "But I forget, or have my Subject lost ...." The poem's feminist emphasis on cultural perceptions of virginity distinguishes Ephelia's poem from contemporary libertine verse. Moreover, the careful phrasing of the poem's title, "Maidenhead, *written at the request of a friend*," suggests Ephelia's attempt to distance herself from the poem's subject altogether. Yet, in this curious and rich little poem, my poet shows an important interest in extending the poetic repertoire for English women writers, even if she herself is merely a *libertin manquée* in this instance. As a writer of *"female poems,"* she cannot fully sustain an artistic rapport with such a subject. Ephelia's refusal to write lines 'unfit for modest Ears' aligns with her insistence elsewhere on respectful deportment between the sexes. The "Maidenhead" poem also is noteworthy for its sexual humor (rare in an English woman writer of this time), and the link it suggests between Ephelia and her contemporaries, especially Rochester, who receives my special attention at the end of this essay.

ADVICE TO HIS GRACE [c. late 1681]. Ephelia's third publication returns her to the sensitive public sphere of Stuart politics, the subject that launched her career in 1678.

Ephelia's *Advice* is a White Letter broadside addressed to James (Scott) Duke of Monmouth (1649-1685), an illegitimate son of Charles II. It concerns the volatile issue of the Stuart succession. This second published broadside of my poet's bears the printed subscription "Ephelia" at the foot of the sheet. The controversy over the Stuart succession produced a rash of occasional pieces and some lengthy serious poems from the pens of professional writers and Grub Street hacks alike. Interestingly, the *Advice*, Ephelia's second broadside on a serious affair of state, is a 50-line poem. This is relevant, as her

49

inaugural publication to a Stuart, an anonymous broadside addressed to Charles II on the Popish Plot, discussed above, also was 50 lines in length. Even though Ephelia later identifies herself as the author of this particular broadside by publishing a slightly revised version of it in her collection of 1679, she may be linking herself to her first published poem by producing a second loyal poem to the Stuarts of exactly the same length.

The *Advice* is among Ephelia's best work: its phrasing, the development of its argument, and the technical management of the couplet display a disciplined, mature talent, not so apparent three years earlier in her broadside to the King. A bold, rousing poem, the *Advice* opens with a command to Monmouth: "AWake, vain Man; tis time th' Abuse to see; / Awake, and guard thy heedless Loyalty." In her direct address to Monmouth, Ephelia shows good rhetorical judgment: she neither attacks nor insults the King's son, but first gains Monmouth's attention and curiosity. She then proceeds with a line of sensible, ethical argument. In strong assertive lines, supported by imperative verbs, Ephelia attempts to reason Monmouth out of his behavior. She emphasizes his disloyalty to his father Charles II and, more so, to the Stuart monarchy. She also drives home Monmouth's naiveté in Whig party-politics.

Behn should have taken a lesson from Ephelia. When Behn penned an epilogue to an anonymous play, *Romulus and Hersillia* in the summer of 1682, she adopted a confrontational posture by harshly pillorying Monmouth on moral grounds as a vile, unrepentant sinner. Behn also exposes this young pretender to the throne as a rebellious son. She hectors Monmouth, and misplaces her emphases by making him deliver moral self-judgments: "Of all treasons, mine was most accurst: / Rebelling 'gainst a KING and FATHER first. / A Sin, which Heaven nor man can e'er forgive." Ephelia's poem more astutely engages Monmouth by emphasizing the effects of his actions on the health of the commonweal. Even while identifying Monmouth as a disloyal son, Ephelia's principal argument is the larger repercussions of his actions to the body politic. This is an appropriate line to take in such a delicate circumstance.

Charles II was offended by the impropriety of Behn's lines. Evidently judging that she had violated royal protocols, the King ordered the Lord Chamberlain to take out a warrant (now found) for the arrest of Behn and also for the actress who spoke her epilogue, Lady Mary Slingsby (*v. True Protestant Mercury* 12-16 August 1682; *Athenaeum* 22 September 1894 396). While no evidence to date exists which documents an actual arrest, Behn evidently was so disgraced by this episode that she briefly withdrew from public view.

Ephelia's model in the *Advice* would have been Dryden's *Absalom and Achitophel* (November, 1681), the most sensitive poem of his professional career. Dryden's poem is the likely parent-text behind Ephelia's *Advice To His GRACE*, just as his *Astraea Redux* and *Annus Mirabilis* guided Ephelia's pen in her broadside to Charles on the Popish Plot in 1678. The most striking parallel between Ephelia's *Advice* and Dryden's great poem is the doctrinal Tory line which informs the thought of both. Dryden and Ephelia emphasize kingly authority, the harmony of the body politic, and the purity of the royal Stuart line. But where Dryden's poem expresses these larger principles through familiar Old Testament typologies, which lend heroic and historic scale to its colorful cast of characters, Ephelia's addresses its subject directly, in the second person. Affronting Monmouth's vanity and ego, Ephelia attempts to embarrass him, by pointing out his exploitation by Shaftesbury's Whig machine, "that busie juggling Crew" of "false Friends." Through a series of pointed questions, she strives to engage and sustain her subject's attention, and to stir his rational faculties. The poem closes not with a castigation of Monmouth's behavior (Behn's tack), but with sensible words of "advice," the operative word in Ephelia's title. Spurring him to constructive action, she asks: "Would you be Great? do Things *Great* and *Brave*: / And scorn to be the *Mobile's* dull Slave ... Prove your high Birth by Deeds Noble and Good; / But strive not to Legitimate your Bloud."

In her closing lines, Ephelia clearly positions herself as Monmouth's superior. He was, after all, a great favorite among English commoners. Further motivating Ephelia's public criticism of Monmouth could have been his suspected liaison with Lady Castlemaine, who may well have been Ephelia's successful rival for Mulgrave in 1674/5, discussed above (p.40). It is entirely possible, furthermore, that Monmouth was an object of Ephelia's ridicule earlier in her career, in her amateur play *The Pair-Royal of Coxcombs*, whose prologue, epilogue, and two songs were published in *Female Poems* in 1679. Reasonably, Ephelia may have harbored a longstanding animus toward Monmouth, dating from the mid-1670s. Her public criticism of him in the *Advice* also suggests her disapproval of the populace which supported him. In this sense, her broadside effectively disassociates her from Monmouth and the social classes which promoted his cause. Ephelia's class bias is a noteworthy feature of the *Advice*, as it aligns with the ethos of privilege and entitlement which typically marks her work. As she asserted in the by-line of her first publication, she was "*a Gentlewoman*."

To date, we know virtually nothing about the publication

history of Ephelia's *Advice*. We recall that Ephelia's first broadside of 1678, on the Popish Plot, was licensed by the royal censor Sir Roger L'Estrange, whose name appears at the foot of the sheet. Nor has any information surfaced on the printer and publisher of the *Advice*. The few institutions which own copies of Ephelia's poem (v. Appendix A) date the poem to c. 1681. Yet, in view of its probable model in Dryden's *Absalom and Achitophel*, published in November, 1681, but possibly in progress during the summer of 1681, the date of late 1681/early 1682 seems more acceptable as the publication date of the *Advice*, regardless of the manuscript date of "6 June 1681" on the Ashmole copy at the Bodleian Library (v. Winn *Dryden* 1987 345).

It is entirely possible, of course, that Charles II was no more pleased with Ephelia's *Advice* then he was with Behn's epilogue of 1682. Records of warrants at this time, however, do not identify anyone who appears to have been Ephelia. Yet the fact remains that Ephelia's broadside to Monmouth was her last published poem.

PORTLAND MS PwV 336, THE UNIVERSITY OF NOTTINGHAM LIBRARY, ENGLAND: A FUNERAL ELEGY ON SIR THOMAS ISHAM [1681]. If indeed an autograph manuscript of Ephelia's, Portland MS PwV 336, an elegy on the death of Sir Thomas Isham, is the last of her known work to date. It is not listed as a published poem in the usual sources. In addition to my observations below, see Appendix D of this edition's apparatus for further details.

Internal and external evidence suggest that this is an authentic literary manuscript of the later 17th century; and, moreover, that it is an autograph manuscript written by the same individual who wrote *Female Poems...by Ephelia* (1679) and the loyal broadsides of 1678 and 1681, discussed above. If this is the case -- and no countervailing evidence has yet surfaced from any quarter -- then this manuscript is incontrovertible evidence of Ephelia's actual existence as a publishing writer of the later 17th century. But, first, a word on the manuscript's subject:

In a two-part article on the Isham family, printed in *The Connoisseur* (1963), Sir Gyles Isham describes Sir Thomas Isham as a romantic figure of impeccable lineage, fine training, and powerful connections (Fig.6). A less attractive image of Sir Thomas, as a debauched, bankrupt aristocrat, appears in some contemporary lampoons and 'session' poems, now available in modern sources (v. *POAS* II: 200; J H Wilson *Court Satires* 1976 44-45, 85). Sir Thomas's recorded enthusiasms in painting and the theater may have involved him in patronal relationships, possibly with Etherege. As documented

Figure 6. *Sir Thomas Isham, 3d Baronet (1657-1681)*
By David Loggan, 1676
Courtesy, Lamport Hall, Northamptonshire

above, a rather unremarkable piece of correspondence between Isham and Etherege is preserved in Northamptonshire. All who knew Sir Thomas, according to Sir Gyles, found him to be a young man of great promise. Unfortunately, his potential was never realized, for he died of smallpox at the age of 24 on 26 July 1681, on the eve of his marriage to Mary Van Bempde (not Barbara Chiffinch, as John Harold Wilson states in *Court Satires* 45). Isham was buried at Lamport on 9 August 1681.

Ephelia wisely grounds her poem in historical allusions to these facts of Isham's biography and reputation. Such references lend a desirable factual balance and veracity to the piece; they also offset the poem's elegiac and sentimental ethos. Given the fact that young Sir Thomas followed the theater circuit and was a documented member of Etherege's circle, some contact between Isham and Ephelia would not be unlikely. Strengthening this possibility is the fact that the two brothers of Ephelia's patroness, Lady Mary (Villiers) Stuart, were educated by Bishop Brian Duppa, who also was a close family friend of the Ishams (*v.* Clark *Correspondence of ... Duppa and Isham* 1894).

My researches into the family backgrounds of the Isham poem identified additional links, between the Ishams and the Verneys. The Verneys are relevant to this discussion since this family owned a copy of Ephelia's *Female Poems* (1679), the copy in fact selected for this edition (*v.* Appendix E). The Isham-Verney connection was formed during the Interregnum, when Sir Ralph Verney and Sir Justinian Isham were fellow-prisoners at St James's Palace during the Civil Wars (*v.* F P Verney *Verney* III 1892 Ch.7).

It may have been Ephelia's patroness who suggested an elegy on Isham to my poet; or perhaps Lady Mary nominated Ephelia to Etherege or to the Ishams, who then made the arrangements. These families were well within Lady Mary's larger social orbit. This broad linkage, then, of Isham-Etherege-Verney-Duppa-Villiers, all staunch royalists, is the connected family background of the Isham elegy. Ephelia was either directly or indirectly associated with this large family-group. While my argument for Ephelia's authorship of the "Isham" manuscript is based on intersecting external and circumstantial evidence, and, so, must remain speculative, my case is not without some persuasive features. We turn now to the manuscript's interesting physical properties.

The physical arrangement of the poem on the manuscript's special writing paper and its author's script are especially pertinent to my case. This is no tidy scriptorium product, but a hastily prepared piece of work. Yet, the layout of the text of the poem and the author's use of interlinear space are entirely professional, and not dissimilar from other literary manuscripts of the 1670s. The fact that the text of the poem is thoughtfully arranged, with two marginal brackets and a catchword -- in the same script as the signature, title, and text of the poem -- suggests that this manuscript may have been preliminary to a fair, printer's copy. Yet, to date, no evidence of publication exists.

The manuscript valuably bears one handmade revision, in line 25, evidently in the author's own hand, as it is in the same script as that of the signature, title, and body of the poem. Interestingly, the author of the "Isham" manuscript inserts a short line (or editorial slash) above the poem's revision in order to visually separate it from the words immediately above it in line 24, "startl'd Fate." This detail is important, as it shows that the author was neither inexperienced in manuscripts, nor unconcerned with the legibility of the manuscript to a printer. As to the nature of this revision, it is a small correction or refinement to the text of the poem, rather than a substantive alteration. Its purpose is to maintain the metrical value of line 25. "Away" is struck from the line "Who from the lovely youth did force away his breath" since "away" introduces two unnecessary syllables in an otherwise correct line of iambic pentameter. This correction shows the poet's concern with prosody and the technical integrity of the couplet.

Of the handwriting, there is much to say, beginning with the reminder to readers that a literary manuscript produced by a woman writer of the Restoration period (as I take this specimen to be) is a special historical artifact; for, at this time, women writers were just beginning to reach print. When they submitted their manuscripts to booksellers or patrons for potential publication or sponsorship, the 'look' of the manuscript -- especially its formatting and script -- were critical factors in its reception. Proper formatting testified to the author's familiarity with manuscripts -- as a reader of others' and as a writer of her own; and handwriting was a reflection of social class and education. In her autobiography of 1667, Margaret, Duchess of Newcastle, admits that her "ordinary handwriting is so bad [that she must] write it Fair for the Press." The script of the Isham manuscript is of a middling-to-high quality. It is not the hand of a professional scribe, nor is the writing as lovely as Behn's; but it is far more calligraphic and sophisticated than that of, say, Katherine Philips, Newcastle, and Elizabeth Polwhele. The handwriting displays features of both formal and informal script at this time (v. Wroth MSS, Huntington; Behn MSS, Morgan; Petti *English Literary Hands* 1977; Whalley *English Handwriting* 1969; *British Literary Manuscripts* eds. Klinkenborg, Cahoon, Ryskamp 1981). One notices, for example, the lovely presentation of the uppercase "A" (very like Behn's), "E," "S," "T," and especially the uppercase "I." The final "d"s (lines 6-9) display the top, backward loop characteristic of the cursive styles of Ephelia's literary contemporaries.

All of the manuscript is in the same hand. There is a consistency and uniformity in the formation of almost all letters. The uppercase "E"s, for example, align with one another, as do the lowercase final "d"s, "t"s, "g"s, and "y"s. The lowercase "p"s are consistently open at the inside circular link, as in the signature "Ephelia," "practise" in line 3, "passion" in line 6, *etc.*

Charles Hamilton, fresh from his work on the Utah forgeries and the Hitler diary forgeries, brought my attention, however, to an inconsistency throughout the manuscript in the formation of the uppercase "H" in lines 12, 22, 23, the Catchword, and line 26. The most conspicuously inconsistent "H"s (in lines 23 and 26) can be explained, I proposed, on the ground of hasty composition. As the title of the poem suggests, this is a "funerall Elegie," written to be read at the funeral ceremony or burial grounds; moreover, it would have been written to meet an imposed deadline set by the Isham family or one of their circle. As I explained to Hamilton, in the hurried act of composition, the poet initially had a different word in mind at the beginning of line 23 and after "when" in line 26. But after the first partial formation of the word's first letter, in both cases, the author rejected the first-choice words in favor of "His" in line 23 and "Hymen" in line 26. The author then returned to these words to restroke the "H" in the interest of legibility. This accounts for the heavier or thicker line in the first downstroke of the "H" in line 23, and of the second in line 26. My poet would have angled her quill-pen to produce a heavier line, as in the bottom half of the first marginal bracket (ll.4-5), and especially in the two flourishes which frame her signature. (True to his nature, Mr Hamilton was interested, but remained skeptical.)

The punctuation in this manuscript is not only conventional for a poem of 1681, but also consistent with the punctuation in other writings by Ephelia. The colon, for example, is employed instead of the period as full-stop punctuation at the end of a couplet (or verse-paragraph) (*v.* line 5 and the closing line). This use of the colon as full-stop end punctuation is also evident in her broadside to Charles II (1678), the epistle-dedicatory in *Female Poems*, and in most of Ephelia's longer poems. Notably, the "Isham" manuscript includes an exclamation mark ("dead!" line 9). Such punctuation evidently appeared in other manuscripts of Ephelia's. Her elegy on the death of Archbishop Sheldon, for example, features two exclamation marks in one line of verse alone (*Female Poems* 1679 pp. 4-5, line 29).

Brevigraphs (y^e, w^{ch}, w^n, *etc.*) do not appear in the text of the "Isham" manuscript (though "S^r" appears in its title). If this manuscript is indeed Ephelia's, then the conspicuous absence of brevigraphs in the body of the poem serves as a 'marker' in determining the attribution of other manuscripts to Ephelia. In some of the scriptorium copies of "*Ephelia*'s Lamentation," identified in Appendix D of this edition's Apparatus, the frequent use of brevigraphs is a principal ground for ruling out their authenticity as holographs, since brevigraphs are not characteristic of the orthography of my poet's work, judging from the "Isham" manuscript.

All of the manuscript appears to be in the same ink, being a common, carbon-based variety. Its transmission, however, from quill-pen to paper appears to be very uneven, suggesting an old or low-quality quill-pen. Among several conspicuous examples, see "Elegies" in line 1; "but" in line 14; "engrose" and "she" in line 32; and "too" in line 36.

The style of the two flourishes which frame the signature is noteworthy. The width of the line at the beginning of each of the flourishes is bold and thick, indicating the writer's familiarity with a more ornate, calligraphic cursive, as well as the writer's familiarity with the presentation of many signatures in literary manuscripts of her day. The use of a flourish in the signature was a conventional calligraphic effect used by some writers when signing their manuscripts. But it also was functional: it directed the printer to set the signature in italic type. And we see that "*Ephelia*" is in fact set in italic type on the closing page of the first issue of her book in 1679 (p.112). The minor detail of the period after the signature "Ephelia" in the "Isham" manuscript is not unremarkable, since a period also follows the name "Ephelia" in three printed subscriptions of her name: after the dedication in *Female Poems*; on the final page of the 1679 *Female Poems*; and after the printed subscription "Ephelia" at the foot of her second broadside, *Advice To His GRACE* (*c.* 1681).

Concerning the paper of the "Isham" manuscript, I received excellent guidance in several classic sources on literary manuscripts of my writer's time, especially William Proctor Williams' "Paper as Evidence: The Utility of the Study of Paper for 17th-century Literary Scholarship" (*v. Essays in Paper Analysis* 1987) and Edward Heawood's "Papers Used in England After 1660" (*v. The Library* 1931; see also other essays by Heawood in *The Library*, 1930-31). The paper of a literary manuscript is critical on several grounds. My particular interest centered on authenticating the manuscript by fixing the relative date of its paper; this, I attempted to do by dating the paper's interesting armorial circle watermark (*v.* hand-traced facsimile, Fig.7). While the University of Nottingham Library does not currently have on premises the technical equipment required to supply a beta-radiographic print

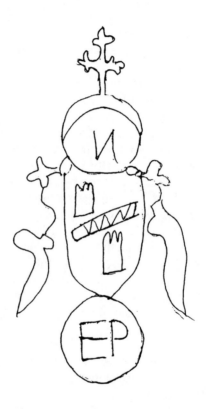

Figure 7. Armorial Circle Watermark of the "Isham" Manuscript
Hand-traced Facsimile
Courtesy, University of Nottingham Library

of the mark, nor was Nottingham (understandably) willing to send out the "Isham" manuscript for paper and ink analysis, its curatorial staff kindly obliged me with a hand-traced facsimile of the mark.

This elegy is written on a single sheet, folded into two folios, measuring 14.5 centimeters by 20 centimeters. The paper is not foolscap, common packing paper, nor account-book paper, but expensive white laid writing paper. It is relatively thin paper (0.11 millimeters), with horizontal chain lines and an elaborate armorial watermark. As detailed below, my researches were able to successfully date the paper by dating its watermark to the period of Isham's death in 1681, at which time this paper was circulating in the London market.

The watermark of the "Isham" manuscript contains four discrete categories of bibliographical information:

> (i) a coat-of-arms on a shield, displaying evidently a bend dexter between two objects (coronets? hands? castles?);
>
> (ii) the initials "E P," displayed below the coat, and circumscribed;
>
> (iii) an uppercase backward "N," displayed above the coat, and circumscribed; and,
>
> (iv) a cross *flory*, above the backward "N," and surmounting the whole.

Scouting through the authoritative sources on watermarks, compiled respectively by Briquet, Churchill, Heawood, Labarre, and Marmol, I located in Heawood's *Watermarks* (1950) three marks which were strikingly similar to the mark of the "Isham" manuscript: Heawood 818, 821, and 822. The most similar of these was Heawood 821 (Fig.8). Its only difference from the mark of the Isham manuscript was the presentation of slightly different initials: "F P."

Among Heawood's brief annotations on these three similar marks, two pieces of information seemed especially pertinent to the watermark of the "Isham" manuscript. First, a specimen of one of the comparable marks, Heawood 822, wherein the backward "N" appears below "E P" (not below the cross as in Heawood 821), had been located among the drawings of the younger Willem Van De Velde (1633-1707), the principal maritime painter at the court of Charles II. Smith's extensive *Catalogue* of 329 of Van De Velde's paintings places him in London, at the Court, during the late 1670s and early 1680s; and we know for certain that the subject of the "Isham" elegy died in 1681. Furthermore, Heawood's annotation on mark 818, wherein the "N" appears below the initials, listed the researches of the English antiquary Rev. Samuel Denne, who had documented such a watermark in a collection of 17th-century letters and documents preserved at the Town

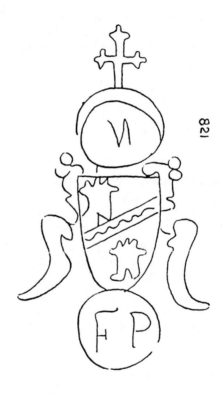

Figure 8. Watermark 821, Plate 129
In Heawood, *Watermarks* (1950)

CRITICAL ESSAY

Hall, Rochester, England (Fig.9). According to Denne's essay on paper-makers in *Archaelogia* 12 (1796), Charles II and members of the Court were known to stay in Rochester en route to Dover. Denne describes Rochester Specimen 41, which he dates to 1679, as "fine, thin, white" paper, properties identical to the "Isham" manuscript at Nottingham; but Denne says nothing more beyond that.

Collectively, these findings date the paper of the "Isham" manuscript to the time Ephelia was active on the London literary circuit, and moreover to the time of Isham's death in 1681.

This special paper may have been manufactured in Genoa or in France, both principal centers of quality writing paper circulating in the London market during the later 17th-century (*v.* Labarre *Encyclopedia of Paper-Making* 1952 342). The case for its manufacture in Genoa is strengthened by the central location of the mark, which was characteristic of Genoese paper exported to English suppliers around this time (*v.* Briquet *Les Filigranes* 324).

With regard to the initials "E P" in the mark of the "Isham" manuscript, I worked from the assumption that these were the initials of the paper-maker, not the patron of the paper-maker, as sometimes is the case. Using the initial of the surname "P," I identified three candidates who manufactured paper for several suppliers and clients throughout the English and Continental markets of the 17th century: the French firm of Estienne Planteau; the Petittou firm, based in Amsterdam; and the Plantin firm in Antwerp (*v.* Churchill *Watermarks* 1935 20).

Further searches beyond these identifications, however, were not yielding. I also was unsuccessful in identifying the mark's coat-of-arms, which most probably is not English, as Gunther Pohl, Chief Emeritus of the New York Public Library Genealogy Department, observed. C R J Humphery-Smith, at The Institute of Heraldic and Genealogical Studies in Kent, suggested the English Plunketts; but this attractive potential lead failed to net certain results. In any case, it is doubtful that an identification of the coat would be explicitly relevant to Ephelia, who could have had access to such paper through her patroness, the Ishams, Etherege, or any of her coterie named or initialed in the *Female Poems*, such as Sheldon, Cary Frazier, Nell Gwyn (of questionable literacy), Edward Ravenscroft ("Damon"), and Rochester, probably the "friend" who requested Ephelia's poem "Maidenhead" and whose reply to her "Lamentation" to Mulgrave must have delighted her. If the "Isham" poet, Ephelia herself could have purchased such high-quality paper from, say, Samuel Mearne, one of several prominent London suppliers (*v.* Davenport *Mearne* 1906). Yet,

Figure 9. Watermark of 1679
Collection of Letters & Documents, Town Hall, Rochester, England
In Denne, "Paper-Makers," *Archaelogia* 12 (1796)

Gould's image of "poor *Ephelia* ragged Jilt" can never be far from mind in any reconstruction of this poet.

Somewhat better luck attended me in the matter of the perplexing backward "N" in the watermark. This feature turned out to be a curious species of negative evidence. Such disappointments can be useful, however, as they rule out other possibilities. Humphery-Smith generously informed me that this interesting backward "N" probably did not suggest "Northamptonshire," as I had naïvely hoped (I had reasoned that the wealthy Ishams of Lamport Hall, Northamptonshire could have engaged their own paper-maker), but rather was apt to be the backward "N" in emblemology for "No Name."

Returning to my sources on watermarks, I saw that this was corroborated in Heawood, for in marks 818 and 822 the circle was empty. Relating this to the "Isham" manuscript, I adduced that this symbol stood for the absence of a particular place-name and manufacturer, making this paper a sort of popular open-stock, high quality stationery, favored by English nobles and their coterie.

As regards the "Isham" poem itself, it is described in its title as "A funerall Elegie." As I mentioned above, the titling is important, as it suggests that the elegy was written (probably in haste) to be read <u>at</u> the obsequies. This might account for several creases in the manuscript, suggesting that it had been folded into a small packet for convenient transport to the funeral ceremony or burial grounds

A computer scan of the language of the Isham elegy, by comparing several of its phrases and images against my concordance of Ephelia's writings set up on WordPerfect 5.1, revealed a number of linked words, phrases, and images in the "Isham" poem which are characteristic of Ephelia's poetic habits in *Female Poems*: "Common Men," line 1 (*cf.* "Great Men," *Bajazet*, line 27); "the Poet's Pen," line 2 (*cf.* "a Female Pen," *Prologue*, line 12); "forward Bud," line 14 (*cf.* "blooming bud," *To... Mary*, line 5); *etc.* Most telling in the "Isham" poem is the following passage, wherein the poet admits that language cannot adequately express profoundly felt emotion:

> but griefs like this can never be confin'd,
> They universally invade mankind:
> Nature herselfe close mourner is become,
> And even the Muses too are stricken dumbe:
> None breath their sorrows in a murmuring verse
> but all in awfull silence waite his Hearse

Similar moments of linguistic breakdown appear in earlier verse of Ephelia's published in the *Female Poems*: in her elegy to Sheldon (lines

29-30) and in the lamentation to *Bajazet* (line 23).

As compared to her earlier performance in elegy, namely Ephelia's poem on Sheldon in 1677, published in *Female Poems* in 1679, the "Isham" poem of 1681 represents a development in my poet's work. Certainly, this is a more sophisticated effort in elegy than the Sheldon poem. The Isham poem displays more control of the subject and more confidence with the couplet. The opening sentiment in the Isham elegy, for example, is carried over five lines before a full stop is indicated by the colon after "thought."

My researches into the provenance of this manuscript disclosed that it was deposited at Nottingham by the then-duke of Portland in 1949. My genealogical researches showed that the Bentinck line (the dukes of Portland) was (and is) related to the Cavendishes. Searches in historical materials showed that Welbeck Abbey, the seat of a great manuscript collection amassed by the Bentincks and earlier family ownerships, was originally owned by the Cavendishes, and thereafter by the Holleses and the Harleys (*v.* p. 239, below, for details and sources). This was key information, as the most celebrated literary writer of the Cavendish line was Ephelia's near-contemporary Margaret (Lucas) Cavendish, Duchess of Newcastle, who produced some 15 volumes of literary and philosophical writings during *c.* 1653-68. I reasonably concluded, therefore, that the "Isham" manuscript may well have came into the Bentinck family through Margaret's relatives. (Her death in 1673 predated the "Isham" manuscript by eight years.) It view of her strong feminism, she may have been a collector of literary manuscripts produced by women. Perhaps this enthusiasm was passed on to her relatives. It is my hope that the fine recent work on Margaret Cavendish, by Kathleen Jones (*Glorious Fame* 1988) and by James Fitzmaurice (*PBSA* 85 1991), will inspire researches into this potential new facet of her literary life.

While I was unable to trace the coat-of-arms and the initials of the manuscript's watermark to a precise source, I nonetheless have traced the mark and some 17th-century specimens of the paper in the work of Edward Heawood and Samuel Denne. Moreover, I have brought to light many relevant particulars of this manuscript's physical characteristics, as well as the interlinked families behind the "Isham" poem, including the Bentinck-Cavendish line. Working from internal evidence, I have demonstrated, through computer-assisted analysis, this poem's similarity to Ephelia's poetic habits and imagery. This cluster, then, of related information makes a reasonably persuasive case for this manuscript as an authentic literary manuscript of the 17th century, probably produced in London, and most probably written by the same Ephelia who produced the *Female Poems* in 1679, and the published broadsides of 1678 and 1681.

CRITICAL ESSAY

The collected writings of Ephelia give us an energetic, versatile young writer. Drawing upon her named models -- Cowley, Dryden, Katherine Philips, Aphra Behn -- as well as those unnamed, such as Donne and Sidney, Ephelia exercises her wit on conventional themes of love, death, friendship, and feminism, while also engaging sensitive affairs of state. Her small body of verse flaunts an impressive diversity of styles and genres; for this young writer is a social commentator, a 'songster,' a playwright, a feminist, a loyal Stuart apologist, and a fine lyric poet on the bliss and betrayal of obsessive love.

We now move from Ephelia's writings to the intriguing traditions of her identity.

"JOAN PHILLIPS"

Skeptical at the outset, I became progressively convinced that the knowledgeable H.B. Wheatley knew what he was about when he contributed to Halkett & Laing's *Dictionary of Anonymous & Pseudonymous English Literature* a single-line identification of Ephelia as one Joan Phillips. This was in 1885. As I began to scour selected literature of Ephelia's day for pertinent references or clues to a Joan, an Ephelia, and a female writer "Phillips" (other than Katherine "Orinda" Philips), I netted four pieces of relevant information corroborating Wheatley:

First was Behn's playful reference to "a Poet Joan" in her survey of the Restoration poetic scene in the Prologue to *Sir Patient Fancy* (1678): "Nay, even the Women now pretend to reign, / Defend us from a Poet *Joan* again!" Second was Thomas Newcomb's reference to a female poet named Phillips, who "in Verse her Passion told" (*Bibliotheca* 1712). Third was the identification of Delarivier[e] Manley's young Court attendant "Euphelia" as a Miss Proud (*Key*, Manley's *Atalantis*, 1714). (Interestingly, Hearne calls her "Froude.") (The *Key's* identification of Manley's "Ephelia," one Elizabeth Laurence, failed to align with available facts on my poet.) Finally, there was Ebsworth's invaluable information that "One of Mulgrave's mistresses was 'humble Joan'," which suggested to me its ironic opposite, 'proud Joan' or Joan Proud (*Roxburghe Ballads* IV 1883:568 n.1).

Recorded Fragments of Ephelia:	Behn's "Poet Joan": 1678, *Sir Patient Fancy* Newcomb's poetess "Phillips": 1712, *Bibliotheca* Manley's "Euphelia" ("Miss Proud"): 1714, *Atalantis* Ebsworth's "'humble Joan'" ("Mulgrave's mistress"): 1883, *Roxburghe Ballads* Wheatley's "Joan Phillips": 1885, Halkett & Laing's *Dict.*

As mentioned at the outset of this essay, I had here a cluster of independent, but intersecting pieces of information, which lent strength to Wheatley's identification of Ephelia as Joan Phillips. As I began culling contemporary information on Ephelia from manuscript notes in 17th- and 18th-century copies of her book, I discovered "Joan Phillips" on pastedowns, flyleaves, and titlepages of both editions of the *Female Poems* (1679, 1682), including my own copy, purchased in 1986 from James Cummins-Bookseller, New York City. *But who exactly was this Joan Phillips?*

This leg of my search began with what I referred to earlier in this Critical Essay as "first principles" (page 19); that is, with what already existed. First, there was Sir Edmund Gosse's "wild rumor" of 1885. Drawing upon Wheatley's undocumented identification of Ephelia as one "Joan Phillips," which he may have gotten from Cunningham or from Stainforth, Gosse rashly suggested that Wheatley's "Joan Phillips" might have been the daughter of the celebrated poet-translator-playwright Katherine "*Orinda*" Philips" (*v.* Annotated Bibliography). The enterprising Gosse even altered the spelling of Wheatley's "Phillips" to coincide with the spelling of his candidate's surname, "Philips." But contemporary evidence challenged Gosse; for I found that Thomas Newcomb, a near-contemporary of Ephelia's, mentioned above, had identified her as a poet named "Phillips" (*Bibliotheca* 1712), and that he, as Wheatley in 1885, spelled her name "Phillips." Yet, Gosse's meddlings have won out: his incorrect "Joan Philips" is recorded in Wing, *NCBEL, NUC, BLC, etc.* Thankfully, information on "*Orinda*"'s daughter, supplied by John Pavin Phillips of Haverfordwest, Wales, dramatically overturned Gosse's hypothesis by identifying "*Orinda*"'s daughter as Katherine Wogan *née* Philips, who was neither a Joan nor a literary writer (*v.* Annotated Bibliography). Gosse's "wild rumor" was happily scratched from my list.

Still holding fast to Wheatley's "Joan Phillips," I next surveyed pedigrees of selected literary Phillips families (all variant spellings). I began with the distinguished Welsh Phillipps (Phillips) line of Picton Castle, Pembrokeshire (Fig.10) for two sensible reasons. First, "Joan Phillips" is a strong Welsh name; and, not surprisingly, the wife of the progenitor of this line, Sir Thomas Phillipps, was an heiress, Joan Phillipps (NLW MSS 12359D 775B 776B 21867B). Second, the Welsh Phillipps line had produced literary patrons, writers, and musicians of the 17th and 18th centuries (*v.* M M Philipps *Phillips of Picton* 1906). Although I located two attractive candidates in this accomplished Welsh line, I could not identify them as publishing writers.

When this trail turned cold, I then shifted my focus from Wales

CRITICAL ESSAY

PICTON CASTLE.

To Sir CHARLES EDWARD GREGG PHILIPPS, Bart., this plate, engraved at his expense, is respectfully inscribed.

Figure 10. *Picton Castle, Pembrokeshire, Wales*
Engraved for Sir Charles Edward Gregg Philipps, Bart. (19th Century)
A Print in the Editor's Collection

67

to England, and began to explore literary English Phillipses, beginning with the line of Ambrose Phillips. I also investigated Phillipses in the booktrade, such as Thomas Phillips at the Black Swan in St Paul's Churchyard, an especially attractive candidate as he had been the steward of Arthur, Earl of Anglesey, a distinguished bookcollector of the time (v. Quaritch *Dictionary* rpt. 1969 323). As Appendix E shows, one of the 19th-century earls of Anglesey purchased Stainforth's copy of the second edition of Ephelia's *Female Poems* (1682). But this promising link did not connect with anything I could ferret out. I then turned to the Edward Phillips line of Shrewsbury, relatives of the poet John Milton. This pedigree included a family named Prowde. A published pedigree of Phillips (Fig.11) and a detailed manuscript pedigree of Prowde drawn up by C S Betton and preserved at Shrewsbury (Fig.12), document an intersection between the Phillips and Prowde families through a marriage in the 16th century between an Edward Phillips and a Katherine (Catherine) Prowde (or "Proud"). This union produced another Edward Phillips, who married Anne Milton, the sister of John Milton. Edward Phillips and Anne Milton were the parents of two sons, Edward and John Phillips, Milton's nephews. The brothers Phillips went on to become professional literary men in London around Ephelia's time, with the elder brother Edward the more respected of the two, and a faithful royalist and supporter of women poets.

This link, then, between Prowde and Phillips galvanized my biographical investigations into Ephelia because it aligned with Mulgrave's mistress "humble Joan" (or, ironically, 'proud Joan') and with Manley's "Euphelia," who was identified in the published *Key* to Manley's *Atalantis* as "Miss Proud." But where within the Phillips-Prowde line was Wheatley's "Joan Phillips"?

In the course of investigating various legal documents, mostly deeds, involving the Shrewsbury Prowdes and Phillipses (Shrewsbury Public Library, Documents 567/2F:1-47), and the Betton manuscript pedigree of the Prowde line, my attention became centered on one Anne Prowde of Milk Street, Shrewsbury. Born in Shrewsbury in 1645, Anne was the only living daughter of Joseph and Anne Prowde *née* Phillips. Her only sister Dorcas died at the age of three in 1655. Her eldest brother Joseph was a graduate of Emmanuel College, Cambridge. Anne Prowde's elder brother Richard, a sea-faring man, was buried at sea, c. 1668. The name Dorcas was immediately relevant, as it brought to mind the name of Dorcas's sister-shepherdess in Shakespeare's *Winter's Tale*, Mopsa, which is Ephelia's name choice for her rival for J.G. in *Female Poems*. Anne Prowde impressed me as an attractive

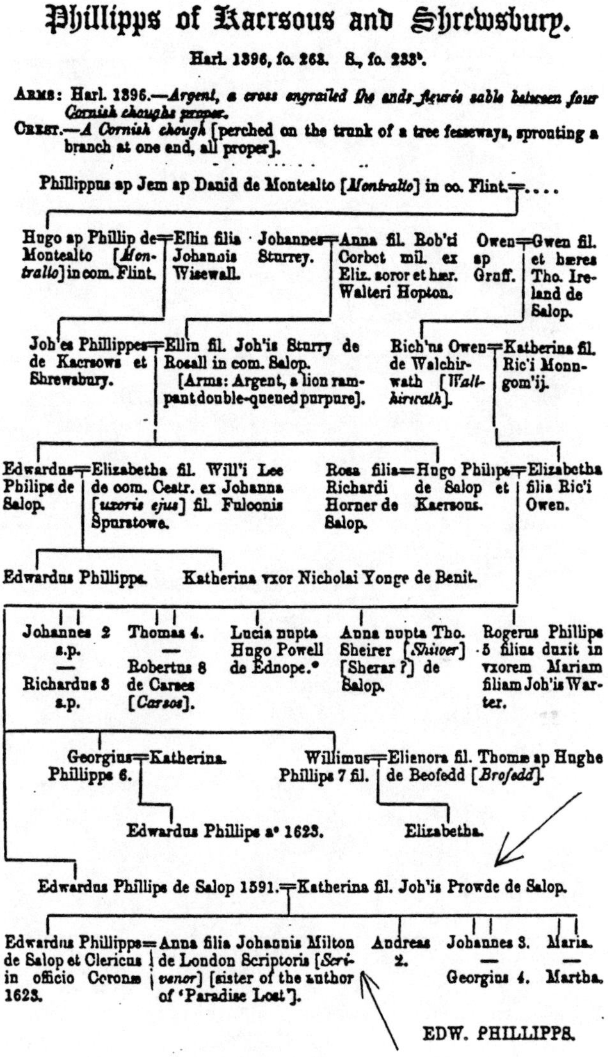

𝔓𝔥𝔦𝔩𝔩𝔦𝔭𝔭𝔰 of 𝔎𝔞𝔢𝔯𝔰𝔬𝔲𝔰 𝔞𝔫𝔡 𝔖𝔥𝔯𝔢𝔴𝔰𝔟𝔲𝔯𝔶.

Harl. 1396, fo. 263. 8., fo. 233ᵇ.

ARMS: Harl. 1396.—*Argent, a cross engrailed the ends figures sable between four Cornish choughs proper.*
CREST.—*A Cornish chough* [perched on the trunk of a tree fesseways, sprouting a branch at one end, all proper].

Phillippus ap Jem ap Danid de Montealto [*Montralto*] in co. Flint.╤....

Hugo ap Phillip de⹋Ellin filia	Johannes⹋Anna fil. Rob'ti	Owen⹋Gwen fil.
Montealto [*Mon-* Johanois	Sturrey. Corbet mil. ex	ap et hæres
tralto]in com. Flint. Wisewall.	Eliz. soror et hær.	Gruff. Tho. Ire-
	Walteri Hopton.	land de Salop.

Joh'es Phillippes⹋Ellin fil. Joh'is Sturry de	Rich'ns Owen⹋Katherina fil.
de Kaersows et Rosall in com. Salop.	de Walchir- Ric'i Monn-
Shrewsbury. [Arms: Argent, a lion ram-	wath [*Walt-* gom'ij.
pant double-queued purpure].	*hirwath*].

Edwardus⹋Elizabetha fil. Will'i Lee	Rosa filia⹋Hugo Philips⹋Elizabetha
Philips de de com. Cestr. ex Johanna	Richardi de Salop et filia Ric'i
Salop. [*uxoris ejus*] fil. Fulconis	Horner de Kaersous. Owen.
Spurstowe.	Salop.

Edwardus Phillippe.   Katherina vxor Nicholai Yonge de Benit.

Johannes 2	Thomas 4.	Lucia nupta	Anna nupta Tho.	Rogerus Phillips
s.p.	—	Hugo Powell	Sheirer [*Shiver*]	5 filios duxit in
—	Robertus 8	de Ednope.*	[Sherar ?] de	vxorem Mariam
Richardus 8	de Carnes		Salop.	filiam Joh'is War-
s.p.	[*Carsos*].			ter.

| Georgius⹋Katherina. | Willimus⹋Elienora fil. Thome ap Hughe |
| Phillipps 6. | Phillips 7 fil. de Beofedd [*Brofedd*]. |

Edwardus Phillips aᵒ 1623.   Elizabetha.

Edwardus Phillips de Salop 1591.⹋Katherina fil. Joh'is Prowde de Salop.

Edwardus Phillipps⹋Anna filia Johannis Milton	Andreas	Johannes 3.	Maria.
de Salop et Clericus de London Scriptoris [*Scri-*	2.	—	—
in officio Coronæ *venor*] [sister of the author		Georgius 4.	Martha.
1623. of 'Paradise Lost'].			

EDW. PHILLIPPS.

Figure 11. *Pedigree of Phillips*
The Visitation of Shrewsbury, 1623
Harleian Society 29 (1889)
Showing Links to Prowde (Proud) & Milton

69

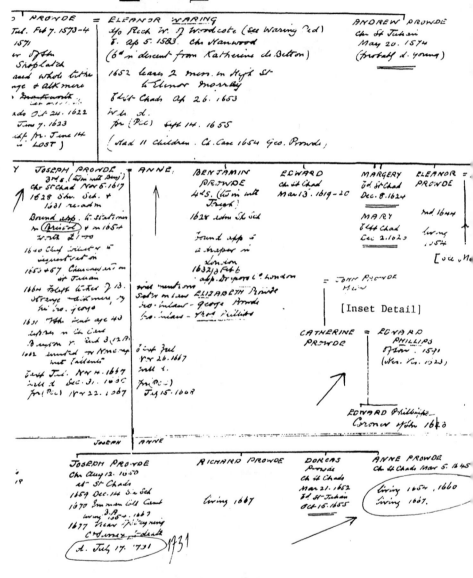

Figure 12. *Pedigree of Prowde (Proud): Detail & Inset Detail*
Showing Links to Phillips of Shrewsbury
Courtesy, Shrewsbury Public Library, MS 2289

CRITICAL ESSAY

speculative candidate for Ephelia, mostly on the ground of intersecting circumstantial evidence.

Of her family, this is known: The Shrewsbury Prowdes were a genteel line of prosperous clothworkers, civic leaders, and churchmen (peerage 1605). Joseph Prowde, Anne's father, was a former stationer in Bristol. After relocation to Shrewsbury, he was the Churchwarden of St Julian's. His brother John Prowde was the Mayor of Shrewsbury in 1650. Many of the Prowdes were prominent Drapers, and active in the Shrewsbury Company of Clothworkers.

The Prowdes were related by marriage to the Edward Phillips line of Shrewsbury and to the John Miltons in London. This large, related family group of Prowde-Phillips-Milton would have enjoyed prestigious connections. If in fact Anne Prowde, Ephelia was a writer of impressive bloodlines, whose early exposure would have pointed her in the direction of a literary life. Her possible attachment to Edward Phillips -- a relative, a professional writer, an historian of women poets -- and thus to the London Miltons, would make Ephelia, *if* Anne Prowde, a newly-recovered member of the Milton-Phillips circle. Is it only coincidental that the incipit of Ephelia's inaugural verse in *Female Poems*, a paean to Charles II on the Popish Plot, salutes the King in an elevated miltonic accent, beginning, "Hail, Mighty Prince!"?

A speculative reconstruction of Anne Prowde's life is possible, based on factual information supplied in documents at Shrewsbury: After the death of her parents, in 1667-68, Anne left Shrewsbury to avoid a marriage to one Richard Plimley, a Shrewsbury mercer. This marriage had been arranged by Anne's maternal uncle and legal guardian, Thomas Phillips of the Strand, London (Shropshire PRO document 567/2F/7). While one Plimley pedigree documents such a marriage (Shrewsbury Public Library document 19559), the more detailed manuscript pedigree of the Prowde line does *not* (Fig.12, page 70). Betton's pedigree of Prowde importantly traces the line down to 1731. *It does not show that Anne married.* Betton's note below her name on the pedigree reads "Living 1654, 1660, 1667." But after 1667, the recorded year of her mother's death, the young Anne Prowde had dropped out of sight. Other sources, such as Shrewsbury marriage records for the principal parishes of Saints Chad, Mary, Julian, and Alkmund, also fail to record a marriage between an Anne Prowde and a Plimley. The extensive *Mormon International Genealogical Index* (2d ed., 1988) records a marriage between a Plimley and an Anne, but the paternal name of this Anne is not recorded. Extant legal deeds of the Prowdes preserved in Shrewsbury do mention one Anne Ford, however, whom Plimley may have married (document 567/2F/7).

71

CRITICAL ESSAY

With a recorded inheritance of 400*l*., which she may have forfeited when she rejected Plimley and fled Shrewsbury, Anne Prowde (if Ephelia) may have set up in London, quite possibly under the guidance and sponsorship of any one of three figures: (1) Edward Phillips, a family relative; (2) Lady Mary (Villiers) Stuart, who reasonably could have known Edward Phillips, since they shared personal links to Wilton House, where Lady Mary resided in the 1630s with her first husband Philip (Herbert), 7th Earl of Pembroke, and where Phillips was a resident tutor in the 1670s (*v.* Godwin *Phillips* 1815).; and (3) Gilbert Sheldon, Archbishop of Canterbury, a recorded family friend of the Phillipses and the Prowdes. As documented above, in my discussion of the family background of Ephelia's "Sheldon" elegy, the Archbishop's signature appears on legal transactions involving the Phillips and Prowde families (Shrewsbury Public Library, Prowde documents 567:2F,2-3; document 1230; R.E. Hone "New Light on the Milton-Phillips Family" *HLQ* 22 1965). As I have pointed out, Ephelia wrote an elegy on Sheldon in 1677, and published the poem two years later in her poetic collection, the *Female Poems*. Vernon Staley, Sheldon's biographer, documents that orphans and writers were special charities of the Archbishop's. If Anne Prowde, Ephelia would have been an orphan after 1667.

My candidate would have begun her career in London as a writer of comic drama, prologues, epilogues, and songs. She may have been attached to the school for ingénues managed by Hart and Banister (v. Appendix B). In view of the feminism of her early work, "The Pair-Royal of Coxcombs" and her gracious encomium to Behn in *Female Poems* (1679), she set up on the feminist model which Behn had brought into vogue. My candidate was active under two covers: In real life, Anne Prowde may have gone under the assumed name "Joan" Prowde. (As Ebsworth stated in 1883, "One of Mulgrave's mistresses was 'humble Joan'.") "Joan," I expect, was a nonce name derived from the shortened forms of her deceased parents' forenames, JOseph and ANne. When Behn publicly disclosed the popularity of "a Poet Joan" (Prologue *Sir Patient Fancy* 1678), she and Ephelia would have enjoyed an inside joke, as nothing had been revealed. The author of *Female Poems*, who enjoyed acrostics, an emblematic frontispiece portrait, and a cleverly encoded pseudonym, did not have to search far for an everyday cover.

Yet, evidently "Joan" Prowde (Proud) was not secure enough: the pseudonym "Ephelia" was selected. My writer would have used a pseudonym for any number of reasons. If in fact Anne Prowde, she was protecting her family from shame, as cultural sentiment against professional women writers was extremely strong during the early years of the Restoration. As the little-known dramatist "Ariadne" explained in her play *She Ventures and He Wins* (1695; comedy LIF), "Nor shall you know, harsh Men, at whom you rail" (*v.* Lyons and Morgan eds. *Female Playwrights* forthcoming 1993).

"Humble Joan Proud," a mistress of a man whom Rochester vilified as "My Lord All-Pride" (Lord Mulgrave), plausibly became known as Joan *Phillips* due to her attachment to the London Phillipses, who were her natural kin. Of this group, Edward Phillips is especially attractive, as he supported the work of women poets. His *Theatrum Poetarum* of 1675 is the first English-language literary history to feature a dedicated section on them. If in fact Ephelia's quiet mentor in her fledgling years in London, Edward Phillips is acknowledged by Ephelia through her curious pseudonym, which may be a cryptonym or encoding for his name as "E.Phillips," adapted and feminized to form the coterie name "Ephelia."

Another possibility, which I find more in keeping with Ephelia's feminism, is that this curious pseudonym refers not to Edward Phillips especially, but to Ephelia's entire maternal line, Phillips. If so, the initial "E" in Ephelia stands for the Latin *ē* or *ex*, meaning "from" or "of" Phillips. The rest of the pseudonym "phelia" would be the pastoral, feminine form of the root of Phillips, "phil." I must acknowledge that another manuscript pedigree of Prowde, drawn in 1663 and preserved at the College of Arms, London (C.35/72), identifies Joseph Prowde's wife as one Anne Guy of Bristol; but the majority of sources, chiefly the legal documents at Shrewsbury, identify her as Anne Phillips of Shrewsbury, and her brother as Thomas Phillips of the Strand, London. It is entirely possible that Thomas Phillips was Mrs Anne Prowde's brother-*in-law*, and that her first husband was kin of the Guy family of Bristol, her second of the Shrewsbury Phillipses. But no recorded genealogical data support this. In Joseph Prowde's will of 31 December 1660, proved 22 November 1667, the young Anne Prowde's guardian Thomas Phillips of London is identified as Joseph Prowde's "brother-in-law," which strengthens my case for Ephelia's maternal line in the Shrewsbury Phillipses.

If Ephelia had been Anne Prowde of Shrewsbury, my speculative hypothesis provides a reasonable explanation for the curious contemporary association of Behn's forename with the name Anne. For example, in the Verney copy of *Female Poems*, selected for this edition, the inscription "Anne" appears in a contemporary hand in the title of Ephelia's elegant encomium to Behn, "To Madame *Bhen*." The title fully reads, in this copy, "To Madame^Anne^Bhen." Even the knowledgeable Luttrell referred to Behn as "Mrs Ann Behn"; and the titlepage of the 1697 edition of Behn's *Rover* identifies her as "Mrs Ann Behn." These locations and several additional examples are identified in O'Donnell's *Behn* (1986; *v.* pp. 37 39-40 58 95 158 257 287 and 401). This contemporary link, then, between Behn and the name Anne may suggest that some of Ephelia's contemporaries knew that my poet's actual forename was not "Joan" but "Anne"; but at some point, they confused her with Behn. This confusion existed into the 19th century. In the catalogue of the Henry Huth library, the description of the Lindsay-Vilders-Huth copy of *Female Poems* identifies its author as Behn (*v.* Appendix E). Reinforcing this interesting tradition of "Mrs Anne Behn" is Gould's passage on Ephelia and Behn as a literary team. This association could have led to a bibliographical confusion between these two handsome young women writers, both feminists, both literary newcomers to London in the 1670s, and both the products of an uncertain background.

Another interesting tradition in historical identifications of Ephelia exists in two poems on friendship in the *Poems On Several Occasions* of Anne (Finch *née* Kingsmill), Lady Winchilsea. She writes of a woman friend named Ephelia, who enjoys "powerful Influence" and who lives in a "large Palace." In light of Gould's portrait of Ephelia as a "ragged Jilt" working the streets of London with Behn, it is unlikely that Winchilsea's Ephelia is the same individual who wrote *Female Poems ... by Ephelia* in 1679. Before her marriage in 1683 to Hineage Finch, Winchilsea had been one of several 'versifying Maid[s] of Honour' at the Court, where she could have known Ephelia or heard about her writings. Perhaps she calls her friend Ephelia in homage to my poet's memory and to the continuum of English literary feminism to which the Ephelia of *Female Poems* contributed. Myra Reynolds, Winchilsea's principal editor, suggests that this later Ephelia may be one of the Thynne women of Longleat (*v. Winchilsea* 1903). In any case, here is a tempting lead which Carol Barash, Charles H. Hinnant, and Ann Messenger may wish to pursue in their valuable probes into the work and coterie of Winchilsea.

Nowhere in the whole of Classical orthography does "Ephelia" derive from the Greek for "freckles," the amusing, undocumented claim of *Kissing The Rod* (1988). While the editorial team of *Rod* wrote off Ephelia in 1988 as a fiction contrived by a cabal of Restoration writers, its editor-in-chief Germaine Greer contradicted the work of her own co-editors a year later, in her *Behn*, when she identified Ephelia, in an endnote, as Cary (Frazier [Fraser/Fraizer]) Mordaunt, Countess of Peterborough, who, according to Greer, "both is and is not Ephelia." Greer's sole evidence is a stanza in "To Capt. Warcup": "Never for Woman was so bad a time, / Falseness in Man is grown a common Crime, / Which Frazier doth lament in tender Rhyme" (*c.*1686; Folger MS m.b.12 f.98). While the Warcup reference errs in identifying Cary as the author of the popular "*Ephelia's* Lamentation," it nonetheless yields, on the face of it, as many as four useful pieces of information, which Greer overlooked:

    (i) it identifies the author of the "Lamentation" as an actual, living female writer flourishing during the 1670s and 1680s;

    (ii) it documents the currency of the "Lamentation" into the 1680s;

    (iii) it mistakes Cary Frazier for Ephelia (both mistresses of Mulgrave at various times), which is a compliment to Ephelia, since "stately Cary Frazier" was a great beauty, though neither a wit nor writer, judging from contemporary references to her; and

    (iv) it illustrates that even a literary gossip of Lenthal Warcup's broad contacts did not know the identity of the woman behind the 'Ephelia' mask (evidently, few in London did; this fact enabled Ephelia to display an image of herself as the frontispiece in *Female Poems*).

Further undermining Greer's identification is Kneller's portrait of Cary, which depicts a woman whose facial planes do not resemble those of the sitter in the frontispiece of *Female Poems*. Also Kneller's subject is a brown-haired woman, not a freckle-faced redhead; and it is difficult to believe that a writer of Ephelia's ego and commitment to authorship would select a pseudonym associated with "freckles."

Moreover, there is a vast difference in personal values between these two young beauties: Ephelia's lengthy verse-essay "Wealth's Power" discloses her disgust of materialism. Cary Frazier, on the other hand, was the living embodiment of it. Contemporary accounts identify her as a conspicuous consumer and the best dressed woman at Court, hardly Gould's "ragged" "Hackney writer" (Rutland MS II 31, 37). Finally, there is a manuscript note in the Verney copy of Ephelia's *Female Poems*, included in this edition, which tentatively identifies the subject of "To Madam *F.*" (probably a mock encomium) as Cary Frazier: "It may be Fraizer." Cary Frazier was a subject of Ephelia's pen, not the writer who held it.

Many blind leads made their way into my biographical searches. Long since scratched, mostly on the basis of biographical fragments and self-disclosures in Ephelia's writings, were all of the following: the highwaywoman Joan Phillips (later Mrs Bracy) of Towcester, Northamptonshire; female kin of Thomas Phillips, bookseller at the Black Swan, St Paul's; three of Mulgrave's mistresses -- Mary "Moll" Kirke,

CRITICAL ESSAY

Frances 'LaBelle' Stuart (a niece of Lady Mary [Villiers] Stuart), and Cary Frazier; Katherine Wogan *née* Philips ("Orinda"'s daughter); the songwriter-lampoonist Katherine Sedley; Anne (Villiers) Bentinck, Duchess of Portland; Mary Mordaunt; Mary Pennington *née* Proud, a writer from Kent; the abandoned wife of Edward Phillips's younger brother, John Phillips; two women in Manley's *Atalantis,* Elizabeth Laurence and Catherine (Cavendish), Countess of Thanet; three red-headed women at Court, Anne Howard, Frances Sheldon, Elizabeth Godolphin (*v.* Wilson *Court Satires*); Elizabeth (Harvey) countess of Stamford; Elizabeth Forster, a mistress of Lord Rochester's; women of Charles Montagu, Earl of Halifax's circle (such as two he names in his verse, "Moll, Countess Dowager of ****" and her rival, a "Mopsa"); and a few attractive candidates from the related Tilly Mowbray-Russell line (*e.g.,* Elizabeth Wriothesley, half-sister of Lady Rachel Russell).

Anne Prowde of Shrewsbury, later "Joan Phillips" of London, aligned more successfully than any of these with the larger configuration of intersecting allusions and genealogical links that grew out of Behn's "Poet Joan," Newcomb's passionate female poet "Phillips," Manley's "Miss Proud," Ebsworth's "humble Joan," and Wheatley's "Joan Phillips." My computerized scan of Ephelia's *Female Poems,* I must add, identified as many as 15 uses of "Proud," 11 of "pride," and 5 of "proudly." In a book of a mere 112 pages, who would not judge such frequency a most attractive 'marker'?

In due course, further researches will either supplement or supplant my speculative case for Anne Prowde of Shrewsbury as the "Joan Phillips" behind the Ephelia mask. If challenged, let the researcher offer a systematic, point-by-point counter-reading of the many allusions and references brought to light in this essay, especially three. The first, J. W. Ebsworth's reference to Lord Mulgrave's mistress, "humble Joan," discussed above. Second, Robert Gould's poetic sketch of my subject as a "poor," "ragged Jilt" and "Hackney Writer," which, in my opinion, rings true. Gould's lines are a brutally candid postscript on the fate of many young women writers of Ephelia's day. For a time they flourished, even with distinguished patronage, but then fell into sore straits, the fate of the literary 'underclass' in any culture. Such were the final days of Behn, the Ephelia of *Female Poems* (I suspect), Elizabeth Thomas, and many others, unknown to us even today, who died miserably in the slums of Grub Street. And third, Ephelia's intimate link to the related Villiers-Herbert-Stuart-Howard line through her patroness. On purely intuitive grounds, I often have thought of Ephelia as an illegitimate daughter of one of the high-born women of this connected lineage. Certainly, this

76

would account for my writer's veiled identity these three centuries and her conspicuous absence on family pedigrees. Until such a broad supposition can be refined and demonstrated, Anne Prowde of Shrewsbury serves as a reasonably attractive speculative candidate, at least for now.

*T*HE PORTRAIT OF EPHELIA

Only a pseudonymous writer utterly secure in her concealed authorship would (a) name her patroness, and (b) display an image of herself in the frontispiece of her own book. As Ephelia discloses in "My Fate," "To My Rival," "To A Proud Beauty," and the lamentation to "*Bajazet*," her face, name, and poetry were well known during her day. Allusions to her by Behn, Newcomb, and Manley attest to this. What was unknown, except to a very small circle of intimates, was Ephelia's identity. And, so, she understandably became confused over the centuries with at least three of her contemporaries, Cary Frazier, Aphra Behn, and Katherine Sedley. 'But, surely, this portrait is fictitious,' I was told by specialists. This observation is understandable, in light of the strenuous 'female' display of the sitter, and the almost generic presentation of the subject. The fact that it is unsigned and undated further detracts from its authenticity. Yet, whether fanciful or ingenious, explanations are possible. Here is my case for this comely frontispiece (*v*. Corbett and Lightbown *Comely Frontispiece* 1979).

Puzzle pictures (so called) always have had special significance, especially if they happen to be frontispiece portraits. In the case of Ephelia's, we have a splendid specimen of the puzzle picture, with its mystification and silent language. Since the portrait is missing in several copies of *Female Poems* (ruthlessly excised from the binding by art collectors, no doubt), we know that it has been a coveted artifact. Not surprisingly, my searches into the provenance of Ephelia's book, identified copies, with portrait intact, in the libraries of two print collectors, Thomas Lloyd of Aston and Frederic Halsey (*v*. Appendix E).

To borrow a phrase from the poetry of Susan Smith Nashe, publisher of *texture press* (Norman, Oklahoma), we have in the frontispiece of *Female Poems* a fully 'embodied page.' While perhaps parodying the languorous beauties of Lely, the portrait distinguishes itself from the charged sensuality, if not vulgarity, of his female sitters by its articulate ensemble of informational clues. Other frontispiece portraits of women writers of Ephelia's day -- say, John Riley's *Behn* for her *Poems*, 1684 -- seem static and mute by comparison. Undated, unsigned, and also lacking a discernible painter's cypher, as Lely sometimes used ("R."), the portrait of Ephelia is a self-inscribed text by the sitter herself. This overtly feminine introduction to a collection of 'female poems' is integral to the book it adorns. Abundantly self-conscious, the sitter in this frontispiece discloses much more than her overripe sexuality: she speaks through the seductive indirection of the portrait's signs and symbols. Assuming that the portrait is in fact an authentic image of the poet whose by-line appears on the facing titlepage, and not a discarded imitation of, say, Lely's *Margaret Hewse* (1672), which it resembles, or retouched apprentice work from the studio of Greenhill, Riley, Closterman, or Wissing, it appears that the sitter has assembled a statement about herself which she invites the spectator to 'read.' I suggest that the message of Ephelia's portrait is a subtly encoded contrast between aristocratic privilege and female debasement. We begin with the its assertion of rank and entitlement.

Just as Ephelia identified herself as a *"Gentlewoman"* in her broadside of 1678, she makes a claim to entitlement in the portrait through physical details, beginning with the armorial badge (or quartering), encased in a roundel at the top of the portrait's frame. The coat in the portrait (Fig.13) appears to be the coat of the ancient Tilly line of France, blazoned *"Argent* a Cross *flory* between four Crescents *Gules"* (v. Papworth's *Ordinary* 1961 637; Mulvihill "Author's Query" *New York Times Book Review* 23 November 1986). As J F Wiffen documents in *Memoirs of the House of Russell* (1833), the Tilly line had died out in the 15th century. Therefore, the engraver, sitter, and possibly the patroness who commissioned the portrait were not violating heraldic law by displaying the abeyant Tilly coat in 1679. Wiffen's pedigree of Tilly (Fig.14) documents a marriage between Tilly and the powerful Russell line in the 14th century. As Hubert Chesshyre at The College of Arms pointed out to me in 1988, the Tilly coat was in fact a quartering on the elaborate Garter stall plate of William (Russell), Earl of Bedford. Wiffen's pedigree also documents a marriage between the Tillys and the Mowbrays in the 13th century. This is relevant, as the Mowbray line, which died out in the late 15th century, devolved to the Howard line, to which Behn was evidently linked in some covert fashion, and into which Ephelia's patroness married in 1664. (Again, we observe a fascinating linkage of family backgrounds behind things ephelian.) In this case, the Tilly coat in the portrait would appear to be an allusion to four powerful related families: Tilly, Mowbray, Howard, Russell. While it is possible that the Tilly coat in the portrait signals Ephelia's connection to one of these illustrious lines through her patronal link to a Howard in-law, who would be distantly related by marriage to the Tilly line through her marriage into the Mowbray-Howard line, it is

CRITICAL ESSAY

Figure 13. *Tilly Coat-of-Arms*
Painted by the Herald Painter, College of Arms, London, 1989
Commissioned by the Editor

LINEAGE OF TILLY.

Arms; *argent* a cross fleury between 4 crescents *gules.*

From MSS. of the Abbé de la Rue, deduced from archives in the Bureau de la
Préfecture at Caen, the Tower of London, and monastic deeds in the Diocese
of Bayeux.

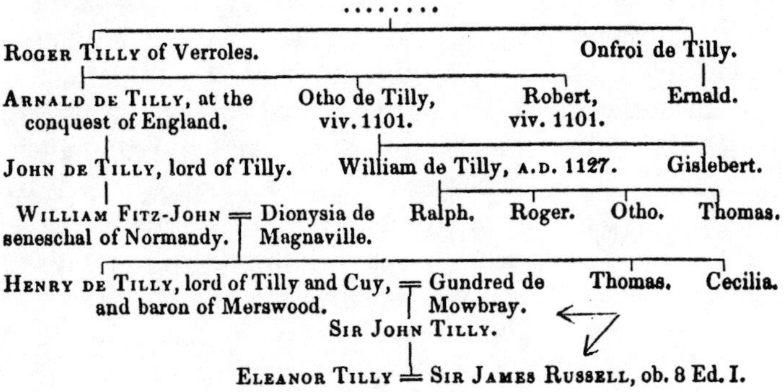

ROGER TILLY of Verroles.   Onfroi de Tilly.

ARNALD DE TILLY, at the   Otho de Tilly,   Robert,   Ernald.
conquest of England.   viv. 1101.   viv. 1101.

JOHN DE TILLY, lord of Tilly.   William de Tilly, A.D. 1127.   Gislebert.

WILLIAM FITZ-JOHN = Dionysia de   Ralph. Roger. Otho. Thomas.
seneschal of Normandy. | Magnaville.

HENRY DE TILLY, lord of Tilly and Cuy, = Gundred de   Thomas.   Cecilia.
and baron of Merswood. | Mowbray.
                        SIR JOHN TILLY.

ELEANOR TILLY = SIR JAMES RUSSELL, ob. 8 Ed. I.

Figure 14. Pedigree of Tilly
From J H Wiffen *House of Russell* (1833)
Showing links to Mowbray (later Howard) & Russell

79

more likely that this heraldic image in the portrait does not refer to *any* of these aristocratic families, but rather to the family which has traditionally been identified as Ephelia's: Phillips.

The coat of the Edward Phillips line of Kaersous, Wales and Shrewsbury, England is structurally similar to the Tilly coat displayed in Ephelia's portrait. The coat of this branch of the Phillips line is blazoned "*Argent* a Cross engrailed the ends *flory* sable between four Cornish Choughs" (Burke *Armory* 1962) (Fig.15). If Anne Prowde, Ephelia is using the abeyant Tilly coat allusively to suggest her maternal line, Phillips. Displaying any coat resembling her paternal line, Prowde, would compromise her carefully guarded pseudonymity.

Of special interest is the fact that the coat in the frontispiece is encircled by laurels. This may quietly allude to the laurel wreath which appears in the bearings of the family with which I associate Ephelia, the Prowdes of Shrewsbury. The coat of this family is blazoned "*Or* three Bars on a Chevron *gules*; crest, a Chaplet of Laurel entwined round a Cross *formée fitched Or*" (Burke *Armory* 1962) (Fig.16). The laurel, a traditional symbol of poetry, is a subject in the *Female Poems*, when Ephelia gives laurels to her lover, J.G. (a distinctly unliterary man) on the occasion of his election to the stewardship of his club (*v.*"To Mr J.G....presented with the Laurel"). Since J.G., as Mulgrave earlier, had jilted Ephelia, and so symbolically declined her laurel-gift, Ephelia confers the laurel upon herself in the portrait. In this visual clue, she has identified herself as indeed the "Poet Joan" whom Behn names in her Prologue to *Sir Patient Fancy* (1678).

My poet's claim to privilege and entitlement in the portrait is further transmitted by her physical appearance. First, she displays the elegant and fashionable coiffure of her day, which features two loose curls (*à négligénce*) at the nape of the neck. This style was introduced to fashionable Londoners by Monsieur Rochfort, and popularized by Nell Gwyn. In literature, it was immortalized by Belinda in Pope's *Rape of the Locke* (1714). Ephelia also displays a single piece of jewelry: not the conventional strand of pearls and matching pearl earrings, so predictable in portraits of women by Van Dyck (*v.* Fig.4, page 32), but rather a portrait-miniature brooch. Dating from the days of Elizabeth I, the portrait-miniature was considered a symbol of true love.

Upon professional magnification of this detail in the portrait (Fig.17), it is possible to discern the head, neck, and shirt collar of a dark-haired man. His facial features are not so discernible. This endearment or memento that Ephelia wears could be an image of one of the two men whom she passionately loved: Lord Mulgrave and J.G. Then, too, it could be a loan from her wealthy patroness, whose prized

Figure 15. *Phillips Coat-of-Arms, Kaersous, Wales & Shrewsbury, England*
Painted by W J F Fenton, Surrey, 1989
Commissioned by the Editor

Figure 16. *Prowde (Proud) Coat-of-Arms, Shrewsbury, England*
Painted by W J F Fenton, Surrey, 1989
Commissioned by the Editor

Figure 17. Magnification of Details in the Frontispiece Portrait of *Female Poems*
By Thomas Todd, Photographer
Taurgo Slides, and the Metropolitan Museum of Art Slide Library, New York

piece of jewelry could have been a portrait-miniature of one of her Stuart relatives.

The very fact that Ephelia's book is introduced by a striking engraved frontispiece portrait is strong evidence of impressive connections at the time the book was produced. Surely it was these same connections which shielded its author from vicious attacks on women writers in the day's antifeminist 'session' satires and lampoons.

Yet, in spite of these details of entitlement and privilege in the portrait, there exists a conflicting sub-text of debasement, beginning with the articulate image of the sitter's dress. She is most assuredly wearing a gown; but what she is *not* wearing is the conventional laced corset and, certainly, the white linen undershift, whose laced fringe is readily observable in female portraiture of Ephelia's day, such as portraits of Behn by Lely, Beale, and Riley (*v.* Laver *Costume and Fashion* 1985 103f; Kemper *Costume* 1979 89f 94f). In light of Ephelia's performance in the poem "Maidenhead" and her criticism of immoral women in her coterie verse, the message of the portrait would not be overtly sexual, as the casual spectator would initially judge from the deep *décolletage* of the sitter's gown. Instead, I suggest that Ephelia gives us a compelling feminist image of stripped-down womankind; for regardless of her pedigree, beauty, and talent, Ephelia has been abused by her lovers and victimized by her adversary "Fate." While her bad luck temporarily abated at the time of her public authorship in 1678, she evidently chose to pose 'in character' for the portrait; and it is this image of Ephelia as a pathetic "ragged Jilt" which Robert Gould fastened on and fixed for posterity in his *Satyrical Epistle.*

Professional magnification of certain details in the portrait (*v.* facing page) led to interesting information, beginning with a curious object on the plinth of the portrait. It appears to be a small ribbon. This may be a fallen ribbon from Ephelia's torn gown, discussed below, or it may be the traditional "true lovers' knot," which sometimes appeared at the top of the coat-of-arms in formal portraits of unmarried English women at this time, to indicate that the sitter was still in the marriage market (*Boutell's Heraldry* 1983 147f.). Such is the case in Faithorne's *Sarah Gilly*, a minor poet of Gould's circle. (As a point of reference, this portrait is erroneously bound in with several copies I have seen of Hannah Woolley's *Gentlewoman's Companion* 1675.) Because Ephelia has committed herself to poetry, her metaphoric or allusive bearings are graced by the more appropriate poetic adornment, a laurel. The conventional lover's knot, withheld from Ephelia through the deceitfulness of Mulgrave and then J.G., now sits as discarded debris on the portrait's plinth, above the second "E" in "EPHELIA."

CRITICAL ESSAY

The frontispiece portrait in *Female Poems*, then, is an autobiographical self-portrait of its sitter, artfully assembled by the sitter herself. The pages following the frontispiece disclose in a different medium -- the printed words of the poet -- the experiences of a young woman writer whose best years were dominated by two men of the world, who exploited her naïveté and abandoned her. Loss -- of parents, "estate," and reputation, as Ephelia discloses in "My Fate" -- marked her early years. Her literary career, though not entirely without achievement, was short-lived.

To the eye of a trained observer there is no denying that the overall presentation of the sitter, in spite of her elegant hairstyle, jewelry, and coat-of-arms, is anything but privileged. In 1989, the knowledgeable Robert W. Karrow, Special Collections Curator at the Newberry Library in Chicago, which preserves the Lindsay-Vilders-Huth copy of *Female Poems* (1679) (*v.* Appendix E), mentioned to me that the gown in the portrait appeared to be torn. Upon magnification (page 82), this seemed plausible. It appears that a break or tear exists in the drapery of the sitter's gown, just to the spectator's right of the portrait-miniature. This tear or rip is clumsily disguised by an unattractive, unravelling bow. A hanging string from the bow is clearly visible, even without magnification. The costume of the sitter, therefore, is dramatically at odds with other symbols and signs of privilege that animate this portrait. Here, I suggest, is the source of Robert Gould's striking description of Ephelia as a "ragged" hack-writer. Since Gould was capturing Ephelia in a few, quick stokes of his splenetic pen in his *Satyrical Epistle* (page 27, above), he naturally would have selected a recognizable contemporary image of his subject. He found one in her own book, no less. Given the detail, high color, and telling veracity of his poetic sketch, Gould's representation of Ephelia was based on first-hand observation.

Thomas Flatman (1637-1680) may have executed this portrait or at least some sketch or likeness of Ephelia, which then served the engraver of the frontispiece. A poet and painter, with a specialty in the portrait-miniature, Flatman was one of Edward Phillips's circle; in fact, so close was their association that their respective canons have been confused for centuries (*v. NCBEL* 2:473). Flatman, as Phillips, was a supporter of women poets; his signed encomium to Katherine "Orinda" Philips was prefixed to her *Works* in 1667. Respectful of his sitter's pseudonymity, Flatman does not lend his name nor initials to the canvas. Yet, according to my reconstruction, he "signed" it nonetheless through the brooch his sitter wears, which could be one of Flatman's own self-portrait miniatures. Some of these have been preserved in the

CRITICAL ESSAY

Dyce Collection and in the collection of the Duke of Buccleuch.

Prince Rupert (d. 1683), husband of Elizabeth Stuart, the unfortunate Queen of Bohemia, is a reasonable candidate for the engraver of this portrait. Attractive evidence exists in the fact of Rupert's intimacy with Ephelia's patroness, Lady Mary (Villiers) Stuart (*v.* Casavetti *Lion & Lilies* 1977 86). Rupert also was a lover of the actress Peg Hughes; and we know from Ephelia's writings that she was active on the theater circuit. As Evelyn's *Sculptura* (1662) documents, Rupert was adept in sophisticated technical procedures of engraving; and Evelyn credits Rupert for introducing Ludwig von Siegen's mezzotint into England. In 1683, Flatman published an affectionate pindaric ode on the death of Rupert, a fact which establishes a firm link between my two candidates. In light of Rupert's documented ties to Ephelia's patroness, he may have been commissioned by Lady Mary to engrave the portrait (or some likeness) of Ephelia, which his friend Flatman had executed.

It interests me that this intriguing frontispiece of Ephelia's book also suggests several features of the ragged, jilted beauty Corinna in Rochester's *Artemisa to Cloe.* Rochester, as well as his wife, wrote poems about a Corinna; and, incidentally, one of Rochester's songs ("What cruel Pains *Corinna* takes") uses the word "proudly," which aligns with my speculative identification of Ephelia as one of the Phillips-Prowde line. Had Germaine Greer and the editorial team of *Kissing The Rod* pursued Greer's casual suggestion that Rochester's Corinna resembled Ephelia, they could have developed some plausible, fresh perspectives on the frontispiece portrait in *Female Poems* and on its sitter. As they did not, I offer my own:

Rochester's *Artemisa to Cloe* was first published as a broadside in 1679, the same year James Courtney published Ephelia's *Female Poems.* Rochester's interesting poem was sold by William Leach at the Sign of the Crown in Cornhill (*BLR* 4 1952-3 183-4). Rochester's verse-epistle includes a lengthy cautionary tale about a beautiful *naïf*, newly arrived in London, who is abandoned by a sophisticated man of wit. She thereafter degenerates into a life of shameful poverty. Rochester's explicit allusion to Corinna's lover as Mulgrave (Ephelia's first lover) would not have been lost on Ephelia and her contemporaries, even if lost on modern readers. A number of details about Corinna suggest the author of *Female Poems.* Rochester's vignette begins:

> That wretched thing *Corinna*, who has run
> Through all the sev'ral ways of being undone:
> ...
> Gay were the Hours, and wing'd with joy they flew,

CRITICAL ESSAY

When first the Town her early Beauties knew:
Court'd, admir'd, and lov'd with Presents fed;
Youth in her Looks, and Pleasure in her Bed:
'Till Fate, or her ill Angel, thought it fit
To make her doat upon a man of Wit;
Who found 'twas dull to love above a day,
Made his ill-natur'd jest, and went away.
Now scorn'd of all, forsaken and opprest,
She's a *Memento Mori* to the rest:
Diseas'd, decay'd, to take up half a Crown
Must Mortgage her Long Scarf, and Manto Gown;
Poor Creature, who unheard of, as a Flie,
In some dark hole must all the Winter lye:
And want, and dirt, endure a whole half year,
That, for one month, she Tawdry may appear.
In *Easter* Term she gets her a new Gown: [*etc.*]

The tale continues with Corinna's plot to avenge herself on all mankind. She begins her plan by ensnaring a wealthy, naïve heir. After exploiting him, she poisons her lover, and, through their bastard son, she inherits his estate. As there is no evidence in Ephelia's work to suggest any proclivity to murder, Rochester must be combining two contemporary scandals. He draws upon the Ephelia-Mulgrave affair in the first section of his story; he then turns in the second half to some other subject of contemporary gossip. Had Ephelia been known as a rank murderess by Rochester and his royalist circle, it seems unlikely that she would have been free to continue publishing, with a signed broadside to a Stuart, no less, in 1681. Rochester's references to Corinna's wardrobe and poverty suggest the debasement subtext in Ephelia's portrait. But absolutely clinching is Rochester's reference in the Corinna tale to his bitter enemy, Mulgrave. In fact, one line in the Corinna tale, "[He] found 'twas dull to love above a day," is a direct allusion to Rochester's answer-poem to "*Ephelia's* Lamentation." In this very answer-poem to the "Lamentation," Rochester begins, in the persona of Mulgrave:

> *Madam,*
> If your deceiv'd, it is not by my Cheat,
> For all disguises, are below the Great,
> What Man, or Woman, upon Earth can say,
> I ever us'd 'em well above a Day?

Rochester's reference in *Artemisa to Cloe* to Corinna's new gown at "*Easter* Term" may refer to the fact that Ephelia's *Female Poems* was published during Easter-Term, 1679 (*v.* Arber *Term Catalogue* I:350).

Money from the sale of her manuscript to Courtney, and a patronal stipend, could have bought her a silk Mantua gown. Yet the gown in the portrait is not new, but "ragged," to use Gould's choice in adjective.

Ephelia may well have been Rochester's model in the first section of the Corinna tale. He took from her experience what was needed to create the first half of a good story. But because he evidently respected Ephelia's pseudonymity, Rochester did not name his ragged jilt "Ephelia," nor does he identify her as a writer (though he *does* say that she "talk'd so fine"). Perhaps sympathetic to Ephelia's treatment from Mulgrave, he did not wish to add to her shame. Yet, I suggest that Rochester cleverly left a valuable link to Ephelia when he called his wretched jilt "Corinna." This name recalls an earlier pseudonymous woman writer of 'female poems,' the Corinna of Pindar's time (5th Century B.C.). As Ephelia, the Classical Corinna was celebrated for her poems to and about women (*v. Oxford Classical Dict.* rpt 1976 290). This background is relevant, since other women writers after Ephelia's time were called "Corinna." Beginning quite possibly with my poet, this name came to be associated with a particular type of woman writer from the London street culture. Dryden, for example, perhaps knowing something of the background of Rochester's Corinna tale, calls the similarly unfortunate poet Elizabeth Thomas "Corinna." (Thomas was born too late to have been the writer of *Female Poems*, of course.) In the 18th century, as Constance Clark has shown, Swift in his verse referred to Delarivier[e] Manley as "Corinna"; and Pope in the *Dunciad* associates Eliza Haywood with the Corinna-type of woman writer (*v.* Clark in *Curtain Calls* eds. Schofield and Macheski 1991).

Rochester's cautionary tale in *Artemisa to Cloe* seems useful to a broader reading of the frontispiece of *Female Poems*. My treatment of his story again underscores the pattern of intersecting contemporary information and allusion which has distinguished the course of my investigations and assisted my formulations. Rochester's story of Corinna aligns with Gould's sketch of Ephelia and with details in her portrait. Surely, no fiction nor hoax prompted Gould and Rochester to lift their pens on these occasions.

In the frontispiece to her book, Ephelia made the choice to leave posterity a candid and characteristic image of herself, one which captured her past, present, and even her unfortunate future, so it seems. While no record exists of the commercial success or print run of *Female Poems* (probably a small coterie printing, given its scarcity), Ephelia evidently flourished long enough to continue her literary pursuits down through August, 1681. Unlike Rochester's Corinna, she did not turn to poison to revenge herself on the men of wit who debased her, such as Mulgrave and then *J.G.*; she turned instead to poetry. The publication of her elegant octavo in 1679 may have been her special triumph over those individuals who, by turns, set her life on a downward path.

Her intriguing biography aside, Ephelia left to the historical record something infinitely more interesting than her personal past, attractive as that has been to researchers these three centuries. Under the protective wing of Lady Mary (Villiers) Stuart, Duchess of Richmond and Lenox, Ephelia left a body of writings -- political broadsides, songs, love-poems, feminist and coterie verse, poems on social issues and manners -- which merit attention for their intrinsic worth, contemporary character, and appealing relevance to the present moment. While reflecting many of the best qualities of Restoration poetry, Ephelia's work also speaks to such modernist concerns as women writers, feminist literature, and the dynamic play between cultural controversy and literary production.

With this first editorial venture on Ephelia's behalf, it has been my special pleasure and mission to restore her to the canon of 17th-century English literature, and to make possible at last the long-overdue status so long denied Ephelia and the legacy of her "female Pen."

II. THE COLLECTED MANUSCRIPT & PUBLISHED

POETRY

OF EPHELIA

A POEM

TO

His Sacred Majesty,

ON THE

PLOT.

Written by a Gentlewoman.

LONDON: Printed for *Henry Brome* at the *Gun*
in
St *Paul*'s Church-yard

Licensed November 23, 1678
Roger L'Estrange

A POEM

TO

His Sacred Majesty,

ON THE

PLOT.

Written by a Gentlewoman.

Hail *Mighty Prince! whom Providence defign'd*
To be the chief delight of Humane Kind :
So many Virtues crowd Your Breaft, that we
Do almoft queftion Your Humanity :
Sure every Planet that o're Virtue Reigns,
Shed it's beft Influence in Your Royal Veins.
You are the Glory of Monarchal Pow'rs,
In Bounties free, as are defcending Showrs ;
Fierce as a Tempeft, when engag'd in War,
In Peace more mild than tender Virgins are;
In Mercy, You not only Imitate
The Heav'nly Pow'rs, but alfo Emulate.
None but Your Self, Your Suff'rings could have born
With fo much Greatnefs, fuch Heroick Scorn :
When hated Traytors do Your Life purfue
And all the world is fill'd with Cares for You,
When every Loyal Heart is funk with fear,
Your Self alone, does unconcern'd, appear,
Your Soul within ftill keeps its awful ftate,
Contemns, and Dares, the worft effects of Fate ;
The Majefty that fhoots from Your bright Eye,
Commands Your Fate, and awes Your Deftiny.
And yet thô Your brave Soul bear You thus high,
Your folid Fudgment fees there's Danger nigh,
Which with fuch Care and Prudence You prevent,
As if You fear'd not, but wou'd crofs th' Event :

Your Care fo Nobly looks, it doth appear,
'Tis for Your Subjects, not Your Self You fear :
Heavens, make this Princes Life Your neareft Care,
That does fo many heavenly Virtues fhare.
If Kings may be allow'd to Copy You,
CHARLES *is the likeft, Nature ever drew :*
Blaft every hand, that dares to be fo bold
An impious weapon 'gainft His Life to hold ;
Burft every heart, that dares but think Him ill,
Their guilty Souls with fo much Terror fill,
That of themfelves they may their PLOT unfold,
And live no longer, when the Tale is told :
Safe in your Care all elfe would needlefs prove,
Yet keep Him fafe too in His Subjects Love ;
Your Subjects view You with fuch Loyal Eyes,
They know not how they may their Treafure prize.
Were You defencelefs, they would round You fall,
And pile their Bodies to build up a wall.
Were You oppres'd, 'twou'd move a generous ftrife
Who firft fhould lofe his own, to fave Your Life :
But fince kind Heaven thefe Dangers doth remove,
We'll find out other wayes to exprefs our Love.
We'll force the Traytors all, their Souls refign
To herd with them, that taught them their Defign.

FINIS.

Licenfed *Nov.* 23. 1678.   *LONDON :*
  Roger L'Eftrange.   Printed for *Henry Brome* at the *Gun* in St. *Paul's* Church-yard.

93

FEMALE

POEMS

On several

OCCASIONS.

_____

Written by *Ephelia*.

_____

LONDON: Printed by *William Downing* for *James Courtney*,
1679

FEMALE
POEMS
On several
OCCASIONS.

Written by *Ephelia*.

LONDON,

Printed by *William Downing,* for *James Courtney, Anno Dom.* 1679.

To the moſt

EXCELLENT PRINCESS

MARY,

Dutcheſs of *Richmond* & *Lenox*.

A S he that *Plants* a tender *Vine*, takes care
To ſhelter it from the cold Northern *Aire*,
And place it where the *Vigour* of the *Sun*
May *Cheriſh* it, will it be ſtronger grown :
So I, that muſt a blooming *Bud* expoſe,
To greater Dangers than the *North* wind blows ;
Under ſome happy Shade wou'd have it grow,
Where it ſecure from *Blaſts* may kindly *Blow* :
Than *Your* great *Self*, none fitter can I find ;
For *You*, to all that need your *Help*, are kind :
So great your *Power* is, none will pretend
T'oppreſs the Smalleſt thing that *You* defend :

A 2   *Your*

The Epistle Dedicatory.

Your Noble Clemency bids me be Bold,
And lay it at Your Feet, Fear bids me hold ;
Asks how I can but hope, that you, who enjoy
Such Mighty Wit, shou'd mind so poor a Toy ?
But Fear I'le Banish, Hope shall be my Guide,
And I will act a Miracle of Pride :
Omit th'Address that all to Greatness use,
And begg you'd Patronize an Infant Muse :
Give leave the front may with your Name be drest,
And then the World will value all the rest.
All know, great Madam, that you do Inherit
Your Noble Fathers far more noble Spirit :
In generosity you've Wonders done,
And Bounty's Prize from all Mankind have won :
Your Face was always Beauty's Standard thought,
Where all Pretenders to be try'd were brought :
Such noble Constancy dwells in your Breast,
Such gen'rous Scorn of Fortune you've exprest,
Ev'n when the greatest of her Ill you've had,
A Fathers fall, as undeserv'd, as sad :
Lost crouds of Noble Friends, a large Estate ;
You bravely bore these sad Effects of Fate :
The Noble Richmond, and Great Howard, are
Losses that nothing ever can Repaire :

Such

The Epiſtle Dedicatory.

Such Valiant, Comely, Loyal, Gallant Men, ⎫
The Court muſt never hope to ſhew agen: ⎬
Yet you with Patience theſe Stroaks ſuſtain. ⎭
More Fortitude's in your Heroick Mind,
Than can be ſhown again by Woman-kind:
Had I a leſs Soul'd Patron, I ſhou'd fear
This idle Trifle would offend your Ear:
But Madam, your Indulgence doth extend,
Not only to Encourage, but Defend

Ephelia.

A POEM

A
P O E M

Prefented to his

SACRED MAJESTY,

on the Difcovery of the

P L O T.

Ail Mighty Prince! whom Heaven has defign'd
To be the chief Delight of human kind:
So many Vertues croud your Breaft, that we
Do almoft queftion your Mortality:
Sure all the Planets that o're Vertue Reigns,
Shed their beft Influence in your Royal Veins:
You are the Glory of Monarchial Pow'rs,
In Bounties free as are defcending Show'rs,
Fierce as a Tempeft when ingag'd in War,
In Peace more mild than tender Virgins are;

B   In

In pitying Mercy, you not imitate
The Heavenly Pow'rs, but rather Emulate.
None but your Self, your Suffrings could have born
With so much Greatnefs, such Heroick Scorn :
When hated Traytors do your Life perfue,
And all the World is fill'd with cares for you ;
When every Loyal Heart is funk with Fear,
Your Self alone doth unconcern'd appear ;
Your Soul within, ftill keeps it's lawful State,
Contemns and dares the worft effects of Fate ;
As the bright Majefty fhot from your Eye,
Aw'd your tame Fate, and rul'd your Deftiny.
Though your undaunted Soul bear you thus high,
Your folid Judgment fees there's danger nigh ;
Which with fuch Care and Prudence you prevent,
As if you fear'd not, but would crofs th'Event.
Your Care fo nobly looks, it doth appear
'Tis for your Subjects, not your Self. you fear :
Heaven make this Princes Life your nearest care,
That does fo many of your Vertues fhare :

If

If Monarchs in their Actions copy you,
This is the neareſt piece you ever drew:
Blaſt every Hand that dares to be ſo bold,
An impious Weapon 'gainſt his Life to hold:
Burſt every Heart that dares but think him ill;
Their guilty Souls with ſo much Terrour fill,
That of themſelves they may their Plot unfold,
And live no longer than the Tale is told:
Safe in your Care, all elſe will needleſs prove,
Yet keep him ſafe too in his Subjects love.
Your Subjects view you with ſuch Loyal eyes,
They know not how they may their Treaſure prize:
Were you defenceleſs, they would round you fall,
And Pile their Bodies to build up a Wall.
Were you diſtreſs'd, 'twould move a gen'rous ſtrife,
Who firſt ſhould looſe his own, to ſave your Life.
But ſince kind Heaven theſe dangers doth remove,
VVee'l find out other ways t' expreſs our Love.
VVee'l force the Traytors all, their Souls reſign,
To Herd with him that taught them their Deſign.

AN

A N
ELEGY

On the Right Reverend
GILBERT SHELDON,
Ld Arch – Bishop of *Canterbury*.

When I heard *Sheldon* had to Fate refign'd,
A fudden Confternation feiz'd my Mind,
Senfelefs I ftood, the dangerous Surprize
Kept back the Pious Tribute of my Eyes:
And tho no words can e're my Grief exprefs,
Yet by their own, all may judge it's Excefs:
For when fo good, fo great a Prelate falls,
The World muft Celebrate his Funerals:
And not a man in the vaft Univerfe,
But fends a Bleeding Heart t'attend his Herfe:
To tell his Vertues would whole Volumes ask,
And were a *Seraph*'s, not a Womans task.

Over

106

Over his Flock, so tenderly Austere,
He taught them both at once, to Love and Fear;
So strictly Pious, that to all that knew
His holy life, his Precepts needless grew.
Despis'd Religion did so Beauteous seem
In this blest Saint, it rais'd its first Esteem:
His head, a Receptacle did contain
More Learning than the world can boast again.
He made his Wealth and large Possessions be,
But humble Handmaids to his Charitie;
VVhich was so great, it might be truly said,
That by his Death the Poor were Orphans made:
VVhen ugly Treason flourisht highest, he
Spight of the danger, own'd his Loyalty.
VVith joy he suffer'd for the Church and State,
And bore with ease the weightiest stroaks of Fate.
Stop! stop a while! fierce Rapture choaks my words,
And no expression to my Thoughts affords:
I am all admiration! and as well
Some heavenly Vision, as his Worth might tell.

B 3   ACROS-

ACROSTICH.

All sev'ral Beauties, Colours, Airs, and Grace,
None ever saw together in one Face:
No? hold a while; I do a Lady know,
Each several Beauty splendidly can show.
But alas! Beauty's but the smallest Grace,
Unless it be i'th' Mind as well as Face:
Rare she is too i'th' Beauties of the Mind;
Young, and yet wise, the wonder of her Kind.

ACROSTICH.

Apollo hence! thy aid I do refuse;
No Nymph will I implore, nor yet no Muse;
No Nectar do I want, to write her praise
Great Subjects, without help our Fancies raise:
In thy sweet Face such charming Beauties be,
Less we at Angels wonder than at thee:
Brighter than Suns thy lovely Eyes appear,
Each look doth a Majestick sweetness wear:
Reign Sov'reign Queen of Beauty, Love, and wit,
Till Death's cold hand shall teach thee to submit.

Loves

Love's first Approach.

Strephon I saw, and started at the sight,
And interchangably look'd red and white;
I felt my Blood run swiftly to my heart,
And a chill Trembling seize each outward part:
My Breath grew short, my Pulse did quicker beat,
My Heart did heave, as it wou'd change its Seat:
A faint cold sweat o're all my Body spread,
A giddy Megrim wheel'd about my head:
VVhen for the reason of this change I sought,
I found my Eyes had all the mischief wrought;
For they my Soul to *Strephon* had betray'd,
And my weak heart his willing Victim made:
The Traytors, conscious of the Treason
They had committed 'gainst my Reason,
Look'd down with such a bashful guilty Fear,
As made their fault to every Eye appear.
Tho the first fatal look too much had done,
The lawless wanderers wou'd still gaze on,

B 4 kind

Kind Looks repeat, and Glances steal, till they
Had look'd my Liberty and Heart away :
Great Love, I yield ; send no more Darts in vain,
I am already fond of my soft Chain ;
Proud of my Fetters, so pleas'd with my state,
That I the very Thoughts of Freedom hate.
O Mighty Love ! thy Art and Power joyn,
To make his Frozen breast as warm as mine ;
But if thou try'st, and can'st not make him kind,
In Love such pleasant, real Sweets I find ;
That though attended with Despair it be,
'Tis better still than a wild Liberty.

The Change or Miracle.

VVhat Miracles this childish God has wrought !
Things strange above belief ! who wou'd have thought
My Temper cou'd be to this Tameness brought ?

I, who the wanton Boy so long defi'd,
And his Fantastick Godhead did deride,
And laugh'd at Lovers with insulting Pride :

Now

Now pale and faint, beneath his Altar lie,
Own him a great and glorious Deity,
And want the pitty that I did deny.

For my proud Victor does my Tears neglect,
Smiles at my Sighs, treats me with difrefpect,
And if I do complain, with frowns I'm check't.

Though all I fue for, be the empty blifs
Of a kind Look, or at the moft a Kifs,
Yet he's fo cruel to deny me this.

Before my Paffion ftruck my Reafon blind,
Such Generofity dwelt in my mind,
I car'd for none, and yet to all was kind.

But now I tamely bend, and fue in vain,
To one that takes delight t' encreafe my pain,
And proudly does Me, and my Love difdain.

To

To a Gentleman that durst not pass the door while I stood there.

SIR,

Passions force compels me now to write,
    And aggravates the wrongs I fain wou'd slight :
They to my Soul in such loud clamours speak,
That Reason to resist them is too weak :
First, Rage or Anger, (call it which you please)
VVhispers my Soul, bear such affronts as these?
Can your great Mind be unconcern'd, when you
VVith your own Eyes did such a passage view?
Can you with Patience hear him say, he dare
Not stir from thence while that fond Fool is there?
Oh! where is all your former Greatness gone?
You in this Act the *Stoicks* have out done :
He calls you fond, and kind, but let him see
You can disdain such petty things as he :
Thus Anger counsel'd me to do,---- but when
I strove to obey her Dictats, ah! then

Some

Something like pitty in your Caufe did plead,
And my faint Anger did in Triumph lead:
Shame pleaded next, and mildly did requeft,
She might not quite be exil'd from my breft,
VVhich fhe muft be, if I fhou'd entertain
But the leaft Thought of loving you again;
For when firft notice of the words I took,
Such heat and blood into my Face it ftruck,
My felf cou'd hardly tell for what it came,
VVhether I blufh'd for anger or for fhame:
But when your face I faw, I ftraight grew cold,
I ftarted, trembl'd, and my Eye-balls roul'd:
The breath I had fcarce ferv'd me to retire,
E're in a Swound I gently did expire.
But my high Thoughts, and too too gen'rous Flame,
Scorn'd to be curbed by a needlefs Shame:
Hate pleaded next, fiercer than all the reft,
And yet a greater ftranger to my breft;
For my calme breft, till now was ne're the Seat
Of Surly Paffion, or unruly Heat,

Hate

Hate urg'd, each Action look'd as done in scorn,
Then asked if I to bear affronts was born :
This and much more She said, but all in vain,
Ill thoughts of you I ne're cou'd entertain ;
Your great Affronts, I witty Jests did think,
And at coy Looks would turn my head, or wink :
Nay, when you gave such proofs of your Disdain,
That I must see't, I gav't another Name ;
I only thought you saw me go astray,
And generously put me in my way.
How strangely is my Life perplex'd by fate !
I wou'd not Love, and yet I cannot hate.

First farewel to *J. G.*

FArewel my dearer half, joy of my heart,
   Heaven only knows how loth I am to part :
VVhole Months but hours seem, when you are here,
VVhen absent, every Minute is a Year :
Might I but always see thy charming Face,
I'de live on Racks, and wish no easier place.

But

But we muſt part, your Intereſt ſays we muſt ;
Fate, me no longer with ſuch Treaſure truſt.
I wou'd not tax you with Inconſtancy,
Yet *Strephon*, you are not ſo kind as I :
No Intereſt, no nor Fate it ſelf has pow'r
To tempt me from the Idol I adore :
But ſince you needs will go, may *Africk* be
Kinder to you, than *Europe* is to me :
May all you meet and every thing you view
Give you ſuch Tranſport as I met in you.
May no ſad thoughts diſturb your quiet mind,
Except you'l think of her you left behind.

To

To Mr. J. G. *on his being chosen Steward of his Club, presented with the Laurel.*

SIr, by your Merit led, to you I bring
   A Laurel-wreath, but 'tis too mean a thing
For your high VVorth and Parts, which we
In vain wou'd Blazon by such Herauldry :
For Laurel, Palme, and Olive, may set forth
Our Love to you, but not express your worth ;
VVhich doth exceed these humble types, as far
As *Titans* Rays out shine a twinkling *Star* :
I'le say no more, lest while I make You best,
I seem Injurious to all the rest
Of this fair Company, who do all by me
Chuse you their Steward, and unanimously
Intreat your care, to make their Club to be
For Honour and Grandure, *The Society.*

To

To *J. G.* in abfence.

DEar Object of my Love! didſt thou but know
The Tortures, that I daily undergo.
For thy dear ſake, thou ſure woud'ſt be ſo kind,
To weep the Troubles that invade my mind;
I need not tell thee that I dearly love,
No, all my Actions will my Paſſion prove:
For thee I've left the wiſe, the great, the good,
And on my Vows, not my Preferment ſtood.
Think then, dear *Strephon*, how unkind thou art,
To prove the Torturer of that tender heart,
That choſe thee out to be its chief Delight,
And knows no real Joy but in thy ſight.
Since firſt thy Courtſhip me to Love inclin'd,
Thou ne're haſt been one hour out of my mind.
How tedious then muſt thy long abſence be
To her, that wiſhes nothing elſe to ſee,
And lives not, but when in thy Company?
Haſte then dear Love! for if thou longer ſtay,
My Griefs will make me ſigh my Soul away.

Prologue

Prologue to the Pair-Royal of Coxcombs, Acted at a Dancing-School.

Gallants,

IF, as you say, you Love Varietie,
 VVe have some hopes, that you so kind will be
To the poor Play, to give it your Applause,
Though not for Wit, nor Worth, but yet because
A Woman wrote it; though it be not rare,
It is not common. VVomen seldom dare
To reach so high, to entertain your Ears,
VVhich strikes our Poets with a thousand fears
Of your displeasure; yet some little Ray
Of hope is left; for womens Pardons may
Be gain'd with ease surely from Gentlemen;
Be kind for once then to a Female Pen.
VVhen you with women in discourse do sit,
Before their Faces you'l commend their wit,
Pray flatter now, the Poet heareth it:
She hopes too, the great VVits, who croud the Age,
Censure the Poets, and undo the Stage,

VVon't

Won't undervalue so their mighty Wit,
To Criticize on what a Woman writ:
Yet if you'l have it so, it shall be Naught,
They that dislike, are welcome to find Fault;
For She protests, She had no other ends
In writing this, than to divert her Friends:
Like, or dislike, She's careless, bid me say,
That you shou'd Censure only when you Pay:
True, they must fawn, that write for a Third day.
She scornes such Basenefs, therefore will not sue:
But yet, bright Ladies, does submit to you;   (blast,
Your Smiles may cherish, what their Frowns wou'd
Then when they Hifs, be pleas'd to Clap more fast:
She knows your Judgments are too clear, and high
To be Deceiv'd, but knows no Reason why
You may not Pardon all the Faults you spy.
Be kind then Ladies to this trifling Play,
Her Wit is now i'th' Bud, when blown, She may
Prefent you with a better; till It come,
This, Ladies, humbly begs a gentle Doom.

C   The

The firſt Song in the Play.

BEgone fond Love, make haſte away,
Duty, not thee, our Souls muſt ſway :
Can thy Almighty Pow'rs
Find out no other Hearts,
To Shoot thy Fatal Darts,
But haplefs Ours,
VVho cannot, though we wou'd, Obey ?
What ſecret Pow'r is it, Controuls
The Empire thou pretend'ſt o're Souls ?
That ſtill thy ſhafts are loſt,
And ſtill thou Shoot'ſt in vain,
For they that feel moſt Pain,
By Duty 're Croſt,
Or elſe unjuſtly meet Diſdain.

Fondly

Fondly Men fay, the VVorld doth move
By Loves Command; for fimple Love,
Alafs! is Subject unto Fate:
Oh Love! Affert thy Pow'r,
And make the Dotards, in an hour
Our Faces hate,
And the young Knights like Swans or Turtles prove.

The Second Song.

COme quickly Death,
    And with thy fatal Dart,
Releafe that Heart
That hath too long been thy great Rivals Slave:
Oh! ftop that Breath
I languifh out in pain;
Let me not Sigh in vain,
But quick and gently fend me to my Grave.

C 2   For

For fince that Swain

That I fo dearly prize,

Doth fcorn my Sighs,

And break thofe Sacred Vows to me he gave ;

I'le not complain of Mans Inconftancie,

But humbly Beg of thee, with fpeed and eafe,

   To fend me to my Grave.

     And Love I'le ftill

     Adore thy Deity,

     And Worfhip thee :

If to my alter'd Shepherd thou'lt Relate,

Since 'twas his will, I fhould not call him mine,

I freely can Refign, and Die for him,

   And glory in my Fate.

       Epilogue.

Epilogue.

The Play is damn'd; well, That we look'd to hear,
Yet Gentlemen, pray be not too severe,
Though now the Poet at your Mercy lies,
Fates wheel may turn, and she may chance to rise.
Though she's an humble Suppliant now to you,
Yet time may come, that you to her may Sue.
Pardon small Errors, be not too unkind,
For if you be, she'l keep it in her mind;
The self same usage that you give her Play,
She'l copy back to you another day.
If you her Wit, or Plot, or Fancy blame,
VVhen you Addresses make, She'l do the same;
But if you'l Clap the Play, and Praise the Rime,
She'l do as much for you another time.

Welcome

Welcome to *J. G.*

Thofe that can tell Heaven's Joy, when News is brought
That fome Poor Sinners dear Converfion's wrought,
Might tell our Raptur'd Extafies, when we
Receiv'd the News, that you were come from Sea :
Each wore fuch Looks, as vifibly expreft   (Breft :
Some more than common Joy, fate fmiling in his
Great as your Friend's Joys, you will nothing find,
Unlefs the Grief of thofe you left behind :
I can defcribe my Joy for your Return
No more, then tell how I your Abfence Mourn :
Both are beyond the reach of words t'exprefs,
And to defcribe them, wou'd but make them lefs :
The Bleffing of young Heirs is mixt with Pain,
And by their Father's Deaths, Princes their Empires
If then all pleafure,meets with fome allay,   (gain)
Forgive me, Deareft *Strephon*, if I fay,
I almoft Grieve to think that thou canft be
Six days in *London*, e're thou Vifit me.

Wealth's

Wealth's Power.

How Happy was the VVorld before men found
Those metals, Nature hid beneath the Ground!
All Necessary things She plac'd in View,
But this She wisely hid, because She knew
That it destructive to her work wou'd be,
And jarr the consort of her Harmony:
No sooner *Steel* was Found, but men began
To find new ways to Death, and cruel man
Made Swords, and Spears, and Bows, and Darts, which
First us'd on Beast ——— (he
VVho fell the Victimes of his Cruelty:
Pride, and Revenge, then Rag'd in every Soul,
And Fiery Passion, Reason did controule.
But when those Mines we're found which we call rich,
Because their Glitt'ring Beauty did bewitch
And please our cousen'd Senses, then with more
Than mean devotion, man did Gold adore:

Deluded

Deluded man did then this Trifle call
The chiefest Good, that cou'd to him befall:
How ſtrangely, Frantick man, didſt thou miſtake,
When of this traſh thou didſt an Idol make?
For tho to it thou did'ſt no Altars rear,
Its Zealous Votary thou didſt appear:
This fatal Poyſon was by Heaven hid
I'th bowels of the earth, and when it did
By chance, i'th' Heſperian Garden ſhoot above,
Heaven, (knowing how miſchievous it wou'd prove)
The paſſage did with watchful Dragons guard,
And made the way to miſery, more hard
To paſs, than that which lead to Blifs:
But all in vain, for had Heaven hidden this
I'th' Verge of Hell, man wou'd have fetcht it thence,
And thought it a ſufficient Recompence
For all his pains; but when he had attain'd,
This much deſired Curſe, he thought he'd gain'd
A Bleſſing Heav'n wou'd Envy, blut alas!
The worth, not in the Metal, but his Fancy was.

No

No Man did needless Merit now regard,
None Vertue fought, none Valour wou'd reward,
None Learning valu'd, none poor Wit did mind,
None honour'd Age, few were to Beauty kind;
All Gold ador'd, all Riches did Admire,
Beyond being Rich, no Man did now aspire.
Gold thus Advanc'd, and all things else neglected,
Justice depos'd, and Wisdom difrespected;
They left the Earth to Wealth's more pow'rful sway,
And fled to Heaven, while Man did Gold obey:
Now Money reign'd in chief, and sottish Man,
A slavish servitude to Wealth began;
Kingdomes to Rule, and Princes to Advise,
Men fondly chose the Rich, and not the Wise;
All lov'd the Man that had a good Estate,
And Poverty was cause enough to Hate;
The Rich might all things do, and Plaudits have
For his worst Acts, but scarce the Poor cou'd save
His best from Censure; now it might be said,
Wealth hid more Faults, than ever Folly made.

A

A Friend, though heretofore a Sacred Name,
Now, nothing but an empty Sound became;
For as Mens Riches did or Ebb, or Flow,
So lefs or more, their Friends did kindnefs fhow:
Honour, that flew fuch noble Flights before,
VVith gen'rous Pinions, now no more cou'd foare
Such Hights, but check'd, to ftoop did not difdain
T'a gilded Lure, and ware a Golden Chain:
Beauty, that all Men did for Heavenly hold,
Forgot its worth, and fold its felf for Gold;
Nay Love, though more Divine than all the reft,
Became a Mercenary, or at beft,
A mingled Compound of defire and wealth,
If any's better, 't muft be had by Stealth:
Marriage is Love and Joynture mixt together,
And yet fometimes it happens that there's neither:
But VVit this glorious trifle did difdain,
VVealth ftrove to make it yield, but all in vain,
More noble Objects gen'rous VVit did chufe
To employ its Thoughts, and did this Trafh refufe.

VVealth

VVealth threatn'd VVit it ever fhou'd be Poor,
Yet VVit the Golden Calf wou'd not adore;
So when both faw their Labour was in vain,
They vow'd to part, and never meet again.

Song.

1.

R Anging the Plain, one Summers Night,
    To pafs a vacant hour,
I fortunately chanc'd to light
On lovely *Phillis* bow'r:
The Nymph adorn'd with Thoufand Charms
In expectation fate,
To meet fuch joys in *Strephon's* Armes,
As Tongue can ne're Relate

2.

Upon her hand She lean'd her Head,
Her Breafts did gently rife,
And every Lover might have read
Her wifhes in her Eyes;

                                         VVith

With every breath that mov'd the Trees,
She fuddainly wou'd Start,
A Cold on all her Body feiz'd,
A Trembling on her Heart.

3.

But He that knew how well fhe Lov'd,
Beyond his Hour had ftaid,
Which both with Fear and Anger mov'd,
The Melancholick Maid.

You Gods fhe faid! how oft he Swore,
He wou'd be hear by One;
And now, alas! 'Tis Six and more,
And yet He is not come.

Loves

Loves Cruelty, or the Prayer.

SPeak cruel Love! what is't thou doſt intend?
Oh! tell me, have thy Tyrannies no end?
Tho to thy Pow'r I have a Rebel bin,
May not Repentance expiate my Sin?
Oh! long e're this, if I had injur'd Heaven,
So true a Convert it wou'd have forgiven:
Four times the Sun his Yearly Race hath run,
Since firſt my Heart was by my Eyes undone;
In all which time, thou ſcarce haſt been ſo kind,
To give one Minutes Quiet to my mind;
Thou takeſt from me the Relliſh of Delights,
My Days no Pleaſure know, no Sleep my Nights:
With wandring thoughts each Pray'r thou doſt pro-
(I offer to my God) and mak'ſt them vain. (phane,
Sometimes with Books I wou'd divert my mind,
But nothing there but *J*'s and *G*'s I find:
Sometimes to eaſe my Grief, my Pen I take,
But it no Letters but *J G* will make.

I ſeek

I feek Diverſion in Company,
But my diſcourſe great Love, is all of Thee;
In Sighs and Sobs, I Languiſh out the Night
And all the day, in Tears I drown my Sight:
Yet I no pity can from thee obtain,
Thou'lt neither Cure, nor mitigate my Pain:
Mercyleſs Tyrant! Since thou wilt not Save,
Quickly Deſtroy, and ſend me to my Grave.

The Reply, by a Friend.

WHat Pray'r inceſſant, to my Ears does fly?
    What proud Preſumption me of Tyranny
Accuſeth? can Love whoſe pow're is ſo Great,
Be taxed with Ingratitude, or Hate?
Fond Girle forbear, and know that your Diſpair
Is want of Courage, cou'd you once but dare
Your Victor, and my Vaſſal, you ſhou'd ſee,
How Heav'n wou'd puniſh his inconſtancy:
But while your Hope on his fond Vows relies,
And thinks Heaven minds thoſe little Perjuries,

                       You

You quit the greater Pow'r, that you may claime
By Beauty's Conquest, the loss of it's your Shame:
When first to you he his Addresses made,
Smiles gave him Life, your frowns, strike him Dead;
But Viper like, being in your Bosom warm'd,
And his chill'd Soul being into Action charm'd.
By th' Influence of your Beams, he straight denies
What gave his Love a Life, and from it flies;
From such a Rebel, as from Plagues i'de run;
'Twixt Love and Hate, is no comparison:
Nor is he worth your Anger, or your Scorn,
Do but forget that ever he was Born:
You can't believe the Gods would e're create
Ingratitude, that Quintessence of Hate.
Think him a *Spectrum*, that had only Shape
Without Substance, and Love did onely Ape,
Then reassume that Pow'r, that Nature's Law
Gives to your Sex; be Wise, keep Slaves in Awe:
Be generous in Love, Love not in vain,
'Tis base to Love, where we're not Lov'd again.

Celadon.

To *J. G.*

TEll me you Hate; and Flatter me no more:
 By Heaven I do not wish you shou'd adore;
With humbler Blessings, I content can be,
I only beg, that you would pity me;
In as much Silence as I first design'd,
To bear the Raging Torture of my Mind;
For when your Eyes first made my Heart your Slave,
I thought t'have hid my Fetters in my Grave:
Heaven witness for me, that I strove to hide
My violent Love, and my fond Eyes did chide
For glancing at thee; and my Blushes hid,
With as much care as ever Virgin did.
And though I languish'd in the greatest pain
That e're despairing Lover did sustain;
I ne're in publick did let fall a Tear,
Nor breath'd a Sigh i'th' reach of any Ear:

          Yet

Yet I in private, drew no Breath but Sighs,
And Show'rs of Tears fell from my wretched Eyes:
The Lillies left my Front, the Rose my Cheeks,
My Nights were spent in Sobs and suddain Shreeks,
I felt my strength Insensibly decay'd,
And Death aproach; but ah! then you convey'd
Soft Am'rous tales into my listning Ears,
And gentle Vows, and well becoming Tears,
Then deeper Oaths, nor e're your Seige remov'd
'Till I confest my Flame, and own'd I lov'd:
Your kinder Smiles had rais'd my Flames so high,
That all at Distance might the Fire Discry,
I took no care my Passion to supprefs,
Nor hide the Love I thought I did possess:
But ah! too late I find, your Love was such
As Gallants pay in course, or scarce so much:
You Shun my sight, you feed me with delays,
You slight, affront, a Thousand several ways
You doe Torment with Study'd Cruelty,
And yet alternately you Flatter me.

D   Oh!

Oh! if you Love not, plainly fay you hate,
And give my Miferies a fhorter date,
'Tis kinder than to Linger out my Fate;
And yet I cou'd with lefs regret have Dy'd,
A Victime to your Coldnefs, than your Pride.

Song.

1.

BEneath a fpreading Willows fhade,
    Ephelia, a harmlefs Maide,
Sate rifling Natures ftore
Of every Sweet, with which fhe made
A Garland for her *Strephons* Head
As Gay as ever Shepherd wore.

2.

She feem'd to know no other Care,
But wether Pinks, or Rofes there,
Or Lillys look'd moft fweet,

Scarce

Scarce thinking on her Faithlefs Swain,
VVho Ranging on the neighb'ring Plain,
A wanton Shepherdefs did meet.

3.

But by Mifchance, he led her near
Th' Unlucky, Fatal Willow, where
His kind *Ephelia* fate;
He told the Kindnefs that fhe fhow'd,
Boafted the Favours fhe beftow'd,
And glory'd that he was ingrate.

4.

The Angry Nymph, did rudely tare
Her Garland firft, and then her Hair,
To hear her Self abus'd:
Oh Love! (fhe faid) is it the Fate
Of all that Love, to meet with Hate,
And be like me, unkindly us'd?

D 2　　　　To

To my Rival.

SInce you dare Brave me, with a Rivals Name,
   You shall prevail, and I will quit my Claime:
For know, proud Maid, I Scorn to call him mine,
Whome thou durst ever hope to have made thine:
Yet I confess, I lov'd him once so well,
His presence was my Heav'n, his absence Hell:
With gen'rous excellence I fill'd his Brest,
And in sweet Beauteous Forms his Person drest;
For him I did Heaven, and its Pow'r despise,
And onely liv'd by th' Influence of his Eyes:
I fear'd not Rivals, for I thought that he
That was possess'd of such a Prize as me,
All meaner Objects wou'd Contemn, and Slight,
Nor let an abject thing Usurpe my Right:
But when I heard he was so wretched Base
To pay devotion to thy wrinkled Face
I Banisht him my sight, and told the Slave,
He had no Worth, but what my Fancy gave:

'Twas

'Twas I that rais'd him to this Glorious State,
And can as easily Annihilate:
But let him live, Branded with Guilt, and Shame,
And Shrink into the Shade from whence he came;
His Punishment shall be, the Loss of Me,
And be Augmented, by his gaining Thee.

Neglect Returned.

P Roud *Strephon!* doe not think my Heart
So absolute a Slave:
Nor in so mean a servile state,
But if I say that you're Ingrate.,
I've Pride, and Pow'r, enough, my Chains to Brave.

2.

I Scorn to Grieve, or Sigh for one,
That does my Tears Neglect;
If in your Looks you Coldness wear,
Or a desire of Change Appear,
I can your Vows, your Love, and you Reject.

D 3 3. What

3.

What refin'd Madnefs wou'd it be,
VVith Tears to dim thofe Eyes,
VVhofe Rays, if Grief do not Rebate,
Each hour new Lovers might Create,
And with each Look, gain a more glorious Prize!

4.

Then do not think with Frowns to Fright,
Or Threaten me with Hate,
For I can be as cold as you,
Difdain as much, as proudly too,
And break my Chain in fpight of Love or Fate.

On a Bafhful Shepherd.

1.

YOung *Clovis*, by a lucky Chance,
  His Lov'd *Ephelia* fpy'd,
In fuch a place, as might advance
His Courage, and abate her Pride:

VVith

VVith Eyes that might have told his Sute,
Although his bashful Tongue was mute,
Upon her gazed he,
But the Coy Nymph, though in Surprize,
Upon the Ground fixing her Eyes,
The Language wou'd not see.

2.

VVith gentle Grasps he woo'd her Hand
And sigh'd in seeming Pain,
But this she wou'd not understand,
His Signs were all in vain :
Then change of Blushes next he try'd,
And gave his Hand freedom to slide
Upon her panting Brest;
Finding she did not this controul,
Unto her Lips he gently stole,
And bid her guess the rest.

3.

She blush'd, and turn'd her Head aside,
And so much Anger feign'd,
That the poor Shepherd almost Dy'd,

D 4   And

And she no Breath retain'd:
Her killing Frown so chill'd his Blood,
He like a senseless Statue stood,
Nor further durst he Woe,
And tho his Blessing was so near,
Check'd by his Modesty and Fear,
He faintly let it goe.

Maidenhead:
Written at the Request of a Friend,

AT your Intreaty, I at last have writ
This whimsey, that has nigh nonplust my wit:
The Toy I've long enjoyed, if it may
Be call'd t'Enjoy, a thing we wish away;
But yet no more its Character can give,
Than tell the Minutes that I have to Live:
'Tis a fantastick Ill, a loath'd Disease,
That can no Sex, no Age, no Person please:
Men strive to gain it, but the way they chuse
T'obtain their Wish, that and the Wish doth lose;

Our

Our Thoughts are still uneasie, till we know
What 'tis, and why it is defired fo:
But th'firft unhappy Knowledge that we boaft,
Is that we know, the valu'd Trifle's loft:
Thou dull Companion of our active Years,
That chill'ft our warm Blood with thy frozen Fears:
How is it likely thou fhou'dft long endure,
When Thought it felf thy Ruin may procure?
Thou fhort liv'd Tyrant, that Ufurp'ft a Sway
O're Woman-kind, though none thy Pow'r obey,
Except th'Ill-natur'd, Ugly, Peevifh, Proud,
And thefe indeed, thy Praifes Sing aloud:
But what's the Reafon they Obey fo well?
Becaufe they want the Power to Rebell:
But I forget, or have my Subject loft:
Alafs! thy Being's Fancy at the moft:
Though much defired, 'tis but feldom Men
Court the vain Blefling from a Womans Pen.

The

143

The Reconcilement.

IF you Repent, can I forgive your Crime,
    Except you Love again, and call you Mine:
What Queftion's this?   Ask fome poor Slave if he
Will take again his former Liberty:
Some greedy Mifer ask, that Gold had loft
If hee'l Receiv't again: one that is toft
In a feirce Tempeft, on the raging Main,
Ask if he wou'd be fafe on Land again:
Ask the Difeafed, if they wou'd be Well
Or ask the Damn'd, if they wou'd leave their Hell:
But ask not me a Queftion So Vain,
As, can you take my wandring Heart again.
No Conqu'ring *Hero* e're did Foes perfue
VVith half the Pleafure, that I took in you;
No Youthful Monarch, of a Glit'ring Crown,
Or prating Coxcomb, of a Scarlet Gown
VVas half fo proud, as I was of your Love;
Nor cou'd great *Juno's* State my Envy move,
VVhile

VVhile in your Heart I thought I Reigned in chief.

Then *Strephon*, think, how killing was the Grief

That I suftain'd, to find my Empire loft,

And fervile *Mopfa* of your Conqueft boaft:

None but a depofd Monarch, made a Scorn

By the rude Slaves that were his Vaffals born,

VVho while th' Imperial Circle grace'd his Brow,

At awfull diftance, to his Feet did bow,

His Scepter fnatch'd by an unworthy hand,

That late was proud to wait his leaft command,

But now th'Infulting wretch dares threat the Head

Of him, whofe Frown but late cou'd look him dead,

Cou'd guefs the horrid Tortures feiz'd my mind,

VVhen I perceiv'd you were to *Mopfa* kind:

That ill-look't Hag! who nere had guilty bin,

(No not in thought) of fuch a dareing Sin,

Had you not broke the Solemne Faith you vow'd,

Made me a Scorn to the Ignoble Crow'd

Of vulgar Nymphs, who now dare loudly prate

Reviling tales, they durft not think of late.

I

I did almoſt to Death this uſage Mourn,
Yet 'tis forgot i'th' Joy of your Return;
Your proofs of Penitence ſhall be but ſmall,
Look kind on me, and not on her at all.

Song.

1.

OBſcure the Glories of your Eyes,
   Or give us leave to Love :
To ſee, and not deſire that Prize ,
Impoſſible muſt prove :
Look not ſo nicely on your Slave,
That at your Feet doth bow,
When ſuch enticeing Looks you gave,
To tempt the Fool ſo low.

2.

Coy wanton Nymph, though you forbid
Your Slaves to ſeek Redreſs,
And force us keep our Torture hid,
Your Guilt is ne're the leſs.

It

It cannnot sure be Pity found,
But barb'rous Cruelty,
VVhen you with Pleasure give a VVound
So deep, you start to see.

To a Lady who (tho Married) could not endure Love should be made to any but her Self.

SAy, jealous *Phillida*, what Humour's this?
No Shepherd can bestow a Smile or Kiss
On any Nymph, but you must pout and vex:
Wou'd you Monopolize the Masc'line Sex?
Is not the sprightly *Damon*'s heart Your Prize,
Securely bound by *Hymens* Sacred ties?
Strephon and *Colon*, your Adorers are,
And bashful *Cleon* does your Fetters wear:
Young *Coridon* did by your Beauty fall;
Infatiate Nymph! wou'd you ingross them All?
Who doth not smile, to see what Pains you take
To watch our private Meetings, and to make

Our

Our Amours publick? and if your lift'ning Ear
By chance foft Amorous Difcourfes hear,
Then raging Mad: with Jealoufie and Pride,
You curfe the Shepherds,and the Nymphs you chide.
But why thus Angry? if we entertain
The Heart and Love of fome poor humble Swain,
VVho never his cheap Thoughts fo high durft lift,
As to prefent you with fo mean a Gift;
What wrong have you? why fhou'd you break your
If they to us prefent a *Linnets* Neft,   (Reft,
A Wreath of Flowers, or a Bunch of Grapes,
Filberts, or Strawberries, or the Roots of Rapes?
When Lambs and Kids, are daily offer'd you
By the great Swains, that for your favour fue;
If any Shepherdefs fo bold dare be,
T'invade thy Right, or proudly Rival thee,
Th'had'ft Reafon for thy Anger; but while we
Content with what you flight and fcorn can be,
Why fhou'd you Envy, or difturb our Joys?
Let us poffefs in Peace thefe little Toys.

ACROS

ACROSTICH.

V ain Girl, thy Muse to be more Modest teach;

E ndeavour not at things above thy Reach:

N o common Pen for this great Task is fit,

I t asks great *Dryden*'s, or sweet *Cowley*'s Wit:

T' express the Beauteous wonders of your Face,

I nimitable Colours, Features, Grace,

A ngelick Sweetness, and a charming State,

C ompounded sweetly, on each Look doth wait:

O h, if my Fancy cou'd but reach your Worth,

O r find fit Epithets to set it forth,

K ings then to thy fair Eyes shou'd Homage pay,

E xpressing Thee more like the Gods than They.

SONG.

S O N G.

1.

YOu wrong me *Strephon*, when you say,
    I'me Jealous or Severe,
Did I not fee you Kiſs and Play
With all you came a neer?
Say, did I ever Chide for this,
Or caſt one Jealous Eye
On the bold Nymphs, that ſnatch'd my Bliſs
While I ſtood wiſhing by?

2.

Yet though I never diſapprov'd
This modiſh Liberty;
I thought in them you only lov'd,
Change and Variety:
I vainly thought my Charms ſo ſtrong,
And you ſo much my Slave,
No Nymph had Pow'r to do me Wrong,
Or break the Chains I gave.

3. But

3.

But when you serioufly Addrefs,
With all your winning Charms,
Unto a Servile Shepherdefs,
I'le throw you from my Arms:
I'de rather chufe you fhou'd make Love
To every Face you fee,
Then *Mopfa's* dull Admirer prove,
And let Her Rival me.

E   ACROS-

ACROSTICH.

R areſt of Virgins, in whoſe Breaſt and Eyes,
A ll that is Vertuous and Lovely lies:
C ou'd I deſcribe but half thy Excellence,
H ow wou'd the Gods with ſpeed Bodies condenſe !
E ternity for Thee they wou'd deſpiſe,
L eave their Divine Abodes, new Shapes deviſe,
L ovelier than that which *Danaë* did ſurprize.

P roud if in any Form they thee cou'd pleaſe,
O r give to their Immortal Cares ſome eaſe;
W hen us, poor Mortals, with your Sight you bleſs,
N one can find words their wonder to expreſs;
E namouring and dazling with your Sight,
Y ou prove at once our Torture and Delight.

The

The Twin Flame.

FAntastick, wanton God, what do'st thou mean
To break my Rest? make me grow pale and lean,
And offer Sighs, and yet not know to who,
Or what's more strange; to sigh at once for two.
Tyrant! Thou know'st I was thy Slave before,
And humbly did thy Deity Adore:
I lik'd, nay, doated on my *Strephon's* Face,
And Sung his Praise, and thine in every place.
My Soul he singly sway'd, alone possest
My Love, and reign'd sole Monarch of my Breast:
Was not all this enough? but thou fond Boy,
Wanton with too much Pow'r, (thy Self t'employ)
Must in my Breast (oh! let it ne're be told)
Kindle new Flame, yet not put out the Old?
Young *Clovis* now, (though I oppose in vain)
Succeeds not *Strephon*, but doth with him Reign:

E 2   And

153

And I, though both I love, dare neither choofe,
Left gaining one, I fhou'd the other loofe:
Both Fires are equal great, Flame equal high,
Yet fpight of this, a difference I defcry;
One wild and raging, furioufly Devours
My Peace, my Reft, and all my pleafant Hours;
The other mild and gentle, like thofe Fires
That melt Perfumes, creates as fweet defires:
That doth with Violence to Paffion tend,
This climbs no higher than the name of Friend.
Yes, greedy *Strephon,* you fhall ever be
My only Love, and fingly Reign o're me:
My Paffion you fhall Monopolize,
You've fuch refiftlefs Magick in your Eyes.
Though *Clovis* Merits yours do far tranfcend,
Yet I'm your Lover, and but *Clovis* Friend;
Blindly I love you, yet too plain difcover,
He'l prove a better Friend then you a Lover.
Accept fweet *Clovis* of that little part
I can prefent of my unruly Heart.

Cou'd

Cou'd I command my Love, or know a way
My Stubborn, lawlefs Paffion to fway,
My Love I wou'd not Parcel, nor beftow
A little Share, where more than all I owe:
This undeferving *Strephon* I wou'd teare
From my fond Breaft, and place your Merit there:
But 'tis not in my Pow'r, fome hidden Fate
Compels me love Him that I ftrive to Hate.
That Love we to our Prince or Parents pay,
I'le bear to you, and love an humble way:
I'le pay you Veneration for your Love,
And your Admirer, not your Miftrefs prove.
Oh! be contented with the Sacred Name
Of Friend, and an inviolable Flame
For you I will preferve, and the firft place
Of all the few I with that Title grace:
And yet this Friendfhip doth fo faft improve,
I dread, left it in time fhou'd grow to Love.

E 3   To

To a Proud Beauty.

IMperious Fool! think not becaufe you're Fair,
That you fo much above my Converfe are:
VVhat though the Gallants fing your Praifes loud,
And with falfe Plaudits make you vainly Proud?
Tho they may tell you all Adore your Eyes,
And every Heart's your willing Sacrifice;
Or fpin the Flatt'ry finer, and perfwade
Your eafie Vanity, that we were made
For Foyles to make your Luftre Shine more Bright,
Aud muft pay Homage to your dazling Light;
Yet know what ever Stories they may tell,
All you can boaft, is, to be pretty well;
Know too, you ftately piece of Vanity,
That you are not Alone ador'd, for I
Fantaftickly might mince, and fmile, as well
As you, if Airy Praife my mind cou'd fwell;

Nor

Nor are the loud Applauses that I have,
For a fine Face, or things that Nature gave;
But for acquired Parts, a gen'rous Mind,
A pleasing Converse, neither Nice nor Kind:
When they that strive to Praise you most, can say
No more, but that you're Handsome, brisk and gay:
Since then my Fame's as great as yours is, why
Should you behold me with a loathing Eye?
If you at me cast a disdainful Eye,
In biting Satyr I will Rage so high,
Thunder shall pleasant be to what I'le write,
And you shall Tremble at my very Sight;
VVarn'd by your Danger, none shall dare again,
Provoke my Pen to write in such a strain.

E 4   SONG.

SONG.

1.

BE Judge, dear *Strephon*, was it kind,
  Through ev'ry fenfe t'invade my Heart ;
And when I had my Soul refign'd,
To play a Cruel Tyrants part ?

2.

Being your Slave, I'm not fo vain
To hope to have one minutes Eafe,
But fhou'd take Pleafure in my Pain,
If my Dear Conqu'rer it wou'd pleafe.

3.

In Sighs, and Sobs, and Groans, and Tears,
And Languifhment I pafs the Day,
My Reft at Night is broke with Fears,
Yet you my Grief with Scorns repay.

4. But

4.

But Since you can fo Cruel prove,
To mock the Suffrings you Create,
Triumph and Boaft how much I Love,
I'le give your Mirth a fpeedy Date.

5.

For know, Infulter, I difdain
To live to feed your Vanity;
My Blood fhall wafh out that fond Stain,
My Honour got by loving Thee.

To

To one that asked me
why I lov'd *J. G.*

WHy do I Love? go, ask the Glorious Sun
    Why every day it round the world doth Run:
Ask *Thames* and *Tyber*, why they Ebb and Flow:
Ask Damask Roses, why in *June* they blow:
Ask Ice and Hail, the reason, why they're Cold:
Decaying Beauties, why they will grow Old:
They'l tell thee, Fate, that every thing doth move,
Inforces them to this, and me to Love.
There is no Reason for our Love or Hate,
'Tis irresistable, as Death or Fate;
'Tis not his Face; I've sence enough to see,
That is not good, though doated on by me:
Nor is't his Tongue, that has this Conquest won;
For that at least is equall'd by my own:

His

His Carriage can to none obliging be,
'Tis Rude, Affected, full of Vanity:
Strangely Ill-natur'd, Peevish, and Unkind,
Unconstant, False, to Jealousie inclin'd;
His Temper cou'd not have so great a Pow'r,
'Tis mutable, and changes every hour:
Those vigorous Years that Women so Adore,
Are past in him: he's twice my Age and more;
And yet I love this false, this worthless Man,
VVith all the Passion that a VVoman can;
Doat on his Imperfections, though I spy
Nothing to Love; I Love, and know not why.
Sure 'tis Decreed in the dark Book of Fate,
That I shou'd Love, and he shou'd be ingrate.

Intended

161

Intended Farewel to *J. G.*

FArewel, Dear Love! may'ſt thou have in Exceſs,
Pleaſure, Delight, Content, and Happineſs :
Oh may thy Joys but equalize my Grief,
Thine great, above compare, as mine beyond Relief:
'Twere vain to wiſh Fate wou'd to thee be kind,
'Twere vain for thee to bribe the Sea or Wind,
'Twere vainer yet to fear a Storm or Fight,
Who know thy Worth, ſuch thoughts as theſe will
The Fates their Duty ſo well underſtand,   (ſlight.
Without my Wiſh, they'l bring thee ſafe to Land;
Thy Merits and it's charge, Heaven ſo well knows,
'Twill guard thee, though unpray'd to, from thy foes,
If thou haſt any; But ſure no one can
Bear hatred to ſo Great, ſo Brave a Man.
But if by chance, thy Princes Enemie
Shou'd hope to make your Ship their Prize to be,
Tell

Tell the Brave Captain, that he need not fear
Their Force, though Strong, for if thou but appear,
With Awful Reverence they'l ſtrait Retire,
And hold it Impious one Gun to Fire:
Sav'd by thy Pow'r, they'l all acknowledge thee
The Guardian Angel of the Ship to be.

Mocked in Anger.

FArewel ungrateful Man, Sail to ſome Land,
   Where Treach'ry and Ingratitude command;
There meet with all the Plagues that Man can bear,
And be as Wretched, as I'm Happy here.
'Twere vain to wiſh that Heav'n wou'd Puniſh thee,
'Twere vain to Invocate the Wind and Sea,
To fright thee with rude Storms, for ſurely Fate
Without a wiſh, will Puniſh the Ingrate
It's Juſtice and thy Crimes, Heaven ſo well knows,
That all it's Creatures it will make thy Foes:

(If

(If they're not ſo already) but none can
Love ſuch a worthleſs, ſuch a ſordid Man ;
And though we've now no publick Enemies,
And you're too ſtrong for private Piracies,
Yet is the Veſſel in more danger far,
Than when with all our Neighbours we had War ;
For all that know what Gueſt it doth contain,
VVill ſtrive to Fire or Sink it in the Main.
Plagu'd for thy ſake, they all will reckon thee
The *Achan*, or Accurſed thing to be.

A Lovers State.

UNthinking Fool ! wrong not thy Reaſon ſo,
To fancy Pleaſures in Loves Empire grow.
Alaſs ! a Lovers ſtate is full of Fears,
Their daily Entertainment, Sighs and Tears :
The Cruel god, in Tortures did delight,
And either Shoots at Rovers, or in Spight.

Amongſt

Amongſt his numerous Slaves, you'l hardly find,
One pair of Lovers mutually kind;
Or if they be, thoſe mighty Bars of Fate,
Int'reſt and Friends, their Perſons ſeparate:
An am'rous Youth, here for a Lady Dies,
Offring his Heart a Tribute to her Eyes:
With thouſand Vows, which proudly ſhe Rejeᶜts,
Sighs for another that her Sighs negleᶜts.
A beautious Nymph, whom Heaven and Nature made
To be by all Ador'd, by all Obey'd:
Though thouſand Viᶜtims ſigh beneath her Feet,
In all her Conqueſts can no Pleaſure meet:
But for ſome Sullen Youth, who proudly Flies,
Dreſſes her Cheeks in Tears, in languid looks her
Here we ſhall Lovers find, poſſeſſing all   (Eyes.
That by miſtake, we Joys and Pleaſures call;
And yet with Jealouſies and Idle fears,
Eclipſe 'em ſo, that ſcarce a Glimps appears.
Men are unconſtant, and delight to Range,
Not to gain Freedom, but their Fetters change:

And

And, what a Year they did with Paſſion ſeek,
Grows troubleſome, and nauſeous in a Week:
And the poor Lady, newly taught to Love,
With Grief and Horror, ſees her Man remove.
Wonder not then thou canſt no Pleaſure ſee,
But know thou ſeek'ſt it, where it cannot be.
Who vainly ſeeks for Joys in Love, as well
Might Quiet ſeek in Courts, and Eaſe in Hell.

A Vindication to angry *Clovis*.

Dear *Clovis*! can'ſt thou entertain one Thought
That I, who've with ſo many Hazards ſought
T'oblige and pleaſe Thee, now wou'd blot thy Name,
Or ſeek t'Eclipſe thy well deſerved Fame?
Shou'd but one word ſlip from my heedleſs Tongue,
Againſt that Vertue I've admired ſo long,
To expiate it's guilt, I'de in thy ſight,
The Impious Criminal in pieces bite.

Knew'ſt

Knew'ſt thou my thoughts, I then wou'd ſcorn to fear
The Envious Tales of any Whiſperer:
But ſince that Object is not in thy ken,
My Heart's true Effigiis take from my Pen;
In my Eſteem, thou haſt ſo high a Seat,
All I think of Thee's, Eminently great:
From thy ſweet Tongue, one word ne're ſlipt away,
That holy Prieſts, or Angels, might not ſay:
Thy Actions ſo juſt, and free from Blame,
Heaven by thy Life it's Sacred Laws might frame:
The ſcatter'd Vertues that all mankind Share,
In thy great ſelf alone united are:
Theſe are my thoughts of Thee, and while they flow
Thus pure, my Tongue can no foul language know:
Thoſe prophane Words cou'd never come from me,
For had'ſt thou Faults, I have no Eyes to ſee:
So faſt the Ties of ſacred Friendſhip bind,
That when I ſhou'd not ſee, I can be blind:
Thou know'ſt I can not wrong thee, if I wou'd;
And *Clovis* know, I wou'd not if I cou'd.

F   Laſt

Laſt Farewel to *J. G.*

FArewell thou ſoft Seducer of my Eyes,
  That, in Loves ſhape, did'ſt Cruelty diſguiſe,
No longer ſhall thy lovely Melting Charms
Bewitch my Soul, to pleaſe it's ſelf in Harms;
No more I'le ſhow'r down unregarded Tears;
No more I'le break my Reſt, with Am'rous Fears;
With Scorching Sighs, I'le blaſt my Lips no more,
No more thy Pity I'le in vain implore;
In Languiſhment, no more my Eyes I'le dreſs,
But reaſſume that Heart thou did'ſt poſſeſs;
For ſince the Gueſt thou wou'd'ſt not entertain,
It was but juſt, it ſhou'd return again:
Now 'tis my own again, with care, and Art
I'le guard each paſſage that leads to my Heart;
Love ſhall Reſign, and Reaſon ſhall command,
And Care and Wiſdome Sentinels ſhall ſtand:
                                        My

My treachrous eyes, nor thy more treachrous tongue,
Shall not betray me as they've done too long:
Nor will I caft one fingle Thought on Thee,
Unlefs my Heart again Aſſaulted be ;
Then I'le remind it of thy Cruelty :
And though the Headftrong Paffion fhou'd prevaile
Againſt my Reafon, yet this barb'rous Tale
Wou'd make the Rebel willingly Submit,
And change the Fever, to an Ague fit:
For who again wou'd venture on that Shore,
Where hee'd been fplit and Shipwrackt once before.

The Unkind Parting.

LOvely Unkind ! cou'd you fo Cruel be
To leave the Land e're you took Leave of me ?
Explain this myftick Act, and let me know
Whether it doth your Hate, or Kindnefs fhow :
Lov'd you too well my Parting fighs to hear ?
Or wanted Strength my kinder Tears to bear?

F 2   Or

Or were you Tend'rer yet, and did decline
A folemn Leave, not for your Sake, but mine?
Left my kind Heart o're charg'd with too much Grief,
Shou'd with my Farewell-fighs breath out my Life.
Or was it (how the very Thought doe's fright!)
To fhow with how much Contempt you cou'd flight?
Or did you love fo little, that no Thought
Of poor *Ephelia* to your mind was brought?
No, no, 'twas none of thefe; I guefs thy mind:
Strephon! thou knew'ft I was fo fondly kind,
That at the News of Parting, into Tears
I ftrait had melted, Thoufand Am'rous Fears
I had Suggefted to my felf, and you
In Complaifance muft needs have done fo too:
You muft have told how loth you were to part,
And vow'd that tho you went, I kept your Heart;
Omitted nothing tender Love cou'd fhew,
From my pale Cheeks have kift the Pearly Dew;
Spoke all the tender'ft things you cou'd devife,
And to the old added new Perjuries;

Vow'd

Vow'd Conftancy in Abfence, and then Swear,
A quick Return fhou'd diffipate my Fear:
All of thefe pleafing Vanities, you knew,
A declar'd Lover was oblig'd to doe:
But to this trouble you wou'd not be brought,
But ftole in filence hence; yet tho you thought
This Tale too long, and troublefome to tell,
You might have grafp'd my hand, and faid Farewel;
At which dire Words, fuch Confternation wou'd
Have feiz'd my Soul, I fenfelefs fhou'd have ftood
'Till you beyond a Sigh's faint Call had fled;
Nay, till *Tangiere*, you'd near recovered:
This way, my Kindnefs cou'd not tirefome be,
Nor your Neglect wou'd not have troubled me.

F 3   Seeing

Seeing *Strephon* Ride by after him I fuppofed gone.

STay lovely Youth ! do not fo fwiftly fly
From her your Speed muft caufe as quick to die :
Each ftep you take, hales me a ftep more near
To the cold Grave : (nor is't an idle Fear)
For know, my Soul to you is chained faft,
And if you make fuch cruel, fatal haft,
Muft quit it's Seat, and be fo far unkind,
To leave my fainting, breathlefs Trunk behind ;
Your Sight unthought of, did fo much furprife,
You might have feen my Soul danc'd in my Eyes;
But the cold Look you gave in paffing by,
Froze my warm Blood, and taught my Hopes to die :
When you were paft, my Spirits foon did fail,
My Limbs grew ftiff and cold, my Face grew pale :
My Heart did Pant, fcarce cou'd I fetch my Breath,
In every part nothing appear'd but Death :

Yet

Yet did my Eyes perfue your cruel Flight,
Nor ever mov'd, 'till you were out of Sight:
But then, alas, it cannot be exprest,
I faint, I faint, my Death shall tell the rest.

S O N G.

1.

KNow, *Celadon* | in vain you ufe
    Thefe little Arts to me:
Though *Strephon* did my Heart refufe,
I cannot give it thee:
His harfh Refufal hath not brought
It's Value yet fo low,
That what was worth that Shepherds Thoughts,
I fhou'd on You beftow.

2.

Nor can I love my *Strephon* lefs,
For his ungrateful Pride,
Though Honour does, I muft confefs,
My guilty Paffion chide.

       F 4   That

That lovely Youth I ſtill adore,
Though now it be in vain;
But yet of him, I ask no more
Than Pity for my Pain.

To Madam Anne Bhen.

Madam! permit a Muſe, that has been long
Silent with wonder, now to find a Tongue:
Forgive that Zeal I can no longer hide,
And pardon a neceſſitated Pride.
VVhen firſt your ſtrenuous polite Lines I read,
At once it VVonder and Amazement bred,
To ſee ſuch things flow from a Womans Pen,
As might be Envy'd by the wittieſt Men:
You write ſo ſweetly, that at once you move,
The Ladies Jealouſies, and Gallant's Love;
Paſſions ſo gentle, and ſo well expreſt,
As needs muſt be the ſame fill your own Breaſt;

Then

Then Rough again, as your Inchanting Quill
Commanded Love, or Anger at your Will:
As in your Self, so in your Verses meet,
A rare connexion of Strong and Sweet:
This I admir'd at, and my Pride to show,
Have took the Vanity to tell you so
In humble Verse, that has the Luck to please
Some Ruftick Swains, or filly Shepherdefs:
But far unfit to reach your Sacred Ears,
Or ftand your Judgment: Oh! my confcious Fears
Check my Prefumption, yet I muft go on,
And finifh the rafh Task I have begun.
Condemn it Madam, if you pleafe, to th'Fire,
It gladly will your Sacrifice expire,
As fent by one, that rather chofe to fhew
Her want of Skill, than want of Zeal to you.

SONG.

SONG.

1.

WHen Bufie Fame, o're all the Plain
     Phylena's Praifes rung,
And on their Oaten Pipes, each Swain
Her Matchlefs Beauty fung:
The Envious Nymphs were forc'd to yield,
She had the fweeteft Face;
No Emulous Difputes they held,
But for the fecond Place.

2.

Young *Celadon* (whofe ftubborn Heart
No Beauty e're cou'd move,
But fmil'd to hear of Bow and Dart,
And brav'd the God of Love:)
Wou'd view this Nymph, and pleas'd at firft
Such Silent Charmes to fee,
VVith wonder Gaz'd, then Sigh'd, and Curft
His Curiofity.

To

To a Gentleman that had left a Vertuous Lady for a Miss.

DUll Animal miscall'd a Man, for Shame
    Give o're your foolish tales of Fire and Flame:
The Nymphs abhor you, and your Stories hate,
Count you a Monster, barb'rously Ingrate:
Your fine sweet Face, in which such Pride you take,
Th' exactness of your clever, easie Make;
Your Charming Meen, bewitching Tongue, nor yet
The fancied Greatness of your boasted Wit,
Can now the meanest Nymph to Pity move,
Though once they taught the great *Phylena* Love:
Phylena, Glory of the *Surrey*-Plain,
The envy'd Wish of every hopeless Swain, (brought
Whose Artless Charms, the Proud and Great had
Upon their Knees, th' Old and Morose had taught
How

How to Languiſh, and they that durſt not ſhow
They were her Lovers, ſilently were ſo :
But you alone, did of her Conqueſt boaſt,
In that one Prize all Natures Wealth engroſs't :
But your inſipid Dulneſs found more Charms,
More Pleaſure in the wanton *Flora*'s Armes ;
With Her you paſt your hours in idle Prate,
While poor *Phylena* unregarded ſate :
Kind heart ! She wept ; and gently She Reprov'd
Your ſtrange Ingratitude, told you, you lov'd
A Shepherdeſs that had a ſickly Fame,
And wou'd bring Infamy upon your Name.
Who can believe ? With unheard Impudence
You own'd your Crime, and urg'd in your defence,
The Nymph ſung charmingly, was very Witty,
Gay, Brisk, had Teeth; oh ! infinitely Pretty :
Ingenious Lime-twigs, to catch Woodcocks on,
Pretty Ingredients to Dote upon !
Can you prefer theſe trivial Toys, that are
As common as their Owner, to the rare

Perfecti-

Perfections dwell in your *Phylena*'s Breaft,
Things too Divinely Great to be expreft.?
Her Vertues, though her Beauty fhou'd decay,
Might Charm the World, and make Mankind obey.
Degen'rous Man ! break this ignoble Chain,
That dims your Luftre, does your Honour ftain ;
Or you'l be judg'd for all your vain Pretences,
Not only to have loft your Wits, but Sences.

S O N G.

1.

EPhelia, while her Flocks were fair,
Was fought by ev'ry Swain,
The Shepherds knew no other care,
Than how her Love to gain :
In Rural Gifts, they vainly ftrove
Each other to Out-vie,
Fondly imagining her Love
They might with Prefents buy.

But

2

But fhe did every Gift defpife,
And ev'ry Shepherd hate,
Till *Strephon* came, whofe Killing Eyes
Was ev'ry Womans Fate:
A while, alas! She vainly ftrove
The Bleeding Wound to hide,
But foon with Pain cry'd out, I Love,
In fpight of all my Pride.

3.

The Wolves might now at pleafure Prey,
On her defencelefs Sheep;
Her Lambs o're all the Plain did ftray,
None in the Fold would keep;
But fhe regardlefs of thefe Harms,
In Paftimes fpent the Day,
Or in her faithlefs *Strephons* Arms,
Diffolv'd in Pleafures lay.

4. But

4.

But as Her num'rous Flocks decay'd,
His Paſſion did ſo too,
Till for a Smile the eaſie Maid
Was forc'd with Tears to woe :
But being Shrunk from few to none,
He left the Nymph forlorn,
Derided now by every one,
That ſhe did lately ſcorn.

Fortune Miſtaken.

THough Fortune have ſo far from me remov'd,
   All that I wiſh, or all I ever lov'd,
And Rob'd our *Europe* of its chief Delight,
To bleſs the *Africk* world with *Strephons* Sight :
There with a Lady Beauteous, Rich, and Young,
Kind, Witty, Vertuous, the beſt Born among
The *Africk* Maids, preſents this happy Swain,
Not to oblige Him, but to give Me Pain :

                                        Then

Then to my Ears, by tattling Fame, conveys
The Tale with large Add.tions; and to raife
My Anger higher, tells me 'tis defign'd,
That *Hymens* Rites, their hands and hearts muft bind:
Now She believes my Bufinefs done, and I
At the dire News wou'd fetch a Sigh, and Die:
But She's deceiv'd, I in my *Strephon* grow,
And if he's happy, I muft needs be fo:
Or if Fate cou'd our Interefts disjoyn,
At his good Fortune I fhou'd ne're Repine,
Though 'twere my Ruin; but I exulte to hear,
Infulting *Mopfa* I no more fhall fear;
No more he'l fmile upon that ugly Witch:
In that one Thought, I'm Happy, Great, and Rich;
And blind Dame Fortune, meaning to Deftroy,
Has fill'd my Soul with Extafies of Joy:
To Him I love, She's given a happy Fate,
And quite deftroy'd and ruin'd Her I hate.

To

To *J. G.* on the News of his Marriage.

MY Love? alas! I muſt not call you Mine,
But to your envy'd Bride that Name reſign:
I muſt forget your lovely melting Charms,
And be for ever Baniſht from your Arms:
For ever? oh! the Horror of that Sound!
It gives my bleeding Heart a deadly wound:
VVhile I might hope, although my Hope was vain,
It gave ſome Eaſe to my unpitty'd Pain,
But now your *Hymen* doth all Hope exclude,
And but to think is Sin; yet you intrude
On every Thought; if I but cloſe my Eyes,
Methinks your pleaſing Form beſides me lies;
VVith every Sigh I gently breath your Name,
Yet no ill Thoughts pollute my hallow'd Flame;

G   'Tis

'Tis pure and harmlefs, as a Lambent Fire,
And never mingled with a warm Defire:
All I have now to ask of Bounteous Heaven,
Is, that your Perjuries may be forgiven:
That She who you have with your Nuptials bleft,
As She's the Happieft VVife, may prove the Beft:
That all our Joys may light on you alone,
Then I can be contented to have none:
And never wifh that you fhou'd Kinder be,
Than now and then, to caft a Thought on Me:
And, Madam, though the Conqueft you have won,
Over my *Strephon*, has my hopes undone;
I'le daily beg of Heaven, he may be
Kinder to You, than he has been to Me.

To

To *Damon.*

Gay Fop! that know'ft no higher Flights than Senfe,
What was it gave thee fo much Impudence,
T' attempt the violation of a Shrine,
That lodg'd a Soul fo Sacred, fo Divine?
Her lovely Face might teach thee to Adore,
But cou'd not tempt thee to a loofe Amour:
Such charming goodnefs in her Eyes appear,
Might ftrike a Satyr with an awful fear;
But thou lefs humane, and more wild than they,
Thy impious Paffion durft before her lay:
Sweet Innocence, how fhe amazed ftood,
To hear fuch Tales, how her affrighted blood
Flufh'd in her Face, and then recoyl'd again,
To hear difcourfe fo horridly Prophane!
She look'd fuch things might teach thee to defpair,
Diffolve thy Being, fright thee into Air:

G 2   But

But thy unpar'llel'd boldnefs durft defpife
The Sacred Lightning that flafht from her Eyes;
And by a fecond Guilt, durft tempt her Tongue
To thunder Vengeance on thee, for her Wrong.
Impious Criminal! for this Offence,
Heaven hardly will accept of Penitence:
In tempting of her Vertue, know that you
Have done more than the Devil dar'd to do:
Audacious Villain! fure, thou next wil't try
Depofing of thy God, to rule the Sky:
That Action hardly can more wicked be,
Than what already hath been done by Thee.
If e're again thy Crime thou do'ft repeat,
Expect thy Ruine to be quick, and great.
With Thunder-bolts thou fhalt be crufh'd to Hell,
There with the Devils, and the Damn'd to dwell:
While that bright Maid, that thou would'ft have (betraid,
Shall be by Angels lov'd, by Men obey'd.

To

To *Phylocles*, inviting him to Friendship.

1.

BEst of thy Sex! if Sacred Friendship can
Dwell in the Bofom of inconftant Man;
As cold, and clear as Ice, as Snow unftain'd,
With Love's loofe Crimes unfully'd, unprophan'd.

2

Or you a Woman, with that Name dare truft,
And think to Friendfhip's Ties, we can be juft;
In a ftrict League, together we'l combine,
And Friendfhip's bright Example fhine.

3.

We will forget the Difference of Sex,
Nor fhall the World's rude Cenfure us Perplex:
Think Me all Man: my Soul is Mafculine,
And Capable of as great Things as Thine.

G 3   4. I

187

4.

I can be Gen'rous, Juſt, and Brave,
Secret, and Silent, as the Grave;
And if I cannot yield Relief,
I'le Sympathize in all thy Grief.

5.

I will not have a Thought from thee I'le hide,
In all my Actions, Thou ſhalt be my Guide;
In every Joy of mine, Thou ſhalt have ſhare,
And I will bear a part in all thy Care.

6.

Why do I vainly Talk of what we'l do?
We'l mix our Souls, you ſhall be Me, I You;
And both ſo one, it ſhall be hard to ſay,
Which is *Phyloſles*, which *Ephelia*.

7.

Our Ties ſhall be ſtrong as the Chains of Fate,
Conqu'rors, and Kings our Joys ſhall Emulate;
Forgotten Friendſhip, held at firſt Divine,
T' it's native Purity we will refine.

To

To the Honoured *Eugenia,* commanding me to Write to Her.

FAir Excellence! such strange Commands you lay,
    I neither dare Dispute, nor can Obey:
Had I the sweet *Orinda's* happy Strain,
Yet every Line would Sacriledge contain :
Like to some awful Deity you sit,
At once the Terrour and Delight of Wit :
Your Soul appears in such a charming Dress
As I admire, but never can express :
Heaven that to others had giv'n several Graces,
Some noble Souls, some Wit, some lovely Faces :
Finding the World did every one Admire,
Resolv'd to raise their Admiration higher :
And in one Piece, every perfection croud,
So fram'd your Self, and of it's work grew Proud :

G 4

Each

Each Rifing Sun faw you more Good, more Fair;
As you alone took up all Heaven's Care:
Such awful Charms do in your Face appear,
As fill Man-kind at once with Love and Fear.
VVho hear you Speak, muft take your Tongue to be
The firft Original of Harmony:
Your Meen hath fuch a Stately Charming Air,
As without Heralds doth your Birth declare:
Your Soul fo Noble, yet from Pride fo free,
That 'tis the Pattern of Humility.
Elfe I had never dar'd to give one Line
To your fair Hand, fo Impolite as Mine.
Pardon, dear Madam, thefe untuned Lays,
That have Prophan'd what I defign'd to Praife.
Nor is't poffible, but I fo muft do,
All I can think falls fo much fhort of you:
And Heaven as well with Man might angry be,
For not defcribing of the Deity,
In its full height of Excellence, as you
Quarrel with them that give you not your Due.

To

To the Beauteous *Marina.*

I.

NAture that had been long by Art out-done,
Resolved a Piece to frame;
So Beauteous, that sawcy Art shou'd own,
She was quite vanquished, and o're-thrown:
And all her mended Faces, after came.
In this Resolve, your lovely Self she made,
And lavish of her Graces,
Out-did her self, exhausted all her Store
Of ev'ry Sweet, till she cou'd give no more;
Bankrupt for ever, to all other Faces.
In Infancy all did the Bud admire,
But when full Blown, it rais'd our Wonder higher,
And Admiration grew into Desire.

2. VVhen

191

2.

When with your Sight the Change you bless,
Or walk the open Street,
A thousand Tongues your Praise express,
While dying Eyes aloud confess,
You have a Captive in each Man you meet.
When bashful *Clovis* chanc'd to spy
Your killing Face, with mine,
So much you charm'd that Shepherds Eye,
That my faint Lights he did despise;
And look'd as I my Empire must resign:
Though his each Look, I challenge as my Due,
He scarce gave one; his Eyes no motion knew;
But fixt as the dull Earth, with Wonder gaz'd on you.

Passion

Paſſion diſcovered.

I Thought, I'le Swear, that I could freely part,
With the ſmall Theft I'de made of *Clovis* Heart.
'Tis true, of Him I ſtill had in my Breaſt,
Some buſie Thoughts that did diſturb my Reſt:
Yet like wild Paſſion it did not ſeem,
But lookt like Friendſhip, or at moſt, Eſteem.
I thought his Heart was a too glorious Prize,
To be a Trophy to my twylight Eyes;
And when with Sighs he has his Paſſion ſhow'd,
A thouſand times I've wiſht, it were beſtow'd
On ſweet *Marrina*; thinking none beſide,
Had Worth enough, to be young *Clovis* Bride:
And beg'd of Love, that he would give her leave;
He ſmil'd to ſee me thus my Self deceive:

Fancying

Fancying that lazy Friendſhip, that (alas!)
Too late I found an active Paſſion was :
To undeceive me, brought that *Shepherd*, where
I, and *Marrina* both together were :
The *Swain* ſurpriz'd, to me did hardly lend
A ſquinting Glance ; but to my Beauteous Friend,
Fierce VViſhing-looks from dying Eyes did ſend.
I turn'd my Head, and ſigh'd at the Diſgrace,
VVhile Love and Jealouſie rag'd in my Face :
Love laught out-right to ſee my Diſcontent;
Now Fool (ſaid ſhe) thy fatal Pray'rs repent.
Malicious God (quoth I) ſo much above
My Self or Intereſt, I *Clovis* love,   (were
That ſtill I wiſh, that lovely Nymph and he united
But wiſh not now the Killing-news to hear.

To

To *Coridon*, on shutting his Door against some Ladies.

Onceited Coxcomb! tho' I was so kind
   To wish to see you, think not I design'd
To force my self to your unwilling Arms,
Your Conversation has no such Charms:
Think less, those lovely Virgins were with me,
VVou'd thrust themselves into your Company;
They've Crowds of Gallants, for their Favours sue,
And to be Caress'd, need not come to you:
'Gainst handsom VVomen rudely shut your Dore!
Had it been *S*erjeants, you cou'd do no more:
Faith, we expected with a horrid yelp,
Out of the VVindow you'd have cry'd, help! help!

                                              VVhat

What Outrage have you offer'd to our Sex ?
That you fhould dread we came but to perplex :
Or fince I faw you laft, what have I done,
Might caufe fo ftrange an Alteration ?
Till now, your wifhing Eyes have at my Sight,
Spoke you all Rapture, Extafie, Delight :
But at the Change, I have a Critick guefs,
So much of Friendfhip to me you profefs,
More than your lazy Tongue can e're exprefs ;
And your performance hath been fo much lefs :
That Debtor-like, you dare not meet my Eyes,
Which was the reafon of your late Surprize.
I'le tell you, Sir ; your kindnefs to requite
A loving Secret, meerly out of fpight :
A Secret four and tweenty Moons I've kept,
I've figh'd in private, and in private wept;
And all for you : but yet fo much my Pride
Surmounts my Paffion, that now were I try'd,
And the Heart fo long I've wifht for, proftrate lay
Before my Feet, I'de fpurn the Toy away :

       And

And tho', perhaps, I wish as much as you,
I'le starve my Self, so I may starve You too:
And for a Curse, wish you may never find
An open Door, nor Woman when she's kind.

My Fate.

OH cruel Fate, when wilt thou weary be?
 VVhen satisfied with tormenting me?
VVhat have I e're design'd, but thou hast crost?
All that I wisht to gain by Thee, I've lost:
From my first Infancy, thy Spight thou'st shown,
And from my Cradle, I've thy Malice known;
Thou snatch'st my Parents in their tender Age,
Made me a Victim to the furious Rage
Of cruel Fortune, as severe as thee;
Yet I resolv'd to brave my Destiny,
And did, with more than Female Constancy.

Not

Not all thy Malice cou'd extort a Tear,
Nor all thy Rage cou'd ever teach me Fear:
Still as thy Power diminifht my Eftate,
My Fortitude did my Defires abate;
In every ftate I thought my Mind content,
And wifely did thy crofs Defigns prevent:
Seeing thy Plots did unfuccefsful prove,
As a fure Torment next, thou taught'ft me Love:
But here thou wer't deceiv'd too, for my Swain
As foon as he perceiv'd, pity'd my Pain:
He met my Paffion with an equal Fire,
Both fweetly languifht in a foft Defire:
Clafpt in each other's Arms we fate all Day,
Each Smile I gave, he'd with a Kifs repay:
In every Hour an Ages Blifs we reap'd,
And lavifh Favours on each other heap'd.
Now fure (thought I) Deftiny doth relent,
And her infatiate Tyranny repent:
But how miftaken! how deceiv'd was I!
Alas! She onely rais'd my Hopes thus high,

To

To caſt me down with greater Violence;
For midſt our Joys, ſhe ſnatch'd my Shepherd hence
To *Africa:* yet tho' I was neglected,
I bore it better than could be expected:
VVithout Regret, I let him croſs the Sea,
VVhen I was told it for his Good wou'd be;
But when I heard the Nuptial Knot he'd ty'd,
And made an *Afric* Nymph his happy Bride:
My Temper then I could no longer hold,
I curs'd my Fate, I curs'd the Pow'r of Gold;
I curs'd the Eaſineſs believ'd at firſt,
And (Heaven forgive me) Him I almoſt curs'd.
Hearing my Loſs, to him was mighty Gain;
I check'd my Rage, and ſoon grew Calm again:
Malicious Fate, ſeeing this wou'd not do,
Made *Strephon* wretched, to make me ſo too.
Of all her Plagues, this was the weightieſt Stroke,
This Blow, my reſolv'd Heart hath almoſt broke:
Yet, ſpight of Fate, this Comfort I've in ſtore,
She's no room left for any Ill thing more.

H

To

To One that Affronted the Excellent *Eugenia*.

THing, call'd a Man ! Ambition cheats thy Senfe,
Or, thou'rt deceiv'd with too much Impudence;
To think that Divine Creature you purfue,
Can be deferv'd, or merited by you :
Dare not to be fo Impioufly Rude,
To tax fuch Goodnefs with Ingratitude ;
One Smile from her will more Obligements pay,
Than fhoud'ft thou live ten Ages, thou coud'ft lay.
Thou talk of Obligations ! that wer't fram'd
To make proud man of his own Sex afham'd :
When in his greateft Pride, he caft an Eye,
On thy ill Manners and Deformity ;
He'l hate himfelf, and rather wifh to be
An Afs, or Owl, than fuch a thing as thee.

Dar'ft

Dar'ſt thou affront Her thou pretend'ſt t'adore?
That Heavenly Mortal, if ſhe be no more;
Becauſe to them better deſerv'd it, ſhe
Shew'd more reſpect, and more Civility?
You rudely muſt Invite her to expoſe
Thoſe God-like Men, unto your barb'rous Blows;
She will not do't; not that thy Arm ſhe fears,
Or thinks thy Valour more refin'd than theirs:
Tho' in their Glory ſhe deſigns no ſhare,
Yet of their Honour ſhe takes too much care,
To let 'em Fight a deſpicable Thing,
That when they've Conquer'd, can no Trophy bring.
Know, Fool too; thee ſhe does too much contemn,
To let thee boaſt thou ever Fought'ſt with them.
To vex thee, they her Favourites ſhall be,
And make their Court ſtill in abuſing thee:
Abuſing thee! what have I vainly ſed?
What Nonſence unawares I've uttered!
The harſheſt *Satyr* that we can invent,
Is *Panegyrick*, when of Thee 'tis meant.

H 2

All

All my Invention cannot reach a Curfe,
For whatfoe're I think, ftill thou art worfe;
Yet I'le endeavour at One: Be't thy Fate
To live the Object of *Eugenia's* Hate.

To *Clovis*, defiring me to bring Him into *Marina's* Company.

CHarming Infulter! fure you might have chofe
Some eafier way than this you now propofe,
To try the boundlefs Friendfhip I profefs;
For if Fate can, this Task will make it lefs.
Clovis, believe; if any Thing there is
I can deny your Merit, it is this :
If I had Rocks of Diamonds, Mines of Ore,
Engrofs'd the Pearls upon the Eaftern-fhore;

VVith

VVith as much Joy, I'de lay'em at your Feet,
As Youthful Monarchs in new Empires meet.
Cou'd you be Happy by my Mifery,
In any fhape but this, I'de wretched be:
VVith ev'ry other Wifh I wou'd comply,
But bright *Marina*'s Sight I muft deny:
That Gift's too prodigal; I'de rather part
With Life its felf, and give my bleeding Heart:
For I with Blufhes own, that Sacred Fire
Once rul'd my Breaft, degenerate to defire.
I thought it Friendfhip; Swore it fhou'd be fo,
Yet fpight of Me, it wou'd to Paffion grow.
When to this worthlefs Heart, you did addrefs,
VVith all the Marks that Paffion cou'd exprefs;
On my foft Neck your Penfive Head wou'd lay,
And Sigh, and Vow, and Kifs the Hours away.
Your Tears, and languifh'd Looks I did neglect,
And wou'd not Love, yet highly did Refpect;
Thought you the beft of Men, and counfel'd you,
To turn your Paffion into Friendfhip too:

Told

Told you, my Heart was cruel *Strephon*'s Prize,
His devout, tho neglected Sacrifice:
Wou'd often talk of sweet *Marina*'s Charms,
And oft'ner wish her lodg'd in your dear Arms.
Ah, fatal Wish ! ye Gods ! why shou'd you mind
The foolish Wishes made by Woman-kind ?
I ev'ry hour saw *Strephon*'s Love decay;
And *Clovis* more Endear'd me every day.
Why at so vast a Rate shou'd he Oblige ?
Or, why so soon shou'd he remove his Siege ?
That Hour that Mine began, Your Love did end,
You took my Counsel and became my Friend:
And by those Ties, did earnestly request,
That I wou'd make *Marina*'s Heart your Guest.
Oh, cruel Task ! you Destinies, am I
In my own Ruine made a Property ?
Yet want the Pow'r the Treason to deny ?
Yes; tho this piece of knotty Friendship be
Hard in its self, and harder far to me;

I'le

I'le try, and in th' Attempt such Vigor show,
I'le make her Yours, tho Fate it self say no:
I'le tell your Merits in such soft, smooth Strains,
Shall leave a Thrilling Pleasure in her Veins;
And when my Tongue no sweeter Words can find,
I'le look, as there were ten times more behind.
Then speak again; nor leave her till I spy
She is Inthrall'd, and loves as much as I.
Then I'le present you with this Beauteous Slave,
The greatest Gift a Lover ever gave:
And when you cannot wish happier to grow,
Then think with how much Pain I made you so.

H 4   In

In the Perfon of a Lady to *Bajazet*, Her unconftant Gallant.

How far are they deceiv'd, that hope in vain
A lafting Leafe of Joys from Love t'obtain?
All the Dear Sweets we're promifs'd, or expect,
After Enjoyment turn to cold Neglect :
Cou'd Love a conftant Happinefs have known,
That Mighty Wonder had in Me been fhown ;
Our Paffions were fo favoured by Fate,
As if fhe meant them an Eternal Date :
So kind he look'd, fuch tender VVords he fpoke,
'Twas paft Belief fuch Vows fhou'd e're be broke:
Fix'd on my Eyes, how often wou'd he fay,
He cou'd with Plcafure gaze an Age away.
When Thought, too great for VVords, had made him
In Kiffes he wou'd tell my Hand his Sute :   (mute,

So

So ſtrong his Paſſion was, ſo far above
The common Gallantries that paſs for Love:
At worſt, I thought, if he unkind ſhou'd prove,
His ebbing Paſſion wou'd be kinder far,
Than the Firſt Tranſports of all others are:
Nor was my Love weaker, or leſs than his;
In him I center'd all my hopes of Bliſs:
For him, my Duty to my Friends forgot;
For him I loſt----alas! what loſt I not?
Fame, all the Valuable Things of Life,
To meet his Love by a leſs Name than Wife.
How happy was I then! how dearly bleſt!
VVhen this Great Man lay panting on my Breaſt,
Looking ſuch Things as ne're can be expreſt.
Thouſand freſh Loves he gave me every hour,
VVhile eagerly I did his Looks devour:
Quite overcome with Charms, I trembling lay,
At every Look he gave, melted away;
I was ſo highly happy in his Love,
Methought I pity'd thoſe that dwelt above.

Think

Think then thou greateſt, lovelieſt, falſeſt Man,
How you have vow'd, how I have lov'd, and than
My faithleſs Dear, be cruel if you can.
How I have lov'd, I cannot, need not tell;
No, every Act has ſhewn I lov'd too well.
Since firſt I ſaw you, I ne're had a Thought,
VVas not entirely yours ; to you I brought
My Virgin Innocence, and freely made
My Love an Offering to your Noble Bed:
Since when, you've been the Star by which I've
And nothing elſe but you, I lov'd, or fear'd : (ſteer'd
Your Smiles I onely liv'd by, and I muſt
VVhen e're you Frown, be ſhatter'd into Duſt.
I cannot live on Pity, or Reſpect,
A Thought ſo mean, wou'd my whole Frame infect,
Leſs than your Love I ſcorn, Sir, to accept.
Let me not live in dull Indiff'rency,
But give me Rage enough to make me die:
For if from you I needs muſt meet my Fate,
Before your Pity, I wou'd chooſe your *Hate*.

To

To Madam F. *A may be Frazer*

Divineſt Thing ! whom Heaven made to ſhew
The very utmoſt that its Skill cou'd do:
If you had liv'd in ancient *Rome*, or *Greece*,
You had had Altars built you long ere this.
Not all the Pow'rs they worſhip'd, e're poſſeſt
Half of the Merit crouds your Noble Breſt.
So Good, ſo Great, ſo Brave, ſo Heavenly Fair;
Princes are proud your Lovely Chains to wear:
So perfect are the Vertues of your Mind,
Not Envy's ſelf, a ſingle Stain can find:
The Vaſtneſs of your Gallant Soul doth move
The World to pay an Univerſal Love.
Yet at an awful Diſtance they admire;
Beyond a Veneration none aſpire.
Oh, may theſe Bleſſings have a laſting Date,
And You be ſafe from all the Strokes of Fate:
My Wiſh is vain, (and Pray'rs are needleſs too)
Heav'n is too Juſt to be Unkind to You.

SONG.

SONG.

KNow, *Strephon*, once I lov'd you more
    Than Mifers do their Wealth;
I took from Heaven you to adore,
And thought no Sin i'th' Stealth :
I knew no Joys, but what you gave,
Nor ever had a Thought
Of any ftate beyond your Slave,
Freedom I never fought.

2.

But fince your ftrange Ingratitude,
Cou'd the foft Favours flight,
For which your Rivals vainly fu'd,
Know you've no longer Right,
To the leaft Joy that I can give,
So unconcern'd I'le prove,
The World fhall eafily believe
That I did never love.

To

To the Angry *Eugenia*.

INcenſed Fair One! if Forgivenefs be
Not in thy Power to extend to Me;
Which to believe, were ſuch an impious Thought,
Heav'n ſcarce wou'd pardon, tho with Tears 'twere
Deſtroy at once the Creature that you hate, (ſought.
And wrack me not with a ſad ling'ring Fate:
Yet e're I Die, permit ſome ſmall Defence,
Not that I will pretend to Innocence;
That were to think that You have been Unjuſt,
Which let me Periſh when I once Miſtruſt.
With all that Rev'rence that a Pious *Jew*
Wou'd name *Jehovah*, I ſhould Speak of You:
But I, prophanely nam'd you in the Ear
Of Crowds unfit ſuch Sacred Sounds to hear:
Yet what I ſaid, if traced, you will find,
Tho ſhort of you, out-did all Woman-kind.

My

My Fault was too much Zeal; this forc'd my Tongue
To tell the Worth it had Adored long.
My Life will witness this; for, Madam, know,
I love too well to Live and Injure You.

SONG.

AH *Phillis* ! had you never lov'd,
Your Hate I could have born
Contentedly, I wou'd have prov'd
The Object of your Scorn.
But you were once as soft, as kind,
As yielding Virgins be;
Gods ! that That Face fhou'd have a Mind
Stain'd with Inconftancy.

2

No Tongue can tell the Mighty Joy
Your Kindnefs did Create;
But the Sweet Rapture you deftroy,
With fuddain caufelefs Hate.

So

So have I seen a Rising Sun
Promife a Glorious Day,
But foon o're-caft, its Brightnefs gone,
Did to rough Storms give way.

To Madam *G.uinn*

S Pight of my Beft Refolves, my Thoughts Afpire
To Speak, what I in Silence fhou'd Admire;
How vainly I endeavour to exprefs,
What none can e're defcribe, but make it lefs !
When your Compofure was as firft Defign'd,
Heaven to a vaft Extravagance was kind;
Beauty and Wit did lavifhly Conteft,
Who fhou'd give moft, which fhou'd adorn you beft :
A Stately Meen, foft Charms, a Face fo fweet;
In You alone do all Perfections meet.

So

So Bright your Beauty, fo Sublime your VVit,
None but a Prince to wear your Chains is Fit.
I wou'd wifh Something, but all Heaven's Store
Cannot afford One Single Blefling more:
Honour nor VVealth you want; nor any Thing,
Unlefs I wifh you a Perpetual Spring
Of Youth and Blooming Beauties; fuch as may
Make all Your Envious Rivals pine away.

Ephelia.

F I N I S.

Advice to His **GRACE**

by

Ephelia

[London, *c.* 1681]

———————

Broadside,

Addressed to *James*, Duke of Monmouth

5⁰⁴

Advice to His GRACE.

A Wake; vain Man; 'tis time th' Abuſe to ſee;
　　Awake, and guard thy *heedleſs Loyalty*
From all the Snares are laid for It and Thee.
No longer let that buſie juggling Crew
(Who to their own mis-deeds entitle You,)
Abuſe Your ear: Conſider, Sir, the State
Of our unhappy Iſle, diſturb'd of late
With *cauſeleſs* Jealouſies, *ungrounded* Fear,
Obſtinate Faction, and *Seditious Care*;
Gone quite diſtracted for *Religion's* ſake;
And nothing their hot Brains can cooler make,
(So great's the deprivation of their ſence,)
But the excluding of their lawful Prince :
A Prince, in whoſe each Act is clearly ſhown,
That Heaven deſign'd Him to adorn a Throne;
Which (tho' *He ſcorns by Treaſon to purſue,*)
He ne'r will quit, if it become His due.
Then lay betimes Your mad *Ambition* down;
Nor let the dazling Luſtre of a Crown
Bewitch Your Thoughts; but think what *mighty care*
Attends the Crowns that *lawful* Princes wear;
But *when ill Title's added to the weight,*
How inſupportable's the Load of State!
Believe thoſe working Brains Your Name abuſe;
You only for their *Property* doe uſe :
And when they're ſtrong ehough to *ſtand alone*;
You, as *an uſeleſs Thing,* away'l be thrown.
Think too, how dear you have already paid,
For the *fine Projects* Your falſe Friends had laid.
When by the Rabbles *fruitleſs Zeal* You loſt
Your Royal Fathers *Love,* Your growing Fortune croſs'd;
Say, was Your Bargain, think ye, worth the Coſt?
Remember what Relation, Sir, you bear
To Royal *Charles* ; Subject and Son You are;
Two Names that *ſtrict Obedience* does require;
What *Frenzy* then does Your raſh Thoughts Inſpire;
Thus by *Diſloyal Deeds* to add more Cares,
To them of the bright Burden that he wears?
Why with ſuch eager ſpeed hunt You a Crown
You're ſo unfit to wear, were it Your own ?
With Bows, and Legs, and little Arts, You try;
A rude, unthinking *Tumults* love to buy :
And he who ſtoops to do ſo mean a *Thing,*
Shows He, by Heaven, was ne're deſign'd for *King.*
Would You be Great ? do Things are *Great* and *Brave*;
And ſcorn to be the *Mobile's* dull Slave :
Tell *the baſe Great Ones,* and *the ſhouting Throng,*
You ſcorn a *Crown* worn in *anothers wrong.*
Prove Your *high Birth* by Deeds *Noble* and *Good*;
But *ſtrive not to Legitimate Your Blood.*

Ephelia.

217

"A funerall Elegie on Sr Thomas

Isham Barronet"

Signed "Ephelia."

[*c.* 9 August 1681]

———

A funerall Elegie on Sr. Thomas Isham Barronet

Folio 1:

Those that write Elegies on Common Men,

who had no worth but from the Poets Pen,

Must practise all that Rethorick has taught,

All moveing arts, by which the soule is wrought

to softest Pitty, and to saddest thought:

to work up passion no such skill I need,

for wou'd I make the world with sorrow bleed,

And Natures selfe hang down her drooping head,

I need to say no more but Isham's dead!

Dead in his blooming years, ere fate had time

to ripen halfe she promis'd us in him:

His early youth did a large hope afford,

of all the worth with which great men are stor'd:

oh! had this forward bud but stay'd t' have blown,

A great Example to mankind hee'd shown,

what gallant, gen'rous things had he not done?

The sweetness of his temper, made him prove

The obiect of an universall love:

So Gracefull, as if Nature ment to shew

in him, the utmost what her art cou'd doe:

his witt, and knowledg, much his years outwent,

to Honour were his lives short actions bent,

His

220

A funerall Elegie on S:t Thomas
Isham Barronet

Those that write Elegies on Common Men,
who had no worth but from the Poets pen,
Must practise all that Rethorick has taught,
All moveing arts, by which the soule is wrought
to softest pitty, and to saddest thought:
to work vp passion no such skill J need
for mine, J make the words with sorrow bleed,
And Natures selfe hang down her drooping head,
J need to say no more but Jshams dead,
Dead in his blooming years ere fate had time
to ripen halfe she promis'd vs in him:
His early youth did a large hope afford,
of all the worth with which great men are stor'd.
Oh! had this forward bud but stagd t'have blown,
A great example to mankind hee'd shown
what gallant gen'rous things had he not done,
The sweetness of his temper, made him prove
the object of an vniversall love:
So Graceful, as if Nature ment to shew
ik him, the vtmost what her art coud doe:
his witt, and knowledg, much his year outwent
to Honour were his lives short actions bent

His

<u>Unedited Transcription (continued):</u>

Folio 2:

His growing courage, did prognosticate

something so great, as even startl'd fate:

                            /his breath
who from the lovely youth did force_∧~~away~~

when Hymen more expected was, then death:

And a bright Virgin ready to be led

In stately tryumph, to his Nuptiall bed:

what words can ere discribe her mighty greif,

as much beyond expression, as releife:

The sorrow all the mourning world doth shew,

she wou'd engrose, and if she cou'd out=doe:

but greifs like this can never be confin'd,

They universally invade mankind:

Nature her selfe Close mourner is become,

And even the Muses too are stricken dumbe:

                                 /verse
None breath their sorrows in a murmuring_∧

but all in awfull silence waite his Hearse,

for hardly any age a man has bred,

so lov'd when living, or so mourn'd when dead.
                        [flourish]
                        Ephelia.
                        [flourish]

Portland MS PwV 336 University of Nottingham Library, Nottingham, England

His Growing courage, Did prognosticate
Something so great as even startld fate:
who from the lovely youth Did force his breath ~~away~~
When Hymen more expected was then Death.
And a bright Virgin ready to be led
In stately tryumph, to his Nuptiall bed.
what words can ere describe her mighty greif,
as much beyond expression as releife:
The sorrow all the mourning world doth shew
She wou'd engrose, and if she cou'd out-doe.
but greiff like this can never be confind
they vniversally invade mankind.
Nature herselfe close mourner is become
And even the Muses too are stricken dumbe.
None breath their sorrows in a murmuring verse
but all in awfull silence waite his Hearse,
for hardly any age a man has bred
so lov'd when living, or so mourn'd when dead.

Ephelia.

III. APPARATUS

225

*A*PPENDIX A: DESCRIPTIVE LIST OF EPHELIA'S POETRY
(with locations, to date)

1. [*c.* early/mid 1670s]. A 'Lost' Play, "The Pair-Royal of Coxcombs. Performed at a Dancing-School."

   Prologue, two songs, and epilogue printed in both editions of Ephelia's *Female Poems.* A specimen of the author's juvenilia. Amateur production, as suggested by title in *Female Poems.* Possibly inspired by the sexual intrigue comedies of the 1670s then in vogue, or by the revival of Fletcher's *Coxcombs* in the late 1660s. Ephelia's 'pair-royal' (the object of her ridicule, as title suggests) may refer to Monmouth, whom she criticized in print in 1681, or to some other of the several 'fitz-roys.' Also a candidate is James, Duke of York, whose adulterous liaison with Katherine Sedley may have stirred Ephelia's pen.

   > 'Lost' or unlocated. No manuscript, no printer's copy identified to date. No further fragments of this play identified to date.
   > Listed in *The London Stage* I:272-273; Milhous and Hume, "'Lost Plays'," *HLB* 25 (1977)

2. 1678. *A POEM TO HIS SACRED MAJESTY, ON THE PLOT. Written by a Gentlewoman.* London: Printed for *Henry Brome* at the *Gun* in *St. Paul's* Church-yard. Licensed Nov. 23. 1678. *Roger L'Estrange*

   Broadside (26.5 cms. x 36 cms.), dual-column format. Text set in italic. 50-line broadside to Charles II on the Popish Plot. Reprinted in Ephelia's *Female Poems* (1679, 1682), under a significantly modified title ("*Presented to* His Sacred Majesty"). Variants, mostly stylistic, to 12 lines. (As both versions are included in this edition, the reader readily can observe these variants.)

   > No manuscript, no printer's copy identified to date.
   > <u>Locations</u>: Bodleian, British Library. Film: Sterling Library, Yale University, and Huntington Library (Luttrell, "Broadsides" III:128); *Early English Books* (University Microfilms)

3. 1679. *FEMALE POEMS ON several OCCASIONS. Written by Ephelia.* [decorative fleur device, 4.5 cms. x 4 cms.] London, Printed by *William Downing* for *James Courtney, Anno. Dom.,* 1679
   Collation: Small 8vo (11 cms. x 17.5 cms.) A³(+/-A1) B-G⁸ H⁸. 112 correctly numbered pages. Engraved frontispiece, designated

"Ephelia," head & bust, in oval frame, in the style of Faithorne, and Lely (his "Beauties" series). With coat-of-arms (or quartering) at top of portrait frame, in a roundel (not shield) and encircled by laurels, apparently Tilly (abeyant by 1679). Frontispiece unsigned and undated, no discernible cypher of engraver nor painter. Epistle-dedicatory, with decorative fleur head (9 x 1.5 cms.), set in italic type, to "The Most Excellent Princess **MARY**, Dutchess of *Richmond & Lenox*" [Lady Mary (Villiers) Stuart, 1622-1685], with printed subscription "*Ephelia*." Last page (p.112) also bears printed subscription "*Ephelia*" (above "*FINIS*"). Discernible watermark (ornate fleur), 4 cms x 3 cms (*e.g.*, A2, octavo position). Vertical chainlines. One incorrect catchword: "Celadon" (C8). Omission of "1," first stanza, D3. Inverted type "Aud" for "And" (E3ᵛ, line 10). Roman type: Great Cannon. Italic type: James.

> No manuscript, no printer's copy identified to date. Price in 1679: 1s. (bound), *Term Cat*.I:350. Last at auction, 1982: Slater copy, Christie's New York, $1800, from Jonathan Hill, who then sold the Slater *Ephelia* to the Clark Library-UCLA
>
> Locations: Bodleian, British Library (2 copies), Leeds; Clark-UCLA, Folger, Harvard, Huntington, Newberry, Texas. In private hands: James Perry copy (unlocated), Mulvihill copy (See **Appendix E**)

4. *c*. 1681. *Advice to His GRACE*. Printed subscription "*Ephelia*."

Broadside. Single-column (slip) format (29 cms. x 17 cms.). Type: White-letter (*i.e.*, Roman, as distinguished from 'Black-letter' or Gothic type). No woodcut, no device. A cautionary 50-line broadside to James (Scott), Duke of Monmouth.

> No manuscript, no printer's copy identified to date.
>
> Locations: British Library, Bodleian, National Library of Scotland (Crawford Collection of English Ballads, no. 158, this collection transferred from John Rylands Library, Manchester, 1988); Clark-UCLA, Folger, Harvard, Huntington, Newberry, Texas, Yale (Beinecke; gift of Yale alumnus Arthur M. Rosenbloom, in 1952). Not at Haigh Hall, Wigan, as Wing records.
>
> Reprinted in *Roxburghe Ballads* IV (1883), ed. J W Ebsworth, as probably the work of another hand. Variants: line 41 leers] legs; line 46 Slave] Slaves.
>
> Reprinted in Reed's *Tracts*: 7

5. [August, 1681]. "A funerall Elegie On Sʳ Thomas Isham Barronet"

Single sheet, folded into two folios, each 14.5 cms. x 20 cms. 40 lines. Evidently, an autograph manuscript, bearing the bold calligraphic signature "Ephelia" at foot of second folio, framed in flourishes. One handmade correction in line 25, in same hand as title, signature, and body of poem. Possibly formatted for printer: 2 marginal brackets and catchword "His." Black, carbon-based ink, with evidence of uneven ink transmission, from a low-quality or old quill-pen. High-quality, white laid paper. Thickness: 0.11 mm. Horizontal chain-lines. Armorial circle watermark, central position, comparably Heawood 821. Possibly commissioned by the Ishams or one of their circle for reading at the obsequies, as title suggests. Signs of multiple foldings, so as to form a small packet for easy transport or posting. (See **Appendix D** for details.)

> Location: Portland MS PwV 336, University of Nottingham. Deposited by the then-Duke of Portland, 1949. Probable first provenance: family of Margaret (Cavendish née Lucas), Duchess of Newcastle (d.1673), literary writer and near-contemporary of Ephelia

6. 1682. *FEMALE POEMS ON Several OCCASIONS. Written by EPHELIA. The Second Edition, with Large Additions.* London, Printed for *James Courtney*, at the Golden horse Shooe upon Saffron Hill, 1682

Collation: Small 8vo (11 cms. x 17.5 cms.), as first edition of 1679; A³(+/-A1) B-G⁸ H⁷ I-L⁸, M⁶ (M2 missigned as M3). With frontis. and decorative details, as in first issue. 169 correctly numbered pages. Reset: titlepage, pp. 111 and 112; the rest, a miscellany of poems by Ephelia's contemporaries. Evidently, not an authorized edition: printed subscription *Ephelia* does not appear on p. 112 of this issue, nor on final page (as in the 1679 issue).

The authors of 20 of the 35 unascribed poems (being the publisher Courtney's "Large Additions") are:

Aphra Behn, "Loves Revenge," "*Jemmy*"
John Dryden, "Farewel to Ingratitude," "But for Hope"
Thomas D'Urfey, "A Nuptial Song," "The Town Blade"
Nathaniel Lee, "Hail to the Myrtle Shade"
Sir Carr Scroope, "Song" ("I cannot change as others do")
     (attributed variously to Scroope and to Rochester)
Lady Rochester, "The Answer"
Rochester: "Expostulation," "Maim'd Debauchee," "Upon His Leaving His Mistress," "Upon a Drinking Bowl," "An Epistle to *Ephelia's* Letter to *Bajazet*," "Song" ("Give me leave to rail at You"), "Song" ("I cannot change as others do") (attributed variously, to Rochester and to Scroope), "The Fall," "Love and Life," "Woman's Honour," "Song" (*Phillis*, be

gentler I advise"); "Song" ("As *Cloris* full of
harmless Thoughts")
"To His Letter" may be a version of Ashmole MS 47 f.47ʳ
"Song" ("*Phillis,* accept a stubborn Heart") may be a
version of Bodl. Rawlinson Poet. 196, f.5, or the
work of Rochester
No manuscript, no printer's copy identified to date.
Locations: Bodleian, British Library; Huntington

See **Appendix D** for information on manuscript copies
of Ephelia's work

---

*A*PPENDIX B: TWO SPECULATIVE ADDITIONS

New Poems, Songs, Prologues & Epilogues. Never before Printed is
commonly recorded as the work of Thomas D'Uffet (Duffett), an
enterprising minor writer of low prestige with a talent for farce,
burlesque, masque, and dramatic adaptation. His *New Poems,* a small
octavo of 122 pages, was published in 1676 by Nicolas Woolfe, a printer
in Cheapside. D'Uffet's collection, now quite rare, prints two juvenilia,
which bear resemblance to some of Ephelia's earlier pieces, with respect
to subject-matter, 'voice,' phrasing, and practice in dramatic verse and
encomium.

Because my researches into D'Uffet's publisher, and into D'Uffet's
biography and writings failed to locate any specific evidence linking him
to Ephelia or to a female poet named "humble Joan," "Proud" ("Prowde")
or "Philips" (all variant spellings), I am introducing these two poems in
the Appendix of this edition, rather than in the text proper, as speculative
additions to Ephelia's canon, based on (1) internal evidence, and (2)
intersecting circumstantial facts. Overall, these two poems are useful for
what they imply about Ephelia's early connections, apprenticeship, and
movements in London.

As Restoration specialists will agree, the poetry miscellanies of
the later-Stuart period were often hastily produced collections of popular
verse. These small, vendible products of the busy literary marketplace
were often described on title-pages as "*Poems on several Occasions.*" Some
of these attractive collections were surreptitious publications, produced
by enterprising booksellers. The second edition of *Female Poems ... by
Ephelia,* published by James Courtney in 1682, was doubtless a pirated,
unauthorized issue. A good many of these miscellanies were rife with
misattributed and unascribed songs, lampoons, love poems, verse-satires,
bawdry, and the occasional prologue and epilogue. The characteristic

eclectic nature of these books was sometimes acknowledged on title-pages as being the work of "several Hands."

D'Uffet's by-line on the title-page of the 1676 *New Poems* does not necessarily authenticate his proprietary authorship of all of the poems printed in this collection. As David M. Vieth has shown in *Attribution in Restoration Poetry* (1963), the so-called Antwerp edition of Rochester's verse in 1680 was neither published in Antwerp, nor exclusively the work of Rochester. The volume freely publishes, without ascription, verse by Aphra Behn, Ephelia, Elizabeth (Mallet) Countess of Rochester, Etherege, Scroope, and several others. Further investigation into D'Uffet's *New Poems* may turn up several pieces of 'lost' or little-known verse by Restoration poets of Ephelia's day. It was doubtless with such publishing practices in mind that Ephelia conspicuously establishes authorship throughout the *Female Poems* by naming herself on the book's title-page, by signing her epistle-dedicatory and the final page of the volume, and (self-portraitist that she is) by placing herself in several pastorals and songs in *Female Poems*.

When D'Uffet's *New Poems* was published in 1676, Ephelia was an ingénue (according to my speculative reconstruction) and writing without patronage. As discussed in my Critical Essay, above, we know for certain that she published anonymously in 1678, and probably earlier. Shortly after her inaugural publication in 1678, however, she secured the patronage of the impressively well connected Lady Mary (Villiers) Stuart. Therefore, it is not surprising that Ephelia's early work, especially her juvenilia, appears without ascription in several of the manuscript and published collections of the later 17th century, as **Appendix D** of this edition illustrates.

The first of these two speculative additions is "Epilogue by a Woman." Now many "she-prologues" and "she-epilogues" of the Restoration tend to resemble one another in their explicit feminism (*v.* Dolan *Feminist Spectator* 1988). This becomes obvious by comparing the prologues and epilogues of, say, Margaret Duchess of Newcastle, Behn, and Ephelia. The overall similarities are striking. Yet, the 30-line "Epilogue" printed on pages 87 through 89 in D'Uffet's octavo aligns rather closely with Ephelia's "Epilogue" published in her *Female Poems* of 1679. In addition to the bold feminism of both pieces, one notices other similarities, such as the superior stance of the (female) speaker, the delightful appeal to humor and reason, and the playful concluding bargain the speaker proposes to an unappreciative male audience. As compared to Ephelia's epilogue and other dramatic verses in the *Female*

Poems, D'Uffet's "Epilogue" is of a lower order, especially with regard to the level of writing and the facility in couplet. If in fact Ephelia's, the epilogue in D'Uffet's collection must have been written quite early in her apprenticeship.

My case is weightier for a second poem in D'Uffet *New Poems*, also an amateur effort. It is a poem of compliment entitled "*To Madam R.P.*," printed on page 26. This 11-line encomium bears a conspicuous resemblance to one of Ephelia's juvenilia, namely her "Acrostich: Rachel Powney." In addition to celebrating women whose names bear identical initials, both poems emphasize identical qualities of their respective subjects: her beauty and virtue. But why would Ephelia write two poems of praise on the same individual? This is understandable in light of the fact that the name Powney may figure in Ephelia's biography and in her literary circle, especially if she were in fact 'kept' by Etherege after her affair with Mulgrave, around 1674/5, as discussed in my Critical Essay. Since Etherege's maternal line was the Powneys of Berkshire, references to Etherege and his kin in Ephelia's verse becomes understandable.

There also is a body of related circumstantial facts, links, and intersecting information which grounds the larger supposition that D'Uffet himself may have been one of Ephelia's circle, especially during her literary apprenticeship in London, during the early-to-mid 1670s, according to my speculative reconstruction. After the death of her parents, a fact she discloses in "My Fate," Ephelia may have established an association with D'Uffet, a poet-playwright of many talents. Four points of potential contact between Ephelia and D'Uffet support this hypothesis:

First, D'Uffet's pen, as Ephelia's, was partial to dramatic burlesque and farce. While Ephelia shares only fragments of her play with us in *Female Poems*, its title alone, *The Pair-Royal of Coxcombs*, suggests a talent in this vein. Temperamentally, Ephelia was a woman of good humor and playful wit, as several of her poems illustrate (*e.g.*, "Maidenhead"). This was a writer who would have found burlesque and farce naturally sympathetic to her personal and poetic disposition.

Second, D'Uffet's profession was originally that of a milliner. It is commonly recorded that he worked out of a shop in the New Exchange. In my survey of the collective provenance history of Ephelia's rare *Female Poems* (Appendix E), I was drawn to an especially interesting ownership signature in one of two copies of the first issue of Ephelia's *Female Poems* preserved at the British Library. What appears on A3^v, in a lovely contemporary calligraphic hand, is "Frances Bullon at Mrs. Vandersprits, a millener, by Londonstone [,] Watlinstreet. 1685." If Ephelia had in fact descended from the prosperous Prowde line of Shrewsbury, which included many clothworkers, she might have had a special rapport with such guildspeople as D'Uffet, Bullon, and their larger circle.

232

Third, the dedicatee of D'Uffet's play, *The Spanish Rogue* (1674), his most indecent effort in drama, is Nell Gwyn, a popular Restoration comic actress and royal mistress. According to a manuscript note in the Verney copy of *Female Poems* in this edition, the "Madam *G.*" of Ephelia's encomium, which closes her collection, is Nell Gwyn.

Finally, there is the recorded fact, from the title-page of D'Uffet's masque *Beauties Triumph* (1676), that this play was originally presented as an amateur production; this also was the case with Ephelia's play *The Pair-Royal of Coxcombs*, which was "Acted at a Dancing-School." Additional information on D'Uffet's title-page states that his play was performed by the "Scholars," namely drama students and protégées of Jeffrey Banister and James Hart, who, the title-page goes on, maintained a new private boarding school for young ladies and gentlewomen in Chelsea. As my researches revealed, Hart was a singer, composer, and Gentleman of the Chapel Royal; and Banister, one of the English Banister family of musicians, and one of the King's Violins (*v.* Spink *Grove* 8:260, 2:117). This new school for dramatic fledglings was the former estate of Sir Arthur Gorge. Since Jeffrey Banister (perhaps *Orinda* Philips's elusive composer "Colonel Jeffries") also was active in Restoration music circles, he may have provided instruction in song-writing at this school; and we know that this was a genre in which Ephelia enjoyed a level of success (*v. Appendix G*). While speculative, it is entirely possible that the orphaned Ephelia, newly set up as a writer in London in the 1670s, may have been quietly associated with this school, and with the D'Uffet-Banister-Hart circle, as an amateur actress, playwright, and song-writer. We know from her work that she produced plays and songs (some set by Snow, Turner, and Farmer); and we also know that she received "loud Applauses" (*v.* "To A Proud Beauty"). The organization, voice, and ethos of her best lyrical poems, especially the lament to *Bajazet*, closely resemble dramatic verse in their aural qualities and accent. There also is the fact of Ephelia's link to the Restoration theater circuit through Nell Gwyn (evidently her "Madam *G.*"), and possibly through Etherege, as discussed above. And certainly Ephelia's theatrical contacts included Aphra Behn, the subject of "To Madam *Bhen*" in *Female Poems*. We know that Behn acknowledged Ephelia (as "a Poet *Joan*") in *Sir Patient Fancy* (1678); and that Robert Gould, a poet-playwright, describes Ephelia and Behn as a literary team. Collectively, these allusions and intersecting circumstances firmly place Ephelia on the Restoration theater circuit and well within the orbit of Banister, Hart, and their ingénues.

Though speculative, my formulations are reasonable, and they carry cumulative weight for Ephelia's association with D'Uffet and his use of her work without ascription in his book of 1676.

The two texts below are unedited transcriptions from D'Uffet's *New Poems* (1676), in *University Microfilms: Early English Books*, FW64, reel 64, Huntington Library copy.

233

Two Speculative Additions to Ephelia's Canon
from D'Uffet's
New Poems, Song, Prologues & Epilogues. Never Before Printed
(1676)

Epilogue by a Woman.

Gentlemen,

OUr mens late disappointments have made known,
Without our Sex no bus'ness can be done;
They treat you just as you deal with us,
You promise fair -----
But if you once get in, ne'r pay a souse,
Women support the World and we the house.
Nature and power teach vile men to rome,
We poor good humour'd things still play at home.
Mens active Legs with one nights dancing grow
Quite dull and tir'd --- Our Tongues are never so:
Their lazy Instruments are out of Tune,
And then forsooth there's nothing to be done.
S'life, out or in we women ne'r lie still,
While our Pit's kept warm and our Purses fill.
Yet, Gallants, you may pardon them for this,
We oft have Play'd when you ne'r came to see's.
Be constanter and less Capricious,
How long shall we weak Vessels teach you thus?
And yet in troth y'are always kind to us;
But we must rail as cunning Lovers do,
Not that y'are false but to preserve you true.
You seem best pleas'd when you are most abus'd,
But fawning wit and easie love's refus'd.
A murmuring Miss revives your faint desire,
And hussing Prologues raise your kindness higher;
As blustring winds increase decaying fire.
Cover our matted Seats but once a day,
And to content you, we'l Act any way.
Then Clap us soundly, while we Play our parts,
Or else ----- a mischief on your stony hearts.

APPARATUS

Speculative Additions to Ephelia's Canon (cont'd.)
Two Verses from D'Uffet's *New Poems* ... (1676)
(unedited transcriptions)

To Madam **R.P.**

*R*Eason and Love, their ancient feud laid by,
Equally strive to raise your power high.
Beauty, Loves never failing dart in you,
Exceeds all praise, and does all hearts subdue.
Cupid in ev'ry careless smile is drest,
Kindling a fire in the beholders breast.
And Reason, if the slave don't straight submit,
Proclaims your Virtue and Victorious Wit;
Love gives the charge, and Reason strengthens it.
Alas what heart can make resistance, where
Youth, Beauty, Wit and Vertue do appear?

———————

235

𝒜PPENDIX C: POSSIBLE CHRONOLOGICAL SCHEDULE OF EPHELIA'S WRITINGS

Determinants: (i) recorded dates of published writings; (ii) internal evidence, such as 'markers' or reference points in the writings, being allusions or references to known personages and events

Some Preliminary Potential Data (Dates, etc.):

Ephelia born *c*. mid-1640s, no later than 1648, the birthdate of her first lover, Lord Mulgrave

Loses both parents *c*. mid-1670s ("My Fate," *Female Poems*, 1679)

Relocates to London, mid-l670s, attached to publisher Courtney, Saffron Hill; later, Chelsea School of literary ingénues

Early beginnings assisted by London Phillips kin and Sheldon (*v.* "Elegy...on SHELDON," *Female Poems*, 1679)

Noticed by the London literary set for her beauty and wit (*v.* first half of Rochester's "Corinna" tale in *Artemisa*, 1679);

Apprenticeship, mid-l670s: anonymous prologues, epilogues, songs

Exposure to court circles, *c*. mid-to-late 1670s to *c*. 1681

Adopts pseudonym "Ephelia"; poems circulating in manuscript

*C.*1674-5 writes *Ephelia's Lamentation* to Mulgrave

Secures patronage of Lady Mary (Villiers) Stuart, *c*. 1677

Reaches print, with licensed broadside to Charles II (1678), "*Written by a Gentlewoman*"

Publishes poetic collection, with frontis., l679; dedicated to Lady Mary (Villiers) Stuart; includes bs. to Charles II in this collection

Publishes broadside against Monmouth, signed "*Ephelia*" (1681)

Writes "Isham" elegy, signed "Ephelia" [August, 1681]

Loses 'protection' of patroness *c*. 1681, falls upon hard times (*v.* Gould, *Satyrical Epistle*)

Possibly dies sometime after "Isham" elegy, precipitating unauthorized second edition of *Female Poems* by the enterprising James Courtney

Date	Poem/Linked Poems	Evidence
*c.*l660s	4 acrostics in *Female Poems* (1679)	1. juvenilia (names untraceable by publication date of *Female Poems*, l679)
early-to-mid 1670s	"Pair-Royal of Coxcombs"	1. similar to feminist dramatic verse of Cavendish, Boothby, early Behn
	"To Madam Bhen"	1. perhaps the occasion of Behn's "Poet Joan" in *Sir Patient Fancy* (1678)

Date	Poem/Linked Poems	Evidence
early-to-mid 1670s (cont'd.)	2 poems in D'Uffet's miscellany (1676)	1. see **Appendix B**
	"Maidenhead"	1. Internal evidence: line 3
*c.*1674-5	*Ephelia's Lamentation*	1. Mulgrave raised to O.G. 1674 2. This, her maiden love affair: "my Virgin Innocence" 3. Poem begins circulating in MS & in handsome scribal copies 4 Earliest MS appearance in the MS miscellany "Wit & Learning...1677" (Beinecke Library) 5 First prtd appearance in *Female Poems* (1679) 6 Begins 4yr. love affair with J.G. after demise of Mulgrave affair, *c.* 1675 ("Loves Cruelty," *Female Poems*, 1679)
	"The Change or Miracle"	1. Speaks as sexual initiate, passion supplanting reason (Mulgrave affair)
c. 1674/5-1679	Some 20 verses to or about "J.G.," aka "Strephon" in *Female Poems*	1. Internal evidence in the poems: a 4-year love affair (*v.* "Loves Cruelty"). Demise of this affair marked by "Song" ("Know, *Strephon*, once I lov'd ..."; Affairs with Clovis & Celadon follow
	Several coterie verses & occasional poems, publd. in *Female Poems*	1. Internal evidence & MS notes, suggesting Nell Gwyn, Cary Frazer, Lady Castlemaine, Ravenscroft, Lady Mary (Villiers) Stuart
c. 1677/8	"Elegy On ... SHELDON"	1. Sheldon d. 9 Nov., 1677, Lambeth (Staley, *Sheldon*, 185) [Publd. in *Female Poems* (1679)]

APPARATUS

Date	Poem/Linked Poem	Evidence
23 Nov. 1678	*A POEM ... ON THE PLOT. Written By A Gentlewoman*	1. Imprint data: licensed broadside 2. Publd. in *Female Poems* (1679) 3. "1678," p.1, *Female Poems*, Newberry co⟩
c. Easter, 1679	"To...MARY" (epistle ded., *Female Poems*)	1. Publd. in *Female Poems* (1679) 2. Allusions to recent deaths of Howard and Richmond, Mary's kin
Easter, 1679	*Female Poems ... Written by Ephelia* (1679)	1. Imprint data on title-page 2. Arber, *Term Cat.*, I:350 3. Plomer, *Dict. of Printers*, 83 4. Morrison, Paul G., *Index*, 73 5. Wing P2030 6. Rochester's "Corinna" tale in *Artemisa to Cloe* ("*Easter* term")
c. 1681	*ADVICE TO HIS GRACE*	1. Monmouth declares open rebellion 2. Height of Exclusion Crisis 3. Written before 1685 (Monmouth executed 1685) 4. "6 June 1681," Ashmole copy, Bodl.
August, 1681	"Funerall Elegie ... On Sir Thomas Isham Barronet" (manuscript; subscribed Ephelia)	1. Isham d. July, 1681, London; buried 9 August 1681, Lamport 2. Watermark of MS dated to this time: *e.g.* a Van de Velde drawing (see Heawood *Watermarks* #821); Sam. Denne essay & Fig.9)
1682	*Female Poems ... Written by Ephelia. The Second Edition, With Large Additions*	1. Imprint data on title-page 2. Wing P2031 3. Paul G. Morrison, *Index* *Varia*: Manual cancel in pub. date in Sather (?)-Arthur-Stainforth-Chew copy at Huntingt⟩ as "1684." Unique cancel in extant copies of edition (see **Appendix E**). This edition proba⟩ unauthorized (see **Appendix A**); possi⟩ occasioned by the death of Ephelia around t⟩ time

APPENDIX D: MANUSCRIPTS OF EPHELIA'S POETRY

I. Autograph Manuscript:
[1681] "A funerall Elegie on S Thomas Isham Barronet"
Portland MS PwV 336, University of Nottingham Library
According to the Library's records, this manuscript was deposited at Nottingham by the then duke of Portland in 1949. Its entry in Nottingham's typescript catalogue is "Mrs Jonn Phillips," owing to a longstanding transcription error. The modern-paper covering note, apparently written by the Librarian of Welbeck Abbey (R.W. Goulding or Francis Needham), attributes the poem to a "Mrs Joan Phillips"; yet "Jonn" was entered into Nottingham's record in error. [It was this information that roused my interest in the abandoned wife of John Phillips; but this search turned up little more than what Godwin supplies in his *Lives* of John and Edward Phillips (John Milton's nephews), 1815.]

This manuscript is a single sheet, moderately fragile, folded into two folios, 14.5 cms. x 20 cms. Special white, laid paper, thickness 0.11mm. With handsome circle armorial watermark (see Fig.7). Horizontal chainlines. In the same ink throughout; a common, carbon-based black ink, unevenly transmitted by an old or low-quality quill-pen. Signs of folding, so as to form a small packet of 7 cms. x 10 cms. One handmade correction (1.25) in the same hand as title, text of poem, and subscription "Ephelia." Formatted, with a catchword and two marginal brackets (perhaps, printer's copy?). No record to date of publication.

Since Welbeck and its great manuscript collection passed through four family ownerships, all interrelated, namely the families Cavendish, Holles, Harley, and Bentinck, and since the name "Cavendish" was in fact added to "Bentinck" by royal license in 1801, after the marriage of Margaret Cavendish Harley to William, 2d duke of Portland in the 18th century, it is possible that the "Isham" manuscript came into the Portland collection via some relation of Margaret (Cavendish *née* Lucas) Duchess of Newcastle (d.1673), a prolific writer and feminist, who freely circulated her own manuscripts and may have quietly collected those of other women writers of her time. No record of any connection between Margaret and Ephelia has been established to date. See Turberville *Welbeck ... 1539-1879* 1938-9; Debrett *Peerage* P944; Burke *Peerage* 2155f.

II. Manuscript Copies:
These are mostly scriptorium products of the popular and variously titled "*Ephelia's* Lamentation" to her *Bajazet* [John (Sheffield) Lord Mulgrave], traditionally attributed to Etherege. Some of the manuscripts listed below ascribe the poem to Rochester. This list is based on information culled from (i) James Thorpe, *Etherege* (1963); (ii) David

Vieth, *Attribution* (1963); (iii) Vieth & Bror Danielsson, *Gyldenstolpe MS Miscellany of Poems by ... Rochester and Other Restoration Authors* (1967); (iv) Peter Beal, *Index of English Literary Manuscripts II* (1987); and (v) further information supplied by the editor.

Recorded data below suggest that (i) Ephelia's poem to Bajazet, and its answer, were popular during their day; (ii) their popularity probably resulted from an actual romantic episode in the eventful lives of Ephelia and Mulgrave; and (iii) the two poems were often paired in printed and manuscript miscellanies of the 17th century.

In the United Kingdom:

Bodleian MS, English misc., e.536, pp.115-6. In a quarto miscellany of poems, late 17th century, as "Ephelia to Bajazet," without ascription. Photo-facsimile, subscribed "Rochester," in Danielsson and Vieth, *Gyldenstolpe* (1967):331, followed by Bajazet's reply, "An Heroicall Epistle ..." (f. 117).

Bodleian MS Rawlinson poet 173, ff.66^v-67^r. In a folio verse-miscellany, *c.* 1670, "Muse's Magazine," 123/8 x 8, 191 leaves, as "Epelia (a Deserted Lover) to Bajaset, which may serve as a Caveat to Women. By L^d Ro.[chester]." Listed in Crum. Vieth suggests this version of the poem may have been copied from one of the A-1680 editions of Rochester's *Poems* (*Attribution*, 466). This miscellany was acquired by John Dunton (d. 1733), a successful English journalist, from a Mr Corbet at the Addison's Head, who may have been its compiler.

British Library Add.MS 28253, ff.158-9. Untitled, no ascription, on two quarto leaves in the Caryll family verse-miscellany (late 17th century). Possibly copied from one of the A-1680 editions of Rochester's *Poems*, according to Vieth (*Attribution*, 466).

British Library Egerton MS 2623, f.78^r&78^v. In small-format, late 17th-century quarto miscellany of poetry manuscripts, as "Ephelia to Bajazett." No ascription.

University of Nottingham, Portland MS PwV 40 ("the Portland Miscellany"), pp. 32-33 in this leather-bound folio poetry miscellany. Includes "Ephelia to Bajacet," no ascription. In the same hand. Volume bears the arms of the first duke of Pomfret (1698-1753) in a small red wax seal. According to Beal, "once used by one James Parks." This MS. fragile. Watermark, apparently, a crown over a *fleur-de-lys*. Followed in the miscellany by "A very heroicall Epistle in Answer to Ephelia," in the same (scribal) hand. No ascriptions, no marginal notes.

University of Nottingham, Portland MS Pw 2V7, ff.66-67. Fine scriptorium copy in this unbound poetry miscellany (quarto), with fine ruled border in red/brown ink. Titled "Ephelia's Letter to her Lover." No ascription, no manuscript notes. Possibly early 18th century.

Herbert Aston family MS, Tixall, Staffordshire, evidently 17th-century. In a miscellany of verse. Apparently, the copy-text of the Ephelia-to-Bajazet poem printed in Arthur Clifford's *Tixall Poetry* (1813). Followed by "An Epistle In Answer to Ephelia." To date, this manuscript has not been located.

Edinburgh University Library MS Dc.1.3/1, pp.22-23, c.1670s. In substantial poetic collection, c.1680s, as "Ephelia to Bajazett." No ascription, no watermark. Acquired before 1900, according to cataloguing data.

National Library of Ireland MS 2093, pp. 70-73. In a poetry miscellany, c.1670s, neat scriptorium product with marginal brackets and watermark (fool's cap with bells), as "Ephelia to Bajasett"; subscribed "Rochester."

Elsewhere in Europe:

Royal Library of Stockholm MS Vu69, pp. 119-122. In a poetry miscellany (quarto), a high quality scriptorium copy, with ruled margins, as "Ephelia"; followed by "A very Heroicall Epistle in Answer to Ephelia." Provenance, perhaps Count Nils Gyldenstolpe (d.1709), Swedish Ambassador at The Hague. A photo-facsimile appears in Danielsson & Vieth, *Gyldenstolpe* (1967).

In the United States:

Harvard University, Houghton Library fMS Eng 602, f. [56ʳ&ᵛ]. In a poetry miscellany, c.1700, as "Ephelia to Bajacet." No ascription. Copied, according to Vieth, from one of the A-1680 editions of Rochester's *Poems* (*Attribution*, 465). Apparently, in two different inks. The answer follows, without marginalia or ascription. Acquired by Harvard, 1926. Provenance: (1) Brian Fairfax family (library auctioned, 1756) (the Fairfaxes are related by marriage to Villiers, the line of Ephelia's patroness); (2) "Sir" Thomas Phillipps (d. 1872), Phillipps MS 9096; and (3) Mr Child of Osterley Pk., Middlesex (Jersey Collection), until the sale of his library by Sotheby's, 1885, to the Earl of Crawford (Lindsay family) (see "Provenance," App.E).

On the last three leaves of this manuscript are contemporary financial records, which conclude with the information that "The cloke maker lives at the Sundile in Fleet Street." Assuming that "cloke" may be a variant spelling of "cloak" (and is not necessarily "clock," as indicated by late-17th-century spellings in Johnson's *Dictionary* and in the *O.E.D.*), this reference may connect with other intersecting pieces of information about Ephelia's association with clothworkers: (i) the milliner Frances Bullon owned a copy of *Female Poems* (B.L. copy; see Appendix E); (ii) D'Uffet's first profession was in millinery (see Appendix B); and (iii) the Prowde family was prominent in this line (see my Critical Essay).

Huntington Library, Ellesmere MS 8736A. In a poetry miscellany (quarto), late 17th century, as "Ephelia to Bajazett," lovely scriptorium copy. No ascription, no marginal notes. Watermark (on all sheets of this miscellany): grapes below name, in bar, (evidently) "I[heart-sharped device]IOVBER," surmounted by a *fleur-de-lys* crown (*cf.* Labarre #443, plate 142 (Paris 1637) and #143 (Paris 1689). Provenance: earls of Bridgewater, the Bridgewater House MSS, acquired by Huntington in a 1917 purchase.

Yale University, Beinecke Library, Osborn Collection b.54, pp. 1180-1181. In bound poetry miscellany, "Collection of Wit & Learning...to...1677," as "Ephelia to Bajazett." No ascription, no marginalia. High quality scriptorium copy.
Substantive Variants, as collated with first printed version of this poem in *Female Poems* (1679):
l.1 who] that
l.15 fierce] strong
l.23 lost alas!] lost --- alas!
l.47 crumbled] shatter'd
l.48-9 Oh! can ye coldness that you shew me now/Suit with ye generous heat you once did shew?] (These two lines not in the first printed text of this poem in *Female Poems*, 1679.)
l.52 of] or
l.52 expect] accept

Yale University, Beinecke Library, b.105, pp. 340-343. In poetry miscellany (quarto), "Songs & Verses" (*c.* 1680), as "Ephelia to Bajazet" in lovely scribal hand. No ascription, no marks. Followed by "A very Heroicall Epistle in Answer to Ephelia," pp. 344-347, in same hand
Substantive Variants: Essentially, as above, including the two (new) lines 48-49, which do not appear in the first printed appearance of the Ephelia to *Bajazet* poem in *Female Poems...by Ephelia* (1679)

𝒜PPENDIX E: COLLECTIVE PROVENANCE HISTORY OF
Female Poems ... *by Ephelia* (1679, 1682)

Determinants: *ownership signatures; ownership bookplates; private library sale & auction catalogues; information from institutional libraries, auction houses, rare-book collectors & dealers; information resulting from the editor's several published queries in British & American journals*

The Book-Plate Of  The Huth Library

This compilation of heretofore uncollected information on Ephelia's work provides a generous amount of data (dates, prices, names, *etc.*), from which the following conclusions can be drawn:

    (i) Ephelia's work was regarded as both valuable and collectible by several distinguished collectors in the U.K. and in the States (some acquiring duplicate copies of her work), from Rawlinson in the 18th century to Thorn-Drury, Huntington, Chew, and Halsey in the 20th century

    (ii) the appreciating commercial value of Ephelia's *Female Poems* has been dramatic. In 1679, according to *The Term Catalogues*, this elegant octavo sold for 1s. bound. As of this writing, a fair copy of this book, with frontispiece portrait and in contemporary boards, and perhaps with a distinguished provenance, would be valued at minimally $2500

    (iii) the *Female Poems* was acquired by print collectors (Lloyd and Halsey), as well as by rare-book collectors, suggesting that the engraved frontispiece portrait of Ephelia, exhibited at New York City's Grolier Club in 1895, may have circulated as a print at one time. Clearly, her lovely book has been appreciated on aesthetic grounds as an artifact of its day

    (iv) several inscriptions and notes in copies of the *Female Poems* lend veracity to the minority view of Ephelia as an authentic, living writer of the 1670s and '80s; they also strengthen H B Wheatley's almost-correct identification of her in 1885 as one "Joan Phillips"; finally, they shed light on such contemporary references to Ephelia as "a Poet Joan" (Behn, 1678), "Mulgrave's humble Joan" (Ebsworth, 1883), and "Phillips, who in verse her passion told" (Newcomb, 1712).

IN THE UNITED KINGDOM:
Bodleian Library, Oxford
    1679 copy: -portrait
        Provenance:
           1. Richard Rawlinson (1690-1755), Fellow of the Royal

Society; Rawlinson auction catalog, 1721:305
2. "Salvy Kinur" (?), calligraphic ownership signature, probably 19th century (front pastedown)

1682 copy: +portrait

Provenance:

1. Sir Thomas Lloyd of Aston, Salop, print & book collector (armorial bookplate). In auction catalog of his print collection (Jones, 1825), Ephelia is (improbably) identified as "Mrs Manley" (1663-1724), since the arms in the Ephelia portrait ("Tilley") suggest Manley's "keeper" "John Tilley, Master of the Mint" (Lot 71)
2. Hurst & Co., New York; purchased Lloyd's copy, one guinea
3. Sir George Thorn-Drury (d.1931), ownership signature
4. Percy Dobell (Thorn-Drury's agent), purchased Thorn-Drury's copy at the Thorn-Drury auction, Sotheby, 1931, Lot 2107 (6 titles), 2 pounds, 10s.

MS Notes:

1. "Tho. Lloyd of Aston: Salop, Esqr."
2. "By Joan Phillips. Same contents as first edition of 1679 to middle of p.112. Balance, a miscellany."
3. "Thorn-Drury. 3/3/0"

British Library, London

Two 1679 copies:

Copy #1, Shelfmark 1078.1.25: -portrait

Provenance:

1. Frances Bullon

MS Note:

1. "*Female Poems*. Frances Bullon at Mrs Vandersprits, a millener, by London stone, Watlinstreet. 1685," a contemporary calligraphic ownership signature

Copy #2, Shelfmark 11631: -portrait

Provenance:

1. William Musgrave, Trustee of the British Museum

MS Notes:

1. ownership signature "W. Musgrave"
2. "Presented by Sir William Musgrave, July 23, 1790"

Varia: Sir William Musgrave's extensive collection of rare books and manuscripts, bequeathed to B.L., 1799, included many 'fugitive' pieces

1682 copy: -portrait
Provenance: Undetermined
MS Note: "897. Fine copy. Rare. 1/1/0" [one guinea]
Varia: Purchased from bookseller Thorpe, 17 Dec. 1846

Leeds University Library, Brotherton Collection
    1679 copy: + portrait
        Provenance:
        1. Edward Allen, Baron Brotherton (bookplate); library catalog, 1913
        MS Note: ink "B.P."; inside of top board (no pastedown)
        Varia: Acquired in 1974 from Minster Gate, York bookseller. Also the title of the poem "Maidenhead" (p.40) is struck, in black ink, yet legible

IN THE UNITED STATES:
Folger Shakespeare Library, Washington, D.C.
    1679 copy: +portrait
        Provenance:
        1. John Verney (most probably Sir John Verney, 1640-1707)
        2. Beverly Chew (1850-1924; Geneva, NY) (bookplate)
        3. Henry E. Huntington (1850-1927; see *Varia*, below)
        MS Notes:
        1. "Joan Philips" in pencil, printed, next to Chew bookplate
        2. "John Verney" (p.1; ownership signature, black ink, contemporary calligraphic hand)
        3. "Joan Philips" (front pastedown)
        4. "The Club Bindery" (free back endpaper)
        5. The following, apparently in the same hand as "John Verney" signature:
            "Anne" (p.72, "To Madam B*hen*")
            "& best" (p.85, line 8, "To P*hylocles*")
            "It may be Fraizer" (p.107, "To Madam *F.*")
            "winn" (or "uinn") (p.111, after "*G*" in "To Madam *G.*")
        Varia: On spine (rebacked, red morocco): "Poems by Joan Philips. London, 1679." Huntington purchased this duplicate Chew copy, in 1924-5, Anderson Gallery, New York. Huntington Library sold it to the Folger in 1949 (the Huntington had acquired the Frederic Halsey copy).

Houghton Library, Harvard University, Cambridge, MA
    1679 copy: +portrait
     Provenance:
      1. Earls of Bridgewater (the Egerton family) (armorial bookplate; free front blank)
      2. Beverly Chew (Chew owned two copies of *Female Poems*, 1679)
      3. Harvard family (bookplate)
     MS Notes:
      1. "[Mrs Joan Phillips]" (front pastedown).
      2. On free front blank, in cursive script in black ink, is Chew's transcription of Thorn-Drury's manuscript note on *Female Poems* in Thorn-Drury's *Little Ark* (1921), according to a printed description of this copy from a sale catalogue (probably Chew's library), pasted to free back blank of this copy: "'In 1679, there appeared a small volume entitled *Female Poems. By Ephelia*. The name has been said, known not upon what grounds, to represent one Joan Phillips. This Joan Phillips, Edmund Gosse thinks, may have been the daughter of Orinda - she had but one - who eventually married Mr Lewis Wogan, a gentleman of Wales; but happily for the credit of the family, Mrs Wogan's name was Katherine, and the author of this book, described by Robert Gould as 'Ephelia, poor Ephelia, ragged Jilt,' must be sought elsewhere.' G. Thorn-Drury in *The Little Ark* 1921."

Varia: The sale catalogue description of this copy, pasted to a free back endpaper, reads: "First edition. The author of this work is not positively known. Edmund Gosse, in his *17th-Century Studies*, says it was written by Joan Philips, and [he] is inclined, from internal evidence, to think she may have been the daughter of Mrs Katherine Philips, 'the Matchless Orinda.' It also has been attributed to Mrs Behn. In 1682, the unsold sheets with some additions, were issued with a new title. This edition contains 64 poems. Mr Chew has written on the fly-leaf a long extract from Thorn-Drury with regard to the authorship." (The latter, quoted above.)

    In addition to the Bridgewater armorial bookplate, this copy bears a memorial bookplate (free front blank°) on which is printed: "Given in Memory of

LIONEL DE JERSEY HARVARD. Class of 1915. Killed in Action, Boisleaux-Au-Mont, France, March 30, 1918." Editor's Note: John Harvard [1607-1638], of this English family, had formed a 320-volume library, which helped form the early Harvard College Library. Significantly, the Harvards were related to the earls of Jersey, some of whom (Edward Villiers, 1656-1711; George Child Villiers, 1773-1859), were related to the Villiers family, the line from which Ephelia's patroness, Lady Mary (Villiers) Stuart, descended.

Huntington Library, San Marino, CA
    1679 copy: +portrait
        Provenance:
        1. Frederic Halsey (1847-1918), prominent print and book collector
        2. Henry E. Huntington, who purchased the Halsey library of 1st editions *en bloc*, Anderson Gallery, New York, 1915
        MS Note: "By Aphra Behn" (on flyleaf)
        Varia: Halsey bought his copy at Sotheby's, 1901, 14/5/0. The sale of the Halsey print collection was judged in the national press to be the largest and most important of its kind in the U.S. to that date
    1682 copy: +portrait
        Provenance:
        1. "Satherby" (?) (ownership signature, free front blank)
        2. Rev. Francis John Stainforth (d. 1866) (armorial bookplate)
        3. Arthur, Earl of Anglesey purchased the Stainforth 1682 *Female Poems*, Sotheby's, Lot 2137, 1867, 1s.
        4. Beverly Chew (bookplate) (from the Anglesey collection)
        5. Henry E. Huntington, purchased Chew copy, 1912
        MS Notes:
        1. On free front blank: "'By Joan Phillips - Second edition Remainder of the sheets of the first edition [1679], with old title canceled and H8 reprinted as HI. There is no H8 in this [second edition] copy. Both first and second editions of this volume are rare. For notice, see Edmund Gosse's *17th-Century Essays*.' - J.S." [probably John Stainforth]

247

Varia: Titlepage of this copy bears a manual ink cancel in publication date. Printed date "1682" appears as "168<u>4</u>." A unique instance of such a cancel in second edition copies. Stainforth had formed a collection of writings by British and American women poets and playwrights (auction catalog, Sotheby, 1867; NYPL copy). Very little attention has been focused on the Stainforth collection. Some mention is made by Myra Reynolds in *The Learned Lady*; see Annotated Bibliography, below.

Newberry Library, Chicago
   1679 copy: +portrait
     Provenance:
     1. Sir John Lindsay, Earl of Crawford & Balcarres
     2. John Vilders (large, perhaps 19th-century, calligraphic ownership signature dominating entire free front blank)
     3. Henry Huth (1815-1878) (bookplate; see copy of, p. 243)
     MS Notes:
     1. "Jn. Lindsay," large calligraphic ownership signature on titlepage". (Identified as John Lindsay in Huth catalogue, 1917 #2669.)
     2. "Jn. Vilders," apparently 19th-century script (identified in Huth catalog as "John Vilders"), in full-page calligraphic ownership signature, dominating entire free front blank
     3. "Joan Philips" under" *Ephelia*" on titlepage
     4. "1678," page 1, which corroborates date of this poem to Charles II on the Popish Plot, first published anonymously by Ephelia ("Written by a Gentlewoman")
     5. Collated as "Perfect. Bernard Quaritch" (back pastedown)
     6. "Mrs Pruitt 10/6/13" [Perhaps "Mrs Proud"?]
     7. "Huth attributed to Mrs Behn" (on free endpaper) in same hand as "Pruitt" note, above
     Varia: Copy purchased by the Newberry at Huth auction, Sotheby, London, 1913, Lot 2669, 7/0/5. The Editor adds: A copy of Ephelia's *Advice To His Grace* (1681) is preserved in the Crawford English Ballads Collection, no. 158, National Library of Scotland, probably deriving from the Jersey Collection of broadsides (Osterley Park), as the Earl of Crawford purchased this collection in 1885.

Clark Library, University of California, Los Angeles
  1679 copy: +portrait
  Provenance:
    1. Dr Gerald E. Slater, MN
    2. Jonathan Hill, NYC bookseller, purchased the Slater copy at the Slater library auction, Christie's, New York, 1982, Lot 124, $1800 + 10% auction house fee. Hill sold the Slater *Ephelia* to the Clark Library, UCLA

University of Texas-Austin, Harry Ransom Humanities Research Center
  1679 copy: +portrait
  Provenance:
    1. "Seth Roule" (?) ownership signature
    2. George Atherton Aitken (Texas purchased the Aitken library in 1922)

Known Copies in Private Hands, as of June, 1992
  1. James Perry copy, 1679 *Female Poems*
     Perry (1756-1821), Scottish journalist and man of letters, resident in London. Perry library auctioned in 1842; his copy fetching 4s. To date, copy unlocated
  2. Maureen E. Mulvihill, Park Slope, Brooklyn, New York
     1679 *Female Poems* -portrait, otherwise complete. Original endpapers and pastedowns. Page 142 inlaid. A2 slightly shaved. Rebacked, brown morocco. On spine (backstrip): Five raised bands. Title, between first & second bands, in gilt and on red leather label, gilt-margins: "*Female Poems* [rule] *Ephelia*." Below fifth band, at foot of spine, "1679," gilt. Purchased, 1986, $650, James Cummins-Bookseller, New York City
     Provenance: According to Cummins, former owner "an unidentified collector in Connecticut"
     MS Notes: "Eplelia" [*sic*]. Joan Philips. Rare, wants portrait. 3/10/0" (free front blank)

*A*PPENDIX F: GENERIC & THEMATIC ORGANIZATIONS OF EPHELIA'S POETRY

I. Generic Organization
types of verse; with some unavoidable overlapping

all page references follow pagination at foot of page

ACROSTIC
Anne Bury 108
Ann Gilbert 108
Venitia Cooke 149
Rachell Powney 152

BROADSIDE
A POEM TO His Sacred Majesty, ON THE PLOT ... 91
Advice to His GRACE [James, Duke of Monmouth] 215

DRAMATIC VERSE
Prologue to *The Pair-Royal of Coxcombs*, Acted at a Dancing-School 118
The First Song in the Play ("BE gone Fond Love, make haste away") 120
The Second Song ("COme quickly, Death") 121
The Epilogue 123

ELEGY
AN ELEGY On ... *SHELDON*, Ld Arch-Bishop of *Canterbury* 106
A funerall Elegie on S^r. *THOMAS ISHAM* Barronet 219

ENCOMIUM (poem of compliment)
To ... Princess **MARY**, Dutchess of *Richmond* & *Lenox* 99
To Madam *Bhen* [Aphra Behn] 174
To *Phylocles*, Inviting Him to Friendship 187
To Madam *F.* [probably Cary Frazier] 209
To Madam *G.* [probably Nell Gwyn] 213

EPISTLE-DEDICATORY
To ... PRINCESS **MARY**, Dutchess of *Richmond* & *Lenox* 99

LYRIC
Love Poem:
        Love's First Approach 109
        The Change or Miracle 110

APPARATUS

APPARATUS

II. Thematic Organization
subjects engaged; with some unavoidable overlapping

all page references follow pagination at foot of page

APPARATUS

APPARATUS

*A*NNOTATED SECONDARY BIBLIOGRAPHY (1883 - 1992):

PROFILES, CRITICISM, AND SELECTIONS OF EPHELIA'S VERSE IN
PRINTED POETRY MISCELLANIES
AND IN
SECULAR SONG-BOOKS;
INCLUSION OF EPHELIA'S PORTRAIT
IN ART EXHIBITIONS

chronological arrangement

Profiles in Reference Works

1920. Reynolds, Myra. "Joan Philips." In *The Learned Lady in England*. Sensitive discussion of *Female Poems by Ephelia* (1679). Names "Joan Philips" as author. No sources cited. Does mention Stainforth's unique collection, now dispersed, of early editions of women poets & playwrights, which included Ephelia's work.

1985. Mulvihill, Maureen E. "Ephelia," with frontispiece portrait from *Female Poems*. In *A Dictionary of British & American Women Writers, 1660-1800*, ed. Janet Todd. Brings attention to conflicting traditions of Ephelia's identity and canon, her robust feminism, occasional misandry, and sexual humor ("Maidenhead"). Mentions the important reference to Ephelia as an authentic personage in Gould's *Epistle* (1691; *Works*, 1702)). See updated profiles below.

1987. _____. "Ephelia." In 2d edition of *Dictionary*, expanded and updated profile (3 cols.). Identifies: Tilly arms in the frontispiece portrait of Ephelia; her literary models; details of provenance and sale prices; contemporary references; characteristic poetic qualities.

1989. _____. "Ephelia." In *British Women Writers: A Critical Reference Guide*, ed. Janet Todd. A further update, superseding author's earlier profiles. Identifies: Lady Mary (Villiers) Stuart as Ephelia's patroness; *J.G.* as possibly a member of the royalist Society of Sea-Serjeants; Ephelia's possible connection to the Phillipps line, Picton Castle, Pembrokeshire, Wales or to the Edward Phillips line, Shrewsbury and London (relatives of Milton); contemporary references to Ephelia as an actual personage; and the inclusion of Ephelia's songs in contemporary song-books.

1990. Grundy, Isobel. 'Ephelia.' In *The Feminist Companion to Literature in English*, eds. Blain, Clements, Grundy. Incomplete, summary treatment, regrettably perpetuating longstanding canonical and historical errors.

Criticism & Commentary

1883. Ebsworth, Joseph Woodfall, ed. In *Roxburghe Ballads* IV. Doubts *Advice To His GRACE* is Ephelia's. Credits *"Ephelia's* Lamentation" to Sir George Etherege on the evidence of one ambiguous reference in Buckingham's "Julian." Supplies invaluable information that "one of Mulgrave's mistresses was 'humble Joan'" (IV:568).

1885. Wheatley, H B. In Halkett & Laing, *Dictionary of Anonymous & Pseudonymous English Literature*, 1882-8. Lists Ephelia as "Mrs Joan Phillips." No source supplied (possibly Cunningham or Stainforth).

1885. Gosse, Sir Edmund. In *Seventeenth-Century Studies*, 2d ed. Suggests Wheatley's "Joan Phillips" may be the daughter of Katherine "Orinda" Philips. This hypothesis overturned by Thorn-Drury, and by John Pavin Phillips of Haverfordwest, Wales (*N&Q* 1958 V:202f).

1888. Verity, A. Wilson, ed. *The Works of Sir George Etherege*. Prints a version of the "Lamentation." Following Ebsworth, credits it to Etherege.

1920. John, Gwen. "Ephelia: An Unknown Poet of the Restoration." In *Fortnightly* v.108. First serious critical treatment of the poems by this prominent British painter-poet-playwright (sister of painter Augustus John).

1927. Prinz, Johannes. *John Wilmot, Earl of Rochester: His Life and Writings*. Confused discussion of the *Bajazet* to Ephelia answer-poem as Rochester's (p.147), but not Rochester's (p.148).

1950. Thorpe, James, ed. In *Rochester's 'Poems On Several Occasions (1680).'* The text of "Ephelia *to* Bajazet" in this collection of 1680 [pp.138-9] follows rather closely the text of this lyric in *Female Poems*, but adds one unremarkable couplet (ll.48-49). Rochester has retained the question mark at the end of the important first couplet, which appears in some MS copies of this verse and in the text printed in *Female Poems*. In an endnote, Thorpe identifies the author of this poem as "[Etherege?]" (p.189). This collection includes Rochester's answer or companion to the "Lamentation," "A Very Heroicall Epistle in Answer to Ephelia."

1953. Pinto, Vivian de Sola, ed. *Poems by John Wilmot, Earl of Rochester*. In an endnote, identifies the *Bajazet* to Ephelia answer-poem as a satire by Rochester on Mulgrave. Asserts that the "Lamentation" is "almost certainly" by Etherege.

1963. Thorpe, James, ed. In *Poems of Sir George Etherege*. Prints "Ephelia to Bajazet" as the first in a linked group of satires on Mulgrave. Valuably collates Ephelia's "Lamentation" to *Bajazet*, crediting it to Etherege. [Thirteen years earlier, Thorpe was not so convinced; *v.* 1950 entry, above.]

1963. Vieth, David M. 1963. *Attribution in Restoration Poetry*. Valuably collates the "Lamentation" to *Bajazet*. Discusses it at some length in Ch.13 as "probably" by Etherege, and as one of a "linked group" of satires on Mulgrave and on Scroope. Valuably collates *Bajazet's* answer to Ephelia, attributing it "probably" to Rochester.

1973. Griffin, Dustin H. *Satires Against Man: The Poems of Rochester*. Supports the traditional attribution of Ephelia's "Lamentation" to Etherege. Overlooks Ebsworth altogether, who introduced this attribution in 1883, and who also brought attention to the linked-group thesis of contemporary satires, later refined and expanded in valuable detail by Thorpe and Vieth. Fails to consider the possibility of an actual writer behind the "Ephelia" pseudonym.

1977. Milhous, Judith and Robert D. Hume. "Some 'Lost' English Plays," *HLB* 25. Lists Ephelia's play, "The Pair-Royal of Coxcombs." Mentions Gosse's hypothesis (see Gosse, above).

1978. Danchin, Pierre. In *Prologues and Epilogues of the Restoration, 1660-1700: A Tentative Check-List*. Lists Ephelia's dramatic verse in *Female Poems* (*v.*#262, p.75) as "possibly by Joan Phillips." Suggests "Epilogue may have been written for a play other than *Coxcombs*.

1981. Rothstein, Eric. In *Restoration and Eighteenth-Century Poetry*. Casts a sympathetic glance upon Ephelia's verse, proposing a "love poetry of cruelty." In Appendix I, understandably confuses the two editions of *Female Poems*, stating that the first issue in 1679 includes verse by Scroope, Rochester, *et al.*

1983. Mulvihill, Maureen E. In "Feminine Portraiture, 1660-1714." Ph.D. diss., Madison, Wisconsin. 453pp., 33 ills. Employs the trope of a 'female anatomy' in a detailed analysis of Ephelia's images of woman's body, heart, and mind. Discusses Gould's reference to Ephelia and Behn in his *Epistle* (1691) as grounding evidence of Ephelia's life in London.

1984. Hobby, Elaine. In "Englishwomen's Writings 1649-1688." Ph.D. diss., Birmingham. See Hobby, 1988, below.

1986. O'Donnell, Mary Ann, comp. *Aphra Behn: An Annotated Bibliography of Primary and Secondary Sources.* Offers a bibliographical description of *Female Poems* (2d ed., 1682). Valuably identifies three poems by Behn among the publisher Courtney's "Large Additions." Mentions the Frances Bullon inscription in the British Library copy, Ephelia's Stuart loyalty, and Gould's reference (1691) to Behn and Ephelia as a literary team.

1986. Mulvihill, Maureen E. 23 November. "Query." *New York Times Book Review.* Identifies the coat-of-arms in the Ephelia portrait as that of the abeyant Tilly line.

1986. _____. "Ephelia Material Sought." *PBSA* 80.

1987. _____. June. "Query" with photo of frontispiece portrait of Ephelia. *The Magazine Antiques.*

1988. _____. "Ephelia and Her Potential Welsh Heritage." *Notes & Queries*, March. Mentions Ephelia's possible link to the Welsh Phillipps clan, Picton Castle, Pembrokeshire, Wales.

1988. _____. Extended note, with query and frontispiece portrait of Ephelia. *Literary Research* 2.

1988. Hobby, Elaine. In *A Virtue of Necessity*. Sensitive feminist discussion of Ephelia's verse, and her several voices and styles in love poetry. Disagrees with Paddy Lyons (Glasgow University), who judges Ephelia a hoax. Questions Ephelia's authorship of "Bajazet," finding it and the last four verses in *Female Poems* out of keeping with the rest of the collection. [Yet, one of these

APPARATUS

addresses "Eugenia," obviously Ephelia's patroness.]

1988. Greer, Germaine *et al.*, eds. *Kissing The Rod*. Unreliable, retrograde discussion of Ephelia as a fiction, constructed by a cabal of Restoration writers. Asserts without etymological documentation that "Ephelia" is Greek for "freckles." Valuably mentions the "Isham" MS at Nottingham, but fails to discuss or print it. Judges Ephelia "a far better poet than she is presently given credit for." See review, Mulvihill, *Scriblerian* (Autumn) 1990.

1989. _____, ed. *The Uncollected Verse of Aphra Behn*. Contradicting *Rod*, asserts in a brief endnote, with one piece of challengeable contemporary evidence [an allusion in "Warcup"], that Cary Frazier both 'is and is not' Ephelia.

1989. Mulvihill, Maureen E. In "Feminism and the Rare-Book Market." *Scriblerian*, Autumn. Surveys the appreciating book-value of *Female Poems* (1679), from 1s. (bound) in 1679 to $1800, at the sale of the Gerald Slater library, Christie's-New York. Mentions Ephelia's possible link to the Phillips-Prowde-Milton line.

1990. _____. Critique of R D Lund, "*Bibliotheca* and the British Dames [1712]" (*Restoration* Fall, 1989). In *Scriblerian* (Autumn). Egregious misinterpretation of Thomas Newcomb's "Phillips, who in Verse her Passion wrote" as Katherine "Orinda" Philips.

1990. Thomas, Patrick, ed. In *The Collected Poems of Katherine Philips: Volume I, The Poems*. Joins two standing identifications of Ephelia -- Wheatley's "Joan Phillips" [which Thomas erroneously attributes to Halkett & Laing]; and the *Atalantis*'s Key's "Miss Proud (*i.e.*, Manley's *Euphelia*), an attendant at Queen Anne's Court -- to form the identification of Ephelia as "Joan Phillips *née* Proud." No corroborating evidence supplied. See review, Mulvihill, *ECS* (Winter) 1993.

1990. Williamson, Marilyn, ed. In *Raising Their Voices*. Pauses over Ephelia, as an intriguing writer worthy of serious attention, in this survey of women writers, 1650-1750.

1991. Mulvihill, Maureen E. In "A Feminist Link in the Old Boys' Network: The Cosseting of Katherine Philips." In *Curtain Calls*, eds. Schofield and Macheski. Mentions Ephelia's possible link to the Prowde-Phillips-Milton line.

1992. Page, Judith. "Ephelia And A Question of Biography." In *exposures* no. 2 (*texture press*, Norman, OK). Pre-publication welcoming notice on this edition.

1992. Mulvihill, Maureen E. In "Casting A Wider Net: The Multimedia Research Initiative." In *Studies in 18th-Century Culture* v. 22. With graphic "Transmedia Tactics for the '90s" and "Appendix of Multimedia Research Sources." Discusses computer-assisted research, by way of electronic scan of Ephelia's writings, to identify characteristic linguistic habits, word-groups, syntactical structures, *etc.* "Proud" appears with conspicuous frequency throughout the writings.

In progress: Page, Judith. M.A. Thesis, University of Oklahoma, Norman. Analysis of Ephelia's *Female Poems* within preceding feminist traditions [*e.g.*, the writings of Lady Mary Wroth, *inter alia*].

Selections of Ephelia's Verse in Printed Poetry Miscellanies

1676. In Thomas D'Uffet, *New Poems, Songs, Prologues & Epilogues. Never before Printed*. Possibly two poems by Ephelia in this collection; see Appendix B, above.

1680. In Rochester, *Poems On Several Occasions*. Prints a version of the Ephelia to *Bajazet* poem, followed by *Bajazet's* answer. Both poems reprinted in subsequent editions. Some 18th-century editions credit the lamentation to *Bajazet* to "the Lady K.S." [Katherine Sedley].

N.B.: This text of the "Lamentation" in Rochester's 1680 collection follows rather closely the text of the poem in *Female Poems*, even retaining the significant question mark after the important opening couplet. The shift in point of view from third person to second person, which appears in the text of this poem printed in *Female Poems*, in Rochester's 1680 *Poems*, and in MS copies of the "Lamentation," also is retained. Subsequent texts of this poem in later collections of Restoration verse, *e.g.*, *Works of...Rochester and Roscommon ...*, 1707, do not reflect this shift in point of view from third person to second person, but employ an essentially second-person point of view throughout the poem.

A critical piece of information exists in the 1707 *Works*, in a footnote on page 71 [F4],: "Having before inserted his Lord's Answer to the following Letter [*i.e.,* the *Bajazet*-to-Ephelia answer-poem, commonly attributed to Rochester], several Gentlemen desir'd us to add the Letter itself [*i.e.,* Ephelia's poem to *Bajazet*]." (Editor's emphasis.) This must be the source of the longstanding tradition of Ephelia as a fiction or literary hoax contrived by a cabal of her literary contemporaries; this tradition is perpetuated even yet, by Paddy Lyons at Glasgow University, the editors of *Kissing the Rod,* and others.

1688. In *The Triumph of Wit.* Prints without ascription a version of the Ephelia to *Bajazet* poem under the title "Memphia to Menacles: or, The forsaken Ladys Epistle to her Wanderer, *etc.* A Poem." Reprinted in subsequent editions, 1692, 1707

1813. In *Tixall Poetry,* ed. Arthur Clifford. Verse collected by the Astons of Staffordshire. Prints without ascription a text of the Ephelia to *Bajazet* poem and its reply from *Bajazet* (commonly attributed to Rochester). Herbert Aston's niece, Elizabeth Thimelby Cottingham, a literary enthusiast and amateur poet, wrote to her uncle of a female playwright's bravery before the critics, possibly referring to Boothby, Polwhele, Behn, or Ephelia. Elizabeth may have contributed the Ephelia-*Bajazet* companion poems to the family collection.

1883. In *The Roxburghe Ballads* IV, ed. Joseph Woodfall Ebsworth. Prints a version of the Ephelia to *Bajazet* poem under the title "Ephelia's Lamentation," which Ebsworth reasonably claims is its original title in manuscript. Asserts on challengeable grounds that Etherege composed the "Lamentation," based solely on one couplet in Buckingham's *Epistle To Julian*: "Poor *George* grows old, his Muse worn out of Fashion,/ Hoarsly she sung *Ephelia's* Lamentation." Ebsworth asserts, without grounds, that the *Advice* was probably written by another hand. The text of "*Ephelia's* Lamentation" in *Roxburghe Ballads* does not follow the point of view in the text of the poem in Ephelia's book, nor in Rochester's, but rather shifts perspective to a second person address throughout, beginning with line 9.

1888. In *The Works of George Etherege,* ed. A. Wilson Verity. Prints the Ephelia to *Bajazet* poem (or "*Ephelia's* Lamentation") as Etherege's. No discussion of its traditions of authorship.

APPARATUS

1936. In *Rare Poems of the 17th Century*, ed. L B Marshall. Reprints one poem from the second edition of *Female Poems* (1682), "Upon His Leaving His Mistress" [Rochester's], and four poems from the first edition of *Female Poems* (1679), "To *Phylocles*," "First Farewel to *J.G.*," "The Change or Miracle," "To one that asked why I loved *J.G.*," and "Love's First Approach." Includes an informative headnote.

1963. In *The Poems of Sir George Etherege*, ed. James Thorpe. See entry for "1963. Thorpe" above.

1970. In *Cavalier Poets*, ed. Robin Skelton. Reprints two songs, from both editions of the *Female Poems* (1679, 1682).

1972. In *Women Poets in English*, ed. Anne Stanford. Reprints three selections. Mentions Ephelia's enthusiastic following during her day, based on internal evidence in *Female Poems ... by Ephelia*.

1984. In *The Whole Duty Of A Woman*, ed. Angeline Goreau. Reprints "To Madam *Bhen*" and "The Prologue." Mentions the "Joan Philips" tradition of Ephelia's identity, but offers no critical response.

1987. In *The New Meridian Anthology of Early Women Writers*, eds. Katharine Rogers and William McCarthy. Reprints from *Female Poems* (1679) "To one that asked why I lov'd *J.G.*" and "To *Coridon*."

1988. In *Kissing The Rod*, eds. Germaine Greer *et al.* Generously reprints, with footnotes, nine choice selections from *Female Poems* (1679): "Love's First Approach," "Prologue ...," "To *J.G.*," "Maidenhead," "To a Proud Beauty," "To one that asked ...," "To Madam *Bhen*," "To *Phylocles*," and "To the Honoured *Eugenia*."

1990. In *British Women Poets 1660-1800*, ed. Joyce Fullard. Prints from *Female Poems* (1679) "To Madam *Bhen*" and "To one that asked ...." Lists Ephelia as Joan Philips. Biographical summary (p.564) incomplete and unreliable. Relies on 19th-century information and later profiles, all unacknowledged. Incorrectly identifies Ephelia's publisher as one "William Dowling."

1991. In *The New Oxford Book of Seventeenth-Century Verse*, ed. Alastair Fowler. Reprints 5 poems from *Female Poems*. Regrettably reprints as Ephelia's a popular song of Rochester's, which was one of the

APPARATUS

"Large Additions" in the 2d ed. of *Female Poems* (1682). [This song first printed in Rochester's *Poems*, 1680.] Misdates this poem to "1679." Mentions Ephelia's "telling directness" (xli) without appreciating her debts to Sidney, Donne, Cowley, Dryden, *et al.*

[forthcoming.] *The Prologues & Epilogues of the Restoration, 1677-1690.* Two volumes. These will be Part II of Pierre Danchin's useful *Complete Prologues & Epilogues of the Restoration, 1660-1700.* Reprints from *Female Poems* the "Prologue" to Ephelia's play "The Pair-Royal of Coxcombs" and "Epilogue." As mentioned above (*v.* "1978"), Danchin suggests that "Epilogue" may have been written for another play, based on the way "Epilogue" is titled, as compared to the full and explicit title of the play's "Prologue ...." [Editor's Note: The very sequence of dramatic verses in Ephelia's collection, however, poses a counterargument.]

Musical Settings of Ephelia's Poems in Song-Books (1683-1719)

"First, then, of Songs, that now so much abound." Mulgrave, *Essay on Poetry* (1682)

1683 (5th ed.). In John Playford's *Choice Ayres & Songs: Being Most of the Newest Songs Sung at Court. The Fourth Book.* Prints without ascription Ephelia's "Song" ("Ranging the Plain one Summers Night"), from *Female Poems* (1679). Set by Moses Snow or William Turner (*v.* editor's Critical Essay, p.15, above).

1683. In *The Newest Collection of the Choicest Songs, as they were Sung at Court.* Prints as "anon." above song. Composer not credited.

1684 (6th ed.). In John Playford's *Choice Ayres & Songs ... The Fifth Book.* Prints without ascription Ephelia's "Song" ("When busy Fame o're all the Plain"), from *Female Poems* (1679). Set by Farmer.

1685. In Henry Playford's *Theater of Music ... The First Book.* Prints without ascription Ephelia's "Song" ("Ah *Phillis*! had you never lov'd"), from *Female Poems* (1679). Set by Turner.

1687. In Henry Playford's *Theater of Music ... The Fourth and Last Book.* (Titlepage, Fig. 18). Prints without ascription Ephelia's "Neglect Returned" ("Proud *Strephon*! doe not think my Heart"), from *Female Poems* (1679). Set by Moses Snow (*c.*1650-1702) (music, Fig. 19.) Snow's setting provides the melody and bass lines. Time signature or tempo is *Alla breve* (quick, duple time).

265

THE
Theater of MUSIC:

O R, A

Choice COLLECTION of the neweſt and beſt *SONGS*
Sung at the COURT, and Public THEATERS.

The *Words* compoſed by the moſt ingenious *Wits* of the Age, and ſet to
MUSIC by the greateſt Maſters in that *Science.*

WITH

A *Thorow-Baſs* to each *SONG* for the *Harpſichord, Theorbo,* or *Baſs-Viol.*

The FOURTH and LAST BOOK.

LONDON,
Printed by B. *Motte,* for *Henry* P*layford,* at his Shop near the *Temple* Church, 1687.

Fig.18. Titlepage, *The Theater of Music ... The Fourth & Last Book*
London: Henry Playford, 1687

Roud *Stre--phon!* do not think my Heart fo ab—fo—lute a

Slave, nor in fo mean and fervile State; but if I fay, That you're ingrate, I've Pride and

Pow'r e—nough your Chains to brave.

Mr. *Snow.*

I I.

I fcorn to Grieve or Sigh for one
That does my Tears neglect ;
If in your Looks my Coldnefs were ,
Or defire of Change appear ,
I can your Vows your Love and you reject.

I I I.

What refin'd Madnefs wou'd it be ,
With Tears to dim thofe Eyes ;
Whofe Rays it Grief doth not rebate,
Each Hour new Lovers might create,
And with each Look gain a more glorious Prize.

I V.

Then do not think with Frowns to fright,
Or threaten me with Hate ;
For I can be as cold as you,
Difdain as much , and proudly too,
And break my Chains in fpite of Love or Fate.

Fig.19. Moses Snow's setting of "Neglect Returned," one of several songs in *Female Poems* ...
by Ephelia (1679). Published without ascription by Henry Playford in *The Theater of Music*
(1687)

1695. In Henry Playford's *New Treasury of Music: or a Collection of the Choicest & best Song-Books*. Prints without ascription Ephelia's "Neglect Returned." Set by Snow. Prints without ascription her "Song" ("Ranging the Plain one summers night"). Set by Snow or by Turner. Both songs in *Female Poems ... by Ephelia* (1679).

1699. In Henry Playford's edition of D'Urfey's *Wit & Mirth; or Pills to Purge Melancholy*. Prints without ascription Ephelia's "Song" ("Ranging the Plain one Summer's Night"). Set by Snow or by Turner. Song printed in *Female Poems* (1679). This setting reprinted in subsequent editions of *Wit & Mirth*, as below.

1707. In *Wit & Mirth*. Prints without ascription two of Ephelia's songs, "Ranging the Plain one Summer's Night," set by Snow or by Turner; and Farmer's setting of "When Busie Fame o'er all the Plain," both from *Female Poems* (1679).

1719. In Jacob Tonson's edition of D'Urfey's *Wit & Mirth*. Prints without ascription the two songs cited above.

[Editor's Note: Day and Murrie's *Song-Books* (1940) errs in listing Ephelia's "Song" ("When Busie Fame, o're all the Plain") as printed on pp. 163-4 of Tonson's edition of D'Urfey's *Songs Compleat, Pleasant & Divertive* (1719). Copy examined: NYPL-Lincoln Center.]

Inclusion of Ephelia's Portrait in Art Exhibitions

1895. Grolier Club Exhibition, New York City. *Engraved Portraits of Women Writers, Sappho to George Eliot*. Includes the frontispiece portrait of Ephelia from *Female Poems* (*v.* frontispiece of this edition). Identified in printed exhibition catalogue as "Joan Phillips" (exhibit no. 259). Copies examined: Grolier Club, New York City, and Brooklyn Public Library - Grand Army Plaza.

INDEX OF NAMES IN EPHELIA'S POETRY
Place Names, Proper Names, Pastoral Names

all page references follow pagination at the foot of page

I. Place Names
Africk (Africa) 115 181 199
Canterbury 106
Dancing-School (probably in London) 118
Europe 115 181
Golden Horse Shoe (bookshop of Ephelia's publisher, James Courtney) 11
London 124
Rome 209
Saffron Hill (location of Courtney's bookshop in London) 11
Surrey-plain, the 177
Tangiere (Tangier) 171
Thames 160
Tyber 160

II. Proper Names
Bhen, Madam (Aphra Behn, 1640-89) 174
Bury, Anne 108
CHARLES (Charles II) (1630-85) 93; as "Sacred Majesty," 103
"Charles, Royal" (Charles II) 93
Cooke, Venitia 149
Courtney, James at the Golden Horse Shoe, Saffron Hill, from *c.* 1671-85
    (*v.*"Courtenay" in Plomer, p.83) 11 97
Cowley (Abraham Cowley, 1618-67) 149
Downing, William (printer of first issue of *Female Poems ... by Ephelia,*
    1679) 97
Dryden (John Dryden, poet-laureate, 1631-1700) 149
F., Madam (probably Cary Frazier, d. 1709) 209
G., Madam (probably Nell Gwyn, d.1687) 213
G., J. (see *J.G.* below)
Gilbert, Anne 108
Howard ("*Great* Howard"; Wm Howard, 1st Viscount Stafford, charged
    and arrested 1678, Popish Plot; executed 1680) 100
Isham, Sir Thomas, 3d Baronet (d.1681) 221
J.G. (see also "*Strephon*," below) 114 116 117 124 131 134 160 162 168 183
MARY ("EXCELLENT PRINCESS") (Lady Mary [Villiers] Stuart, 1622-85,
    Ephelia's patroness "Eugenia") 99
[Monmouth, James Scott or Fitz-Roy, Duke of ("His Grace" and "vain
    Man"; executed 1685] 217
[Mulgrave; see *Bajazet* below]
[Philips, Katherine 'the Matchless *Orinda'* (see *Orinda*, below)]

III. Pastoral Names

INDEX OF TITLES

Index of First Lines

273

FINIS

A Note on the Editor

Maureen E. Mulvihill is a member of The Princeton Research Forum, Princeton, New Jersey. In the 1980s, she was an Associate Fellow of New York City's Institute for Research in History, founded by Arthur Schlesinger and others in the early 1970s.

She earned a Ph.D. in Restoration & 18th-Century English Literature at the University of Wisconsin in 1983, with a dissertation on ideologies of woman in later-Stuart England as a model of the rise of liberal thought. At the post-doctoral level, she studied at the Rare Book School of Columbia University, the Yale Center for British Art, and the Metropolitan Museum of Art. As an undergraduate, she attended Monteith College, Wayne State University, Detroit, where she earned a Bachelor of Philosophy in Humanities, with a baccalaureate essay on the Expressionism Movement in the arts. Her M.A. thesis, at Wayne State's English Department, examined the satiric caricature in Pope and Swift within Classical and 18th-century literary and pictorial traditions.

Dr Mulvihill has taught literature, humanities, and women writers at Wayne State University, the University of Detroit, where she studied with Sir Tyrone Guthrie (Visiting Artist, 1969-70), Hunter College-CUNY, New York University, and Touro College-Manhattan.

Her publications to date include *Poems by Ephelia (c.1679)*; several original essays, "Casting A Wider Net: The Multimedia Research Initiative" (*Studies in 18th-Century Culture* 1992), "A Feminist Link in the Old Boys' Network: The Cosseting of Katherine Philips" (*Curtain Calls: Women & the Theater, 1660-1820* edited by Schofield & Macheski, Ohio 1991), "Feminism and the Rare Book Market" (*Scriblerian* Autumn 1989), "Essential Studies of Restoration Women Writers" (*Restoration* Fall 1987); and several first profiles, in Janet Todd's *Dictionary of British & American Women Writers* (1985), Todd's *British Women Writers* (1989), Katharina Wilson's *Encyclopedia of Continental Women Writers* (1990), Wilson's *Medieval Women Writers* (1993), and *British Publishers To 1830* (*Dictionary of Literary Biography* series, 1993).

In 1992, she was the recipient of a Frances E. Hutner Award from The Princeton Research Forum. In 1990, she was an NEH Fellow and a member of the James Clifford Award Committee of the American Society for 18th-Century Studies.

She has been a Visiting Scholar at Metropolitan State College, Denver, Colorado, and at Utah State University, Logan Utah. Her guest lecture engagements to date have been at the Brooklyn Museum, Georgian Court College (New Jersey), McMaster University (Ontario), New York University, Princeton University, and the Honors Institute of the New Jersey Institute of Technology.

Her developing collection of rare books includes writings by Anna Maria Van Schurman, Katherine Philips, Aphra Behn, Ephelia, Lady Winchilsea, Robert Gould, Delarivier[e] Manley, Hannah More, Mary Wortley Montagu, and John Gay.

Her work in progress is *Stewardess of Culture: Englishwomen Writers & Patronesses, 1660-1714*, a multimedia source-book and prototype of its kind (NY: Garland Publishing, Inc. [1995]). Since 1983, she has resided in Park Slope, Brooklyn, with her husband, composer-musician Daniel Harris.

Poems by Ephelia (c. 1679)

Second Printing - 1993

———

Critical Essay and Apparatus set in 10/12 Palatino
Decorative initials in Zapf Chancery
Printed on acid-free, permanent, 60-pound Boise
by Thomson-Shore, Inc., Dexter, Michigan
Bound in BookCloth by Thomson-Shore, with silver spine stamp
Book and dustjacket design by Maureen E. Mulvihill